LANCPOL99

Comparative Politics

To the memory of Aaron Wildavsky: a great scholar and a true friend

Comparative Politics

An Introduction and New Approach

JAN-ERIK LANE AND SVANTE ERSSON

Polity Press

First published 1994 by Polity Press
in association with Blackwell Publishers.

Editorial office:
Polity Press
65 Bridge Street
Cambridge CB2 1UR, UK

Marketing and production:
Blackwell Publishers, the publishing imprint of Basil Blackwell Ltd
108 Cowley Road
Oxford OX4 1JF, UK

238 Main Street
Cambridge, MA 02142, USA

ISBN 0 7456 1256 3
ISBN 0 7456 1257 1 (pbk)

A CIP catalogue record for this book is available from the British Library and from the Library of Congress.

Typeset in 11 on 12pt Sabon
by Best-set Typesetter Ltd, Hong Kong
Printed in Great Britain by Hartnolls Ltd, Bodmin, Cornwall

This book is printed on acid-free paper

Contents

List of Figures

List of Tables

Preface

The study of comparative politics is certainly not a novelty that has to fight for recognition in the field of political science. An interest in understanding the range of variation in political macrostructures between countries may be traced back as far as Aristotle. Comparing polities more or less systematically for a period of a few centuries since Montesquieu has resulted in a number of distinctions that offer guidance in the interpretation of similarities and differences between the political systems of present-day countries. One may ask why states are different as well as why they are similar. Which concepts are typically used when comparing the political institutions of states? And are there some recurrent topics?

Our purpose in writing this textbook is to make a contribution to the field of comparative government by looking at the major *models* used in the analysis of the states of the world. We try to identify and test some general hypotheses about macropolitics: are there a few generalizations about states that constitute a core body of knowledge in this field, which has been much dominated by area studies? Besides looking at the institutional web of government we analyse the relationship between society and the state. We start from the traditional structural approaches and then move towards the emerging institutionalist framework, trying to present comparative politics as a model-based discipline.

The study is based on a selected set of some 130 countries, for which we have managed to gather a small set of data concerning political and social variables. The perspective is *state centred*, looking at states during the post-Second World War period, i.e., from 1945 until 1990, with a population larger than one million. The level of exposition has been kept elementary, so that the volume may be used in undergraduate courses in comparative politics – or, as it is often called, 'comparative government'.

The structure of the book follows from its aim to base the presentation of comparative politics on an examination of the models in this field of knowledge. Behind different concepts and approaches in comparative politics there are two main issues that constantly arise: state stability and state performance. States are dissolved and disappear, and new ones are created. Which factors enhance *state stability*? States are valued because of what they do. The set of state activities is very large, including both peace and war activities, or decisions and programmes that range from welfare provision to genocide. The performance records of states vary tremendously in relation to such classical values in political theory as liberty and equality. Why such marked difference in *state performance*?

Comparative politics is not only description but also explanation. From our two dependent variables – state stability and state performance – we turn to analyse the conditions that bear upon them – to the so-called independent variables. What could be the logic in terms of which such independent variables may be derived in accordance with the methodology of comparative enquiry? Relevant to the understanding of states are sets of structural and institutional conditions. However, states are not simply functions of major structural or institutional factors. There exist degrees of freedom for the major actors, the political elites and their followers. Thus we also look at actors and their relevance for understanding state stability and state performance.

The next step involves models that combine structural, institutional and actor-related conditions in order to find out which kind of factors matter most. State stability and state performance are aggregative properties that depend, on the one hand, on the efficiency with which states may mobilize resources and execute policies and, on the other, on the amount of legitimacy which the citizens bestow upon the state. Finally, the problem of regime transition is examined, looking at what role general factors play for the creation of democratic regimes or stable democracies.

Little of what is presented here has been published before. Only in chapters 5, 6 and 7 have we used some material published elsewhere, namely 'Behaviouralism', in *The Blackwell Encyclopedia of Political Institutions*, ed. V. Bogdanor (1988) and 'The Political Trinity', in *Comparative Politics: New Directions in Theory and Method*, ed. H. Keman (Amsterdam: Free University Press, 1993). We have utilized data made available by the Inter-University Consortium for Political and Social Research from Polity II: Political Structures and Regime Change (Gurr, 1990), for the interpretation of which we are solely responsible.

We must thank both the anonymous reviewer of the publisher for substantial guidance when struggling with various versions of the manuscript and Clive Napier, Murray Faure, Kieren O'Malley and Pierre Hugo at the Department of Political Sciences at the University of South Africa for their advice when the book was finalized.

Jan-Erik Lane, Svante Ersson
Oslo and Umeå

Introduction: The Art and Craft of Comparative Politics

A lot has been written on the status of comparative politics as a field of knowledge. Usually, this literature is both hesitant and ambiguous concerning the means and ends of comparative politics as a body of knowledge (Mayer, 1989; Wiarda, 1991; Macridis and Burg, 1991; Almond et al., 1993). Comparative government or comparative politics is said to be in a crisis, or will face a crisis, or has passed through a crisis. On the one hand, it is stated that not much that is really valid has come out of all the efforts that have been poured into the discipline. On the other, it is argued that, to some extent, comparative politics has not been able to resolve its methodological issues, which hampers the whole enterprise. In this introductory chapter we look at some of the problems that have been raised in the debate over the art and craft of comparative politics. Perhaps expectations have been too high, which explains why the prevailing mood in the evaluation of what has been done is overly pessimistic. Why study comparative politics? One reason used to be: description, as in the traditional approach.

The traditional approach

Comparative politics as a discipline is a loosely structured body of knowledge where alternative frameworks, approaches and methodologies compete with one another (Chilcote, 1981; Blondel, 1990; Bebler and Seroka, 1990; Rustow and Erickson, 1991; Needler, 1991; Hague, Harrop and Breslin, 1992). A number of distinctions may be made in order to unpack such a complex phenomenon.

It should be explicitly stated from the very begining that comparative politics has no unique or established methodology in terms of which enquiry should be conducted. What is called the 'traditional' mode has been considered inadequate since the late 1950s, but there exists no single paradigm or approach that has replaced it.

The traditional approach characterized much conventional research until the late 1950s. It involved the following elements (Macridis, 1955; Bill and Hardgrave, 1973):

1 *Configurative description*: the study of political systems was oriented towards a detailed description of some countries without the use of any explicit conceptual framework.
2 *Parochialism*: there was a typical Western bias in the selection of relevant countries to be studied, e.g., the United Kingdom, France, Germany, the United States and the Soviet Union – and in the relevant variables to be employed for description.
3 *Formal-legalism*: the constitutional orientation was prevalent in much of the work, as it comprised detailed descriptions of the rules supposedly governing the operations of cabinets, legislatures, courts and bureaucracies.
4 *Empiricism*: models or theory were non-existent in traditional comparative politics, at least at the level of intention and recognition. Concepts were often employed with little methodological discussion as to their definition and measurement.
5 *Non-comparison*: most of the texts in the field of comparative government either studied one single country or engaged in parallel descriptions of a few countries.

Yet one must remember that not all comparative work has been identical since the coming of modern political science around 1900. Moreover, it may be questioned whether comparative politics as it stands today is as different from the traditional approach as has been claimed (Sartori, 1991). The rejection of the traditional approach was strong enough to offset highly demanding requirements on the emergent new discipline, both theoretically and empirically. Another answer to the question about the purpose of the study of comparative government was to look upon it as a craft or a tool for guiding policy-making in the newly independent states of the world. Still others wished to create an abstract art.

The overemphasis on craft

The strong leaning towards development studies entailed a determined call for a statement of action implications. If one knew the craft of comparative politics, then one would also be able to spell out the practical consequences for reforms that would help new states achieve their development objectives. The search for immediate applications of comparative politics to urgent social, economic and political problems in the world placed a tremendous burden on the discipline.

Translating the theoretical steps ahead in the emerging field into really practical solutions to the issues in the 1960s, when many new states set out for a course towards so-called development, was a hopeless task. There was bound to be disappointment and a search for alternative models, because the discipline was not capable of launching safe prescriptions about how institutional reform and policy programmes could guide the Third World states towards the achievement of their highly ambitious objectives. The strong demand for a craft of comparative politics was expressed at the same time as the traditional approach was abandoned. Yet the search for a strong dose of scientism interpreted along positivistic notions should be distinguished from the search for a political developmental approach.

In his overview of the evolution of comparative politics as a discipline Wiarda underlines the two crucial roles played by the developmentalist approach, as it first achieved a dominant position in the 1960s then later, in the 1970s, became the common target of all kinds of criticism (Wiarda, 1991: 221–50). The developmentalist approach was far from monolithic. Wiarda noted several differences:

> First, there are the disciplinary differences: the more deterministic approaches of economists such as W. W. Rostow or Robert Heilbroner, for example; the sociological – but sometimes also deterministic – studies of Karl Deutsch, Marion Levy, or Seymour Lipset; and the generally nuanced, subtle, and multifaceted political science approaches of David Apter, Lucian Pye, Dankwart Rustow, Myron Weiner and others. (p. 226)

Within political science the Almond perspective was derived from structural-functionalism and Talcott Parsons's pattern variables, but as a matter of fact *The Politics of the Developing Areas* (Almond and Coleman, 1960) never had the dominant role later attributed to it. Thus Samuel P. Huntington, in his *Political Order in Changing Societies* (1968), stated a critique of so-called functionalist approaches, although he remained faithful to the developmentalist perspective.

The overemphasis on craft orientated towards the magic concept of development resulted in deep-seated methodological contentions, the emerging underdevelopment-dependency approach claiming that the entire developmentalist perspective was not simply wrong in the sense of resulting in false explanations, predictions and observations, but also in the meaning of social injustice (Frank, 1967). The attempt to identify what was development for a country came to be regarded as a question about political and economic values, where the developmentalist perspective was looked upon as biased, ethnocentric and capitalist (Wiarda, 1991: 3–30).

Taking a step back and looking at the fierce battle in the 1970s and 1980s between the adherents of the developmentalist perspective and their critiques within dependency theory (Cardoso and Faletto, 1979), corporatism (Wiarda, 1981), Marxism (Chilcote, 1981) and bureaucratic-authoritarianism (Collier, 1979), one may underline the distinction between knowledge and action or theory versus praxis. Evidently, this battle was fought not only about the standard canons of social science research; it also involved a great deal of political conflict concerning the concrete implications of development.

The scholars of the developmentalist perspective were accused of being tied up with the propagation of American individualistic values, whereas the critiques searched for an altogether different developmental path, a supposed third alternative between capitalism and communism. In particular, Rostow's model, expounded in *The Stages of Economic Growth* (1960), of three stages for the transition from a traditional agricultural economy to a modern industrialized society gave rise to the accusation that it implicitly propagated capitalist values.

The sharp confrontation between the developmentalist school and the emerging alternative approaches resulted from an overemphasis on craft in comparative politics. What came out of the heated debate was a predicament that has been referred to by Stanley Hoffman as 'islands of theory' (Wiarda, 1991: 245). It is hardly surprising that a premature search for the action implications or moral consequences of comparative politics as a discipline would end up in disappointment and eclecticism. The alternative perspectives replacing the developmentalist approach soon ran into difficulties of their own; there is no one single widely accepted paradigm for the conduct of comparative research into macropolitics today. Paradoxically, one may note that the developmentalist approach has seen a comeback in the early 1990s: some of its ideas may be found in the emerging literature of transition politics (Diamond et al., 1990b; Hyden and Bratton, 1992).

Some of the approaches replacing the developmentalist framework also had a strong craft orientation. Thus the dependency school recommended very different action as means in a strategy for the long-term development of peripheral countries in relation to core countries. Again, the link between theory and praxis was conceived in a simplistic fashion.

The question should really explicitly be raised as to whether comparative politics is or should be a craft. The relationships between the theoretical and practical aspects of social science research are far from clear or extensively known. The application of social science to the solution of practical problems depends on the availability of usable knowledge, which in itself is a controversial concept (Wildavsky, 1979; Lindblom, 1990; Lijphart, 1990; Allison and Beschel, 1992). The derivation of usable theories is an open-ended enterprise where it is far from obvious that clear-cut or unique solutions will be arrived at. Since the concept of development is an essentially contested notion, it is not productive for comparative politics to focus on political or social development as if they were its key reference point.

Typical of the perspective on comparative politics as a craft is the belief in a close correspondence between knowledge and action. However, it is really difficult to spell out the action implications of hypotheses in a theoretical manner. For example, suppose one finds a positive correlation between an Islamic culture and a lack of civil and political rights; what kind of actions would one recommend to rulers in a country that faces increasing support for Islamic fundamentalism, such as Algeria and Egypt? Such questions involve moral issues that cannot be settled within the framework of comparative government.

The relationship between knowledge and action, theory and praxis is far more complicated than was realized in the developmental approach. Not only must the place of values be recognized; practical knowledge also has characteristics of its own that comparative politics as a discipline may not fulfil. Stating recommendations and suggesting means to various goals involve access to hypotheses concerning highly predictable and concrete events. It is far from obvious that this knowledge orientation is what comparative politics can deliver.

Even if the practical aspects are reduced and it is not regarded as a major craft in the service of mankind, there remains a set of hotly debated issues concerning comparative politics as an art, theoretically speaking. Rejecting the traditional approach, the drive for the greater application of scientific method into the discipline did not actually imply that action implications or moral overtones should be at the heart of comparative politics. Yet a third reason for conducting comparative research in macropolitics is to conceive of its aiming at interpretation or explanation.

The uneasiness about art

We must remember that it was not long ago that scientism gained ground in the discipline, Macridis calling in 1955 for a non-parochial, non-formalistic, non-legalistic and analytic comparative politics. The concept of science contained two very different models of concepts and propositions. One school argued that a general theory could or should be formulated, whereas the other argued in favour of middle-range theories. What united these two different methodological perspectives was their adherence to scientism.

When the traditional approach was abandoned scholars began to look on comparative politics as a basically nomothetical enterprise that, as an art, should have a strict structure comprising well-defined concepts and a hierarchical net of hypotheses to be corroborated in cumulative research. The difference between the generalists and the middle-range scholars concerned the range and scope of comparative concepts, where the middle-range alternative was adhered to by those influenced to some extent by a positivistic methodology. The middle-range school developed as a reaction to the many attempts to formulate one single general framework of concepts for the entire field of comparative politics. Although the two approaches differ, they were related to each other not only in time but also logically. In the words of L. C. Mayer:

> The survey of existing attempts at theory building has revealed that political science is at what might be called a pre-theoretic stage of development. Most of the existing theoretical work has been concerned with establishing logical

relationships between nonempirically defined concepts or imprecisely defined classes of phenomena. (Mayer, 1972: 279)

The middle-range approach argued that macropolitical theory along the lines of Parsonian sociology bypassed the empirical aspects of social science, which the school would tap by means of the full use of indicators and measurement strategies. However, one may raise the question whether comparative politics can be described by means of Kuhnian concepts such as normal science and paradigmatic changes. The uneasiness and hesitance about methodologies stemmed from an overambition to be truly scientific. The grand social theory frameworks and the positivistic school both displayed this vacillation concerning what comparative politics as an art was really about.

It should be mentioned that the controversy concerning comparative politics as a craft is unrelated to the alternative interpretations of the discipline as an art (see figure 1). Actually, many of the contributions to the discipline following the demise of the traditional approach were either conducted in terms of model II or along the lines of model III. No wonder there was a tremendous gulf between theory and praxis. The reaction to the prevalence of type III led scholars to type I. It should be mentioned that type IV was not excluded, because some theories predicted the major developmental trends in Third World countries from highly abstract concepts such as modernity, modernization and rationalization or secularization.

The search for the essence of comparative politics

Comparative politics is not the same as the comparative method. 'Comparative politics' means the study of politics at the macrolevel, referring to units denoted by words such as 'political system', 'state' or 'nation-state' and 'government' (Scarrow, 1969). The comparative method, on the other hand, is a methodology for the study of any kind of social unit, for example, political parties or societies, diachronically or synchronically (Roberts, 1972; Collier, 1991; Öyen, 1990; Bartolini, 1993).

If comparative politics is not simply the employment of comparative research techniques in political science, then what is its substance? Actually, a number of attempts have been made to identify its essence, but they seldom meet with agreement from the discipline. The search, although very interesting in itself, spurns unnecessary conflict, because at the heart of comparative politics there can only be what is actually accomplished at various periods of time.

Peter H. Merkl, in his *Modern Comparative Politics* (1977), gives a few suggestions concerning the nature of comparative politics. He states:

		Craft	
		Weak emphasis	Strong emphasis
Art	Middle-range	I	II
	General theory	III	IV

Figure 1 The art and craft of comparative politics

> Not only are some nations much richer and more powerful than others, but some parts within most nations – a certain class of people, the cities, or a certain ethnic group – are likely to be richer and more powerful than the rest. It is the task of the discipline of comparative politics to describe and analyze these differences and similarities among states and within them and to explain the political conflicts that arise from them. (Merkl, 1977: xii)

There can be no argument that this definition contains vital aspects, but is it really wide enough? Merkl goes on to mention the time dimension, the spatial dimension and the sociocultural dimension of comparative politics, where the last comprises the matrix of personality and culture of a society. He also speaks about various kinds of structure and process: the system of political parties and interest groups, the formal structure of governmental institutions and the policy process (Merkl, 1977: xii). This is a plausible identification of what comparative politics is all about, but one may, of course, wish to include other things or question the meaning of some of the crucial terms, such as 'structure', 'system' and 'formal governmental institutions'.

Comparative politics consists of the theories about macropolitics that are present in the discipline at different points of time. As sets of theories come and go or hypotheses change, it would hardly be rewarding to identify once and for all the essence of the discipline, although it is vital to discuss its basic assumptions. The main offspring of such endeavours is that it opens one's eyes to important phenomena that are *not* covered by the prevailing definition.

Causality in macropolitics

In *Redefining Comparative Politics* (1989), Mayer underlines how crucial the comparative method is for the entire enterprise of comparative politics. Actually, it is claimed that the conduct of comparative analysis is the *sine qua non*:

> The central theme of this chapter is that comparative analysis should be considered as a method that plays a central role in the explanatory mission of political science itself. (Mayer, 1989: 56)

It may be worth while here to employ the distinction between ends and means. The use of the comparative method – we shall see that this concept is by no means clear-cut – is not an end in itself but a means to basic objectives such as understanding or explanation.

Crucial to these two objectives is the mastering of a great deal of information in terms of the principle of causality. Generalizations do not only play a role in explanation, they also afford a convenient way of organizing the data. If some connections could be found concerning the workings of macropolitics, then that would help to structure the knowledge. Since models provide convenient ways in which to express generalizations, model-building is particularly important in comparative politics.

The Humean theory of knowledge, emphasizing the notion that the principle of causality involves regularities or generalizations, seems highly adequate for comparative politics at its present stage. The rule that the same cause is accompanied by the same effect, or that a different effect is preceded by a different cause, may be applied to macropolitics. And it just so happens that comparison is the chief tool for arriving at and testing such generalizations. Thus the various methods in comparative research are valuable because they enhance model-building, which is conducive to the organization of knowledge by means of generalizations.

It is often argued that general theory in comparative politics turned out to be the particularism of the universalism in Western knowledge. The various theoretical frameworks suggested after the critique of the traditional approach are accused of carrying a basic Western bias. When a general theory of comparative politics stated in value-loaded concepts was combined with a strong dose of craft, the discipline seemed nothing more than an aspect of cultural imperialism or an extension of the foreign policy of the USA (Wiarda, 1991: 224). The search for indigenous concepts or non-ethnocentric models can be looked on as a reaction to the culture-bound perspective inherent in several of the grand theory perspectives.

However, this is an overreaction, because indigenous concepts also have to be employed in causal interpretation if they are to be truly useful. Thus ethnocentric approaches should be done away with, but this does not imply that a causal perspective is invalid. Models or generalizations about relationships between properties, entities or variables is of the utmost importance if the discipline is to arrive at some elementary state of knowledge. It has been argued that concept formation is the most vital task for comparative politics in the 1990s (Bebler and Seroka, 1990). True, concepts are important, but it is through model-building that concept formation really pays off.

The Humean perspective, developed into an emphasis on model-building, does not imply a heavy commitment to the craft interpretation of comparative politics or some kind of positivistic scientism. It is only through the structuring of knowledge by means of model-building that one may arrive at an overview of scattered pieces of knowledge. What are the practical implications of models is a separate matter that will have to be reflected upon by additional criteria. And generalizations about causal relationships in macropolitics need not imply general theory and its highly abstract correlates.

An outline of the book

In the first chapter an attempt is made to derive a set of core problems that comparative politics has tried to tackle over the years. Chapter 2 surveys the states of the world today and presents the sample which will be analysed. Chapter 3 looks at various notions of statehood, in particular state persistence. State stability in general and regime longevity in particular are discussed in Chapter 4. In Chapter 5 state performance is analysed, including the democratic records of state as well as policy outputs and social outcomes.

In Chapter 6 we turn away from the two dependent variables – state stability and state performance – in order to discuss the conditions that bear upon them – the so-called independent variables. First we consider the logic in terms of which such independent variables may be derived in accordance with the methodology of comparative enquiry. Chapter 7 focuses on the set of structural conditions and their consequences as either sufficient or necessary conditions. Employing various typologies for the presentation of the institutional conditions, Chapter 8 discusses the causal impact of some salient institutional properties, stating how they may be measured. Chapter 9 turns to actors and their relevance for understanding state stability and state performance.

In Chapter 10 models combining structural, institutional and actor-related conditions are tested on the basis of a theory about legitimacy and efficiency as crucial for state stability and state performance. Finally, in Chapter 11 the problem of regime transition is brought up: we look at what general factors play a role in the creation of democratic regimes or stable democracies, and an attempt is made to draw some policy conclusions in relation to the debate about how system transitions could be governed or at least partially influenced.

It may well be the case that a multiplicity of area studies in countries in various parts of the world could give a richer picture of the state and its macropolitical properties. Case studies would provide for an opportunity for a careful and minute analysis of the social and economic environment of the state, the state institutions themselves and the key actors. The advantage of taking a totally different approach, a general comparative perspective based on a systematic analysis of data from almost all the state countries of the world, is that it allows for explicit model-building and model-testing. And models lie at the heart of systematic knowledge.

Conclusion

The purpose of the study of comparative government is to understand the logic of macropolitical systems such as the state. Thus the focus is upon establishing generalizations about the state which may be used for explanations of the past and predictions about the future (Collins, 1986; Collins and Waller, 1993). If the study of comparative politics can help us in the interpretation of major events, such as the collapse of regimes or the conditions for regime transitions on the basis of a recognition of crucial links between social, economic and institutional factors on the one hand, and fundamental state properties on the other, then it would be a blend of both art and craft.

Trying to find a reasonable answer to the question of why one should engage in comparative politics, one may underline the likelihood or the prediction of the probability of an increase in the number of democratic states (Modelski and Perry, 1991). Or one may put the emphasis on feasibility, that is, specifying the action conditions for a policy to enhance the prospects of democracy (Lijphart, 1990; Allison and Beschel, 1992). In his *Preparing for the Twenty-First Century* (1993), Paul Kennedy attempts to identify some of the main social, economic and political frameworks that structure the actions of men and women. Comparative government could contribute here by identifying the variety of conditions that impact upon state stability and state performance. It may not be able to predict accurately single events of historical importance, but it can display what is feasible or likely in macropolitics.

1

Comparative Approaches

Introduction

Comparative politics as a discipline may be described as the study of the similarities and differences in the macropolitical institutions of the countries of the world, including the attempt to account for the patterns of country variation (Eckstein and Apter, 1963; Keman, 1993). We undertake here an overview of a few approaches to comparative government in order to pin down how two main topics in the comparative analysis of political systems – state stability and state performance – have been studied. The overview is selective and makes no claim to be comprehensive or to present an analysis of the evolution of major theories. The purpose is to see how the stability and performance of states have been modelled explicitly or implicitly in comparative politics.

Legitimacy

Max Weber engaged in a number of comparative studies, one of which is his analysis of historical structures of authority (Weber, [1922] 1978). Compared with his broad comparative analysis of various religions and their consequences for economics and politics, the analysis of political regimes in *Wirtschaft und Gesellschaft* is short but succinct.

It seems that, to Weber 'Autorität' has the same meaning as 'Herrschaft', standing for obedience relationships. People obey leaders in authority structures, one of which is the state. Weber defines 'Staat' as the organization that successfully upholds a claim to the monopoly on the legitimate exercise of force. And people may obey leaders out of expediency, minimizing the costs of non-compliance, or out of a belief in the legitimacy of authority; there exist three reasons for the belief in legitimacy: tradition, charisma or legal rationality.

The Weber model focuses on stability, claiming that authority structures are stable to the extent that such structures are institutionalized. Relationships based on naked power or authority exercised by means of coercion or threats of coercion are unstable, whereas the belief in the legitimacy of authority – considering the authority structure to be valid – is conducive to its stability. And typical of Occidental societies, in contradistinction to the Oriental ones, is the systematic rationalization of all belief-systems, including the political interpretations about the legitimacy of authority.

Weber's basic idea is that the overall trend is towards the legal-rational type of systems of political authority. Traditional authority systems, though legitimate, are not grounded on rational deliberations but stem from supernatural ideas which cannot withstand the seminal rationalization trend as expressed in the development of Western capitalist institutions in the economy. Charismatic rule is capable of breaking the spell of traditional authority, but it requires the routinization of charisma as everyday life returns after the period of change.

Weber's model of state stability was an attempt to come to grips with dynamic aspects at the macrolevel of politics. Weber's paradigm influenced both comparative enquiry and the historical investigation of systems of rulership, ancient, medieval and modern (Wittfogel, 1957; Eisenstadt, 1963; Bendix, 1978).

Democracy, constitutional government and power

Weber looked at historical categories of regimes, but typical of much of the evolution of comparative politics in the twentieth century has been the preoccupation with one type of regime: democracy. Besides engaging in configurative studies of a parochial set of political systems, James Bryce attempted in *Modern Democracies* to arrive at some principles concerning the nature of a democratic regime by means of an inductive method looking at the 'facts' (Bryce, 1921).

Bryce employed the comparative method describing a number of political systems – ancient Athens, the republics of Latin America, France, Switzerland, Canada, the United States, Australia and New Zealand – in order to arrive at what he considered constant in human behaviour: a set of psychological principles promoting democracy.

The basic question is whether democracy can work, and the argument is that a successful democracy requires a moderating legislature such as the British House of Commons, which in turn depends on the moral character of the people in the country. A legislature of the British type means that sharp and divisive conflict is avoided and that government expediency is emphasized to the exclusion of caucuses and opportunists.

A number of structural factors are adduced as conducive to the type of national spirit that fosters a consensus-orientated oligarchy governing a

democracy: a small size of polity, a homogeneous social structure, an agricul-
turally based economy, and a history of successful resolutions of conflicts in
a democratic fashion.

The Bryce model of the conditions for successful democracy may be
interpreted as an attempt at understanding both state stability and performance, both perspectives combined in the frequently used concept of a stable
democracy. Bryce's strong preference for British democracy – adversarial or
Westminster-type democracy – has been challenged by scholars who argue
that there are other models relevant to the interpretation of the stability of
the democratic state. Bryce initiates the search for models that either look
upon institutions as being in the Lijphart tradition (1968, 1984) or see
economic factors (affluence) and social conditions (industrialization, urbanization) as being conducive to a viable democratic state, as in the Lipset
tradition (1959).

When focusing on the internal structure of democracy, Carl Friedrich saw
democracies as species of constitutional government. The label 'constitutional' has a strong performance ring, as it denotes legality, division of
power and civic rights. A variety of mechanisms may be identified with
constitutional rule.

In *Constitutional Government and Democracy* (1950) Friedrich underlines three requisites for this type of regime: institutional properties, social
conditions and cultural characteristics. To the first category belong a responsible bureaucracy, an effective diplomatic service, an efficient and powerful
judiciary, a deliberating legislature, separation of powers and a constitutional arbitration system. That conditions such as responsibility, efficiency
and deliberation may enhance democratic rule is hardly a surprising
statement. We need to look at the operation of alternative institutional
arrangements. Friedrich himself mentions a two-party system and a plurality
election system, but why should only these institutions matter crucially?

The second category comprises economic affluence, informative media of
communication and extensive political integration of various interests in
society, and the third consists of a viable political tradition where democracy
feeds on consent between diverging groups and is impaired by animosity
between major social interests. What is required is a sort of balanced heterogeneity in society and politics – democracy being threatened by the intensity
of political and social conflict, particularly concerning fundamental procedures and ultimate objectives.

Arguing that the study of comparative government had to be based on
an explicit deliberation about fundamental concepts, Karl Loewenstein
favoured the concept of power. He claimed in *Political Power and the
Government Process* that the distinction between democracy and autocracy
was essential to the understanding of modern political systems. The modern
democratic-constitutional state tries to establish an equilibrium between the
various competitive and pluralistic forces within society. In modern autocracy, social control and political power are monopolized by a single power

holder, subordinating the individual to the ideological requirements of the group dominating the state (Loewenstein, 1965: 7).

How are we to measure the distinction between authoritarian and democratic states? We may wish to identify degrees of democracy – meaning that the distinction involved is more than a simple dichotomy. Is it possible to move from qualitative observations about different kinds of political systems to a quantitative representation of system properties?

Herman Finer's *The Theory and Practice of Modern Government* presented a synthesis of reflections on several major themes in comparative politics (Finer, 1950). Although his analysis is much influenced by the conflict between democratic ideology and authoritarianism during the interwar years, it covers not only the governments of Britain, the United States, France, Germany, Fascist Italy and the Soviet Union, but also themes that were bypassed in the traditional approach to comparative politics, such as the consequences of economic systems.

Finer states that two things are necessary to a 'complete act of government': to resolve and to execute. The centres of the first, the resolving branch of government, are the electorate, the political parties, the legislature (parliament or congress), the cabinet and the chief of state. The centres of the second, the executive branch, are the cabinet, the chief of state, the civil service and the courts of justice (Finer, 1950: 109). The identification of both politics and administration as the targets for enquiry in comparative politics no doubt increased the scope of comparative analysis of the state (Peters, 1987; Rowat, 1988).

Finer's model of the state comprised seven dimensions in a political system across which the institutions may vary: (1) the electorate, (2) parties, (3) the legislature, (4) the cabinet, (5) the presidency, (6) the administration and (7) the courts of justice. Here, Finer identifies institutions of central importance in the analysis of politics at the macrolevel. But he rests content to concentrate on only two fundamental polar types beneath the variety of manifestations of these basic seven entities, namely, the democratic regime and the authoritarian regime. How much do various regime typologies in comparative politics differ?

Functionalism

A major political science methodology popular in the late 1950s and 1960s was the functionalist approach, which influenced comparative enquiry. Its typical focus, if not its bias, was stability. Functionalism grew out of anthropological (Malinowski, 1922; Fortes and Evans-Pritchard, 1940) as well as cultural studies (Kluckhohn and Leighton, 1946; Radcliffe-Brown, 1952), which broadened the study of politics to include so-called stateless societies (Cohen and Middleton, 1967).

Functionalism as a general methodology in sociology was based on the hypothesis that the operation of a variety of behaviour structures led to or resulted in the same outcomes or 'functions' (Parsons, 1951; Levy, 1952; Jones, 1967). The comparatist would first try to identify invariant functions, presumably present in all social systems. Second, he/she should proceed to analyse how structures could vary from one polity to another but result in the same omnipresent or invariant functions.

Gabriel Almond (1960) conceived of the political system as fulfilling functions in terms of structures. On the one hand, there are input functions: political socialization and recruitment, interest articulation, interest aggregation and political communication. On the other hand, there is the set of output functions: rule-making, rule application and rule adjudication (Almond and Coleman, 1960: 17). Structures were the institutions or behaviour patterns whose operation resulted in one of these six basic functions.

'Multifunctionality' referred to the basic tenet in functionalist models that different structures could fulfil the same functions, placing the analysis of structural variation across space or through time at the heart of comparative politics. In Almond and Bingham Powell's *Comparative Politics* the model, though basically functionalist, incorporated a systems approach derived from David Easton (see pp. 17–19). Almond and Powell speak of inputs and outputs. Political systems have a varied capacity for handling inputs and outputs as conceptualized in the idea of system capacity (Almond and Powell, 1966: 29).

Political systems vary with regard to their internal functioning: conversion processes which consist of the transformation of demands and support (inputs) into authoritative decisions to be implemented (outputs) (Almond and Powell, 1966: 29). In addition there are system maintenance and adaptation functions. Almond and Powell identify four types of challenge to a political system: state building, nation building, participation and distribution. Political development was specified as the degree of specificity with which concrete structures fulfil omnipresent functions as well as the extent to which political structures are distinct from one another.

Almond and Powell suggested a comparative theory of the political system where its crucial notion about political development refers to three aspects: differentiation, autonomy and secularization. Their model claims that the more modern or developed a system is, the more it is characterized by structural differentiation, subsystem autonomy and secularization in the political culture. And it stated that the development of higher levels of system capabilities was dependent on greater structural differentiation and cultural secularization (Almond and Powell, 1966: 323). Political development implied both increasing state stability and better state performance records.

Attempts to clarify the troublesome concept of political development resulted in definitions that identified various characteristics, for example, those involved in the political prerequisites of economic development or the politics typical of industrial societies; factors in political modernization and the operation of a nation-state; those in administrative and legal development or mass mobilization and participation; and factors in the building of democracy or in stability and orderly change such as mass mobilization (Pye, 1966). How could so many factors in complex processes of social and political change be called 'political development'?

James S. Coleman singled out differentiation and capacity, alongside equality, as typical of political development. He regarded political development as the acquisition by a polity of the capacity to be manifested in the institutionalization of (1) new patterns of integration regulating and containing the tensions and conflicts produced by increased differentiation, and (2) new patterns of participation and resource distribution adequately responsive to the demands generated by the imperatives of equality (Coleman, 1965: 15).

The addition of equality and participation to system capacity and differentiation made the concept of political development even more labyrinthine, as these aspects need not accompany the two other aspects of political development. Any hypotheses about ties between system capacity and structural differentiation may be questioned, just as the claim that political participation and equality were related to these two features of a political system.

The concept of political development has been a matter of contention because it was approached differently in several models (Weiner and Huntington, 1987). In addition, there exist a number of interesting change phenomena that fall outside the functionalist approach, such as conflict and revolution. Around the whole notion of modernization there built up a body of theory which was open to the accusation that it was based on concealed value premises about what is to count as modern. The literature on political change processes remains amorphous in that some employ empirical indicators and statistical tools, whereas others remain confident in presenting theoretical arguments (Leftwich, 1990).

Samuel Huntington argued that institutionalization is basic to state stability involving increased adaptability, complexity, autonomy and coherence of the polity. Political development is not the smooth and harmonious development of Western-type institutions modernizing unadaptable traditional ones. Instead he launched an institutionalist model focusing upon the conflictive introduction of modernized leadership, whether democratic or authoritarian, which was not necessarily in agreement with some Western blueprint of 'modern' government.

Yet the measurement of the process of political institutionalization entails a complex procedure (Huntington and Dominguez, 1975). Autonomy could be measured by the distinctiveness of the norms and values of the organization and by the extent to which the organization controls material resources. Coherence could be tapped by the number of contested successions in relation to total successions, by the number of cleavages among leaders and members, and by the occurrence of alienation and dissent within the organization as well as by the loyalty of organization members (Huntington, 1965: 404–5).

The models of the functionalists involved a number of problems for comparative research that were never resolved. For example, when political development is identified with system capacity and system differentiation, the functionalist model implies that political development is somehow a function of increase in statehood: the stronger the state the more political development. However, when political development is identified with autonomy and system differentiation, there is a sort of contradiction in so far as it means less state involvement: the more subsystem autonomy, the more developed is the political system.

The dependency school

The functionalist theory about a natural development towards a modern polity for the Third World countries was strongly rebutted by scholars adhering to the so-called underdevelopment theory. The state of under-development was not the starting-point for Third World countries but the end-state or outcome of centuries of economic exploitation and political domination by the European powers as well as the United States. The entire framework of modernization theories, with its Marxist theories of imperial-ism, was criticized as biased and incapable of explaining why countries in Latin America had actually started to underdevelop with the penetration of the Western capitalist economic system into the hinterland of the world (Frank, 1967; Szentes, 1983).

Theories of comparative politics often neglect the impact of international politics in general, and international regimes in particular, upon state stab-ility and performance. A number of scholars have tried to close this all too wide gap by suggesting models of international systems. Perhaps the best-known ones are the core-periphery model, the centre-hinterland model and the world-systems model (Galtung, 1971; Wallerstein, 1974).

The so-called *dependencistas* emphasized the implications of economic conditions upon state stability and performance, in particular the conse-quences for the Third World countries of the development of capitalism (Smith T., 1991: 119). Although the dependency school may be traced back to Hobson's theory of imperialism, much work in the 1970s and 1980s paid attention to the variety of economic developments in different Third World countries as well as to their political correlates, as, for example, with that of Henrique Cardoso (Cardoso and Faletto, 1979). The dependency framework opened up important perspectives on the political consequences of increasing indebtedness and highly uneven economic growth processes in various parts of the Third World.

The systems approach

The systems perspective was launched in Easton's well-known books *A Framework for Political Analysis* and *A Systems Analysis of Political Life*

(1965). His systems approach belongs to general social theory. Firstly, Easton provided a new coherent perspective for comparative politics – the framework of the political system as an input–output system. Secondly, he suggested a special theory about the conditions for the persistence of political systems.

The general model suggested by Easton placed the polity in a dynamic context, the political system receiving inputs from the environment in the form of demands on the one hand and support on the other. These inputs are handled by means of the conversion processes of the system resulting in the outputs of the polity: decisions and actions. These performance outputs are monitored back to the polity by means of an information feedback loop, new demands and support reacting on the outcomes of these actions and decisions, all affecting the stability of the political system (Easton, 1965a).

Easton used the model to illuminate the question of how political systems persist, asking how any and all political systems manage to prevail in a world of both stability and change. Ultimately he tried to reveal the 'life processes of political systems': the fundamental functions without which no system could endure and the typical modes of response through which systems sustain themselves (Easton, 1965b).

Easton was preoccupied with the problem of polity stability. A distinction is often made between the *genetic* problem of how a regime comes into existence and the *persistence* problem of how stable a regime proves to be. Both problems are interesting in comparative enquiry, but they require different treatment. Easton focused heavily on system persistence, almost stating that persistence was some kind of natural equilibrium that political systems would tend towards.

Easton's model amounted to a general theory because it covered all political systems, stating necessary or sufficient conditions for regime persistence. For example, if a political system of any kind – democratic, authoritarian, traditional, primitive – persists, then some conditions are satisfied, such as a certain level of support for the regime or not too many demands on the leaders. However, Easton mixed the polity survival problem (first problem) with another problem, namely the conditions for social order in general.

Easton's objective was to extract from the total political reality those aspects that are the fundamental activities without which no political life in society could continue. This (second) problem can be formulated in the following way: what are the necessary conditions for social order? There are some necessary conditions for social order, for example, that the society persists biologically and that it is not characterized by anarchy or anomie. If these conditions are satisfied, then there is a framework for variation for different kinds of political systems or regimes.

If a regime or a state ceases to exist, there may be alternative political systems to replace it. Consequently there are two different types of persistence conditions: (1) those necessary conditions which, if they are not present, exclude social order; (2) those necessary conditions which, if they are not

Regime	Social order in a society	
	Existing	Non-existing
Persisting	USA, United Kingdom, China	Marginal cases: Kabul regime, Bosnia 1992–
Non-persisting	France 1958, Spain 1975, USSR 1991	Lebanon 1980s, Somalia 1991–, Cambodia

Figure 1.1   Political system persistence and social order

present, exclude one regime or a specific state. A political system may perish, even though the necessary conditions for political life are satisfied, because it may be replaced by another system. The distinction is illustrated in figure 1.1.

Systems theory underlined notions such as system persistence and regime survival. Can we deal with an important macroconcept such as state stability without the notion of a teleological drive towards a steady state or equilibrium? In *Modern Comparative Politics* Merkl pointed out the bias in functionalism and systems analysis, in particular in the notions of 'pattern maintenance', 'stable equilibrium' or 'system persistence'. Rather than stability and equilibrium, instability and disequilibrium are far more typical of contemporary societies, whether they be developing or already highly developed (Merkl, 1977: 19).

Crisis theory and revolutions

One approach that focused heavily on instability was presented in Joseph LaPalombara's *Politics within Nations* (1974), which looked at how states face specific challenges which must be met if they are to survive. Instrumental in the variation in comparative politics are the degrees of freedom of states when they react to a set of crisis phenomena.

Nation building is an ongoing process in several countries where other ties compete with national identification – tribal, rural or local (identity crisis). It involves, first and foremost, a belief in legitimacy directed towards political institutions from among those affected by the exercise of political power. A stable polity tends to be one where considerable legitimacy is accorded the basic institutions of government (legitimacy crisis). Then there is the question of the organizational capabilities of the state to maintain control over its territory and manage its internal affairs (penetration crisis). Furthermore, a society channels the quest for participation in its various expressions where the institutionalization of mechanisms for elite representation and mass involvement are important (participation crisis). Finally, a state has to meet the material and immaterial expectations of the people in a country, and this constitutes the most omnipresent crisis phenomenon of the states of today. The question of equality in the distribution of life opportunities is highly relevant from a political point of view (distribution crisis).

Governments today are confronted with crises phenomena (LaPalombara, 1974: 568). Do different kinds of government perform differently in relation to these? A state perspective includes the making and implementation of public policies as well as their social and economic outcomes.

Another approach referring to change in general and violent transition in particular is to be found in Ted R. Gurr's comparative work. In *Why Men Rebel* Gurr emphasizes state instability, approaching macropolitics as sequences of revolutionary processes involving various kinds of political violence (Gurr, 1970). Basically, Gurr points out poor state performance as a major cause of state instability, which may be tapped by measuring economic deprivation and political repression. One cannot take for granted that states have a natural tendency towards stability. On the contrary, political conflict and its sources in poor state performance must be at the heart of comparative politics (Gurr, 1980).

Towards institutionalism

Around 1970 there evolved in comparative politics what has come to be called the modern approach. It displayed a strong urge to make the study of government truly comparative – embracing all kinds of states to be analysed by means of abstract models to be tested by quantitative data. After the functionalist and systems analysis frameworks, which were orientated towards functions, inputs and outputs, there was again a strong interest in political institutions at the macrolevel.

Blondel

Jean Blondel's *An Introduction to Comparative Government* (1969) made norms the crucial element, as they pattern how government behaves and what it accomplishes, comprising three crucial aspects: participation, means of government and purpose of government. Whereas typologies often build on models that remain implicit in comparative enquiries, here we had an explicit framework of comparative concepts focusing on performance.

Norms specify how processes managing social conflicts are structured: who participates, what tools are employed when conflicts are resolved and, finally, what policies are implemented. The modes of participation include elite versus mass participation; the modes of government operation involve liberal versus authoritarian tools; and the modes of government policies can be classified as either radical or conservative.

In the revised edition of his earlier work, *Comparative Government* (1990), Blondel identifies a few essential aspects of contemporary states. *Participation* is the extent to which there is a mass society, or a continuum from monarchy to democracy. The *means of government* vary in a monolithic or pluralistic society according to the freedom of the press, meetings and political parties. The *ends of government* are defined by the probability that citizens can move up the social ladder as well as the degree to which resources are owned privately, or degree of radicalism or socialism.

The combination of these three dimensions gives a number of categories that Blondel employs to derive a list of five types of political or state regimes (1990: 25–32): (1) liberal-democratic regimes, (2) egalitarian-authoritarian regimes, (3) traditional-inegalitarian regimes, (4) populist regimes and (5) authoritarian-inegalitarian regimes.

Whereas communist systems score low on participation and high on radicalism, regimes in developing countries are characterized by somewhat more participation but less radicalism, while at the same time being less harsh than the communist regimes when it comes to means of government. On the other hand, according to Blondel, the rich Western countries offer high levels of participation and liberal means of government without being either conservative or radical concerning the ends of government policies.

It may be argued that the Third World countries form much too amorphous a set to be described as medium on participation, with semi-authoritarian tools of government as well as rather conservative policy-making. Among the Third World countries we find very different types, from the liberal-democratic touch of India to military junta suppression in Argentina, or a regime involving genocide, such as that of the Khmer Rouge in South-East Asia. And we may also wish to make distinctions in the set of Western liberal countries with regard to performance record, some scoring higher on radicalism than others in terms of, for example, welfare spending or actual income equality.

Finer

Another well-known comparative volume was published by Samuel E. Finer in 1970. It starts with a separation between private and public government, government in general being standardized arrangements for taking decisions affecting the group and for giving effect to them. All groups, whether face-to-face groups such as the family or a religious group such as the church, have government procedures, but public government stands for the government of the 'territorial state' (Finer, 1970: 37). A task for comparative government is to establish first how, and then, as far as possible, why, states vary along a number of different dimensions (Finer, 1970: 38).

1) *Participation versus exclusion* Even if all government is the exercise of power by an elite over the population in a country, what may vary

is the involvement of the masses in government by the few or the many. On the one hand, we have the extreme form of direct democracy in the shape of the referendum and, on the other, the polar extreme type of popular submission. In between there is the representational mode, which provides the masses with a mechanism of popular control.

2) *Coercion versus persuasion*   Some rulers rely on coercion and rule by means of fear. A less repressive form of rulership is the combination of manipulation and deference in traditional societies, where tribal chiefs, sheikhs, religious leaders or noblemen rule. Among the developing countries one type of rulership is to regiment the population by monopolistic groups, as in, for example, a one-party state relying on new nationalistic symbols. Finally, there is bargaining based on the cognition of interests among various social groups, the typical way of governing a liberal democracy.

3) *Sub-group autonomy versus sub-group dependence*   The overall position of societal groups in relation to those in power may vary. In some societies, groups may constitute themselves freely, express their particular interests and viewpoints and intervene in the political process up to the point of criticizing or even hindering the activities of the government (Finer, 1970: 49). In others, groups can express their views and interests only to the extent that the government allows. Far from criticizing, let alone frustrating, the activities of the government, collective action is expected to conform to and actually further its policies in every way (Finer, 1970: 48).

4) *Representativeness versus order*   Public government may enhance the maintenance of law and order, bringing about predictability. However, the notion of representativeness means that government changes its operations to fit with public opinion. What is necessary is a trade-off by states between these two demands, emphasizing either order or representativeness.

5) *Present goals versus future goals*   When a government makes policies it is under pressure to consider both present-day goals according to the responsiveness theme and future goals as they may currently impinge on policy-making. And these goals may not be in agreement with one another. Thus some governments make promises for the future whereas others rely on present-day goals (Finer, 1970: 53).

The Finer framework (see figure 1.2) is a combination of institutional properties of the state, dividing the states of the world into five main kinds of system: (1) the liberal-democratic state; (2) the totalitarian state; (3) the quasi-democratic regime; (4) the façade democracy; (5) the military regime (Finer, 1970: 55). Such a state typology remains relevant for the understanding of comparative government in the early 1990s.

A crucial question in relation to these regime types concerns their viability. Whereas the military regime tends *ipso facto* to be unstable, the sources of

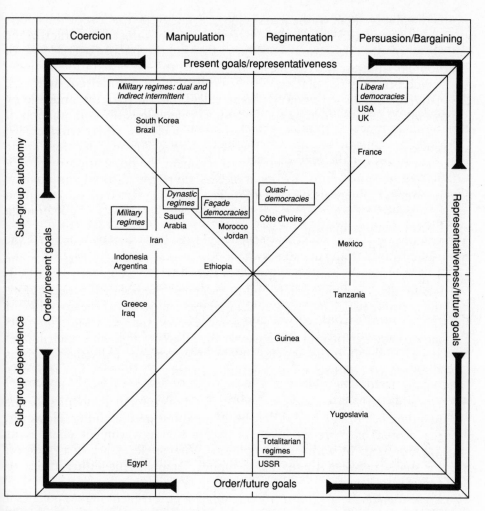

Figure 1.2 The Finer framework

the stability of a democratic state need to be researched among a broad set of social, economic and institutional factors.

Linz

Which states belong to the set of non-democracies? How are they to be identified and can we speak of various types of non-dictatorship? Juan Linz has dealt in particular with the problem of sorting out the basic kinds of non-democratic types, as, for example, in 'Totalitarian and authoritarian regimes' (1975). There is in fact considerable agreement as to which political systems are to be designated the 'stable democratic' polities. Only in regard to countries such as Mexico, Sri Lanka and Colombia is there real disagreement.

Linz's basic argument is that to state that a political system is non-democratic does not amount to much if one does not also state something positive concerning what actually characterizes such a system. An authoritarian political system is not simply a dictatorship in the sense of one-man rule; a dictatorship is a transitory polity which may develop into an authoritarian regime when the exercise of power is institutionalized. Nor is authoritarianism the same as totalitarianism; a totalitarian regime is one in which (1) power is monistic but not monolithic; (2) there is an elaborate ideology which provides for the legitimization of the regime and a Weltanschauung for cultural life; and (3) citizens participate and are highly mobilized in terms of the ideology of the single ruling party.

An authoritarian regime may be a stable system of rule, according to Linz. It is a mixture of democracy and totalitarianism. In terms of performance the authoritarian polity stands between the pluralism of democracies and the monism of totalitarian rule, in between the moderate multi-ideological belief system of the former and the ideological penetration of the latter, and without the intensive political participation of the masses in totalitarian systems and the openness of power elite groups in democracies. Authoritarianism is different from the contestation and participation typical of a democratic polity, yet not identical with the one-dimensional nature of the power systems in totalitarian regimes, with their heavy mobilization of the masses.

Authoritarian regimes differ along three basic dimensions: the extent of limited pluralism, the degree and type of participation and the extent of ideological penetration of one single belief-system. They are easily separated from democratic regimes, but the border-line with totalitarian ones is less strict (O'Donnell, 1988).

We find bureaucratic authoritarianism in Latin-American countries during various periods of time alternating in a peculiar circular fashion with democracy or semi-democracy. Bureaucratic authoritarian regimes may be created by military coups, as in Brazil in 1964 and in Argentina in 1966, or they may emerge out of earlier Fascist experiences, as in Spain and Portugal at the end of the Franco and Salazar periods. Typically such regimes involve limited participation channelled in a manner that has been set up as a reaction to radical movements threatening both the established order and the future of a democratic polity. Such regimes may develop a more comprehensive supporting ideology, such as organic statism or what Schmitter calls 'state corporatism' (1983).

Comparative public policy

The performance perspective in comparative government has been much researched in the emerging field of comparative public policy. Traditionally nothing was said about what governments actually did, as the focus of interest was on the structure of the state. To look at policy outputs or governmental programmes and policy outcomes or social results in a comparative perspective added a new dimension to the discipline.

The orientation of comparative politics towards public policy was based on the attempt to understand what different states propose (policy outputs) and what they actually accomplish (policy outcomes) (Heady, 1979; Heidenheimer, Heclo and Adams, 1990; Wildavsky, 1986). Granting the institutional differences between various states in terms of governmental structures, citizens' rights and political party or trade union operations, are these distinctions relevant for the understanding of allocative and redistributive differences (Castles, 1982; Castles, Lehner and Schmidt, 1988)?

The intersection between comparative politics and public policy is the focus on state performance. Do regime properties matter for policies and outcomes? Regimes may be valued for their own sake or for their value as instruments for the accomplishment of social goals. Questions about state performance are of crucial importance in the evaluation of various political systems. There is a large set of problems here for comparative research dealing with policy outputs and outcomes.

There are a number of models that offer explanations of the consequences of government operations. State effects may relate either to general performance dimensions, such as polity durability, civil order, legitimacy and decisional efficacy (Eckstein, 1971; Gurr and McClelland, 1971), or to specific policy outputs or policy outcomes (Wilensky, 1975; Frey, 1978; Whiteley, 1986).

Actually, a number of polity performance or public policy models were suggested as the comparative analysis of the output side of the state gained momentum. These models pointed out policy determinants among such nonpolitical factors as affluence, urbanization and industrialization, but it was also argued that politics matter, whether in the form of institutions or by actions of the major actors in the state.

Policy outputs are typically measured by means of public finance data stating the per capita cost of a programme or the percentage of the budget or GNP allocated to an item of expenditure. Aaron Wildavsky's *Budgeting: a Comparative Theory of Budgetary Processes* (1986) suggests a conceptual schema for the analysis of differences in national budgeting systems (see figure 1.3). Budgeting involves three variables: resources, goals and situations. Since budgeting involves the allotment of resources it treats issues concerning taxation and economic policy. As it deals with goals it becomes a mechanism for the resolution of conflicts about priorities.

The classification is based on two pairs of variables: certain–uncertain and rich–poor. The first pair relates to the input–output of allocation systems: the degree of probability that predicted resources will flow into the system and that resources will leave the system in the way predicted. The second pair

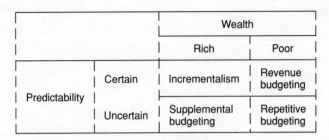

Figure 1.3   Types of budgetary structure

relates, of course, to the availability of funds. Repetitive or supplemental budgeting would tend to occur in Third World polities, whereas incrementalism or revenue budgeting would occur among the OECD countries. In order to take the comparative analysis of state activities one step further, it is necessary to formulate models about polity performance, polity outputs and polity outcomes.

Some major problems in comparative politics

Comparative politics, or the study of the governments of the countries of the world, has developed in a striking fashion during the postwar period. As described in the Introduction, the traditional approach has been abandoned both theoretically and empirically. It is now recognized that the discipline needs the elaboration of explicit and abstract concepts. And advance in comparative knowledge is dependent on the use of measurement procedures and systematic data analysis.

Comparative politics deals with a more or less specific set of questions. Here we have identified a set of crucial problems: (1) stability of authority, (2) democracy and democratic prerequisites, (3) political system functions and structures, (4) political development, (5) institutionalization, (6) polity persistence, crises and revolution and (7) political performance.

The list could easily be enlarged, for there is neither any limit to what should be included in comparative politics nor any method that allows us to select *the* most appropriate framework for comparative enquiry.

Implicitly or explicitly, comparative politics discusses questions about the institutional structure of the state as it affects stability and performance. The causes of the wide differences in the stability and performance of states are sought in a variety of conditions. Generally speaking, there are several highly salient problems in comparative politics, one of which focuses on state stability and its very varied modes, and another looks at state performance and its different expressions.

Conclusion

Comparative politics, we suggest, is basically an attempt to interpret states, how they persist and how they perform. Is it possible to look at the field of comparative politics in terms of state models, that is, hypotheses about the factors that have an impact upon the variation in stability and performance of states? Our purpose is to make a contribution to the field of comparative government by looking at the major models used in the analysis of the states of the world, explaining the variation in state stability and state performance.

There is no generally accepted conceptual paradigm in comparative government. Rather there is sharp competition between models and alternative approaches. Often the presentation of various pieces of knowledge is rather eclectic, starting from the input side of the political system and moving to the output side by way of analysis of the basic institutions at the macrolevel of politics. An alternative to the input–output scheme so typical of much of comparative politics is to start from the identification of a set of models that systematize the knowledge in this field of research by looking at interrelationships between the state and conditions that have an impact on stability and performance. What are the basic characteristics of states today? Let us begin the empirical analysis of identifying them.

2

States in the World

Introduction

Comparative politics has to decide what its universe of discourse is to be. What is the unit of analysis when modelling various properties and relationships in the conduct of comparative enquiry? There are a few alternatives, but here we argue that, rather than 'political system', 'polity', 'government' or 'nation', 'the state' is the best choice.

However, the concept of the state is an essentially contested notion. The theoretical debate around the meaning of the word 'state' or 'Staat' is extensive, to say the least (Jellinek, 1966; Skocpol, 1979; Held, 1989). The basic problem is to identify the typical properties of the set of states, very large ones in terms of population, such as China, India, the United States and Brazil, as well as tiny ones, such as Iceland, Botswana, Costa Rica and Papua New Guinea. We focus on one well-known definition of the concept of the state, and in this chapter we identify the states that the analysis in the volume will cover.

Politics may be interpreted as a general phenomenon concerning the exercise of power, occurring in all kinds of social systems: primary groups, kinship, neighbourhood groups, large villages or small towns and small cities, big cities or metropolitan areas, small states, medium-sized states, large sub-states, giant nation-states or huge multi-ethnic states, and finally large interest organizations and the big international organizations such as the UN, WHO, ILO and FAO. Political systems may be identified in all kinds of social systems (Easton, 1965a).

A polity is a more specific political phenomenon as it is tied to the following concepts: country or nation, the political body as a set of citizens, or a specific territory organized politically. Comparative politics looks at politics at the macrolevel or at the polity level, or as denoted by the label we prefer: 'states'. In this chapter we enter into a preliminary discussion regarding the states of the world.

State definitions

Much speculation has focused on the nature of the state. What its fundamental characteristics are is closely tied up with the difficult question about the state concept, its meaning or connotations. What are the typical properties of the state? To constitutionalists the state is a law-orientated organization, creating rules as well as following them. To power realists the basic property of the state is the use, or threat of use, of physical force. Some definitions of the 'state' underline legitimacy whereas others emphasize power and might.

The search for a definition of the concept of the state has resulted in a number of state theories which are not in agreement with regard to the necessary and sufficient properties that would identify such a concept (Vincent, 1987; Dunleavy and O'Leary, 1987). Yet talking about the reference or denotation of 'state' or 'Staat' is not as puzzling as the discussion about the connotation of 'state'.

Whether a state may be said to exist or not in a given society is most of the time quite clear-cut, since there are standard indicators that provide guidance. True, in marginal cases it may not be easy to tell whether there actually is a state. A state may cease to exist, as in Lebanon in the early 1980s, for example, or as in Somalia in the early 1990s, resulting in anarchy. Or it may not be clear whether an organization can really be called a 'state': is there literally a Vatican state? Or one state may be broken up into several states, as in the former Yugoslavia, where claims to territorial sovereignty are a cause of civil war.

As long as one demands only what the word 'state' stands for in reality, specifying a few necessary or sufficient criteria that allow us to apply the concept in the real world, things are not that difficult. Several standard reference books list the number of existing states. Speaking generally, a state is a phenomenological concept, that is, an organization that is labelled 'state' by various actors.

If the problem of the concept's present-day reference is not a major one, because it may be solved by means of standard identification criteria, then its historical application shows up more of the difficulties. When did states first appear? Were there states in a similar sense among the Romans, in ancient China, in the Middle Ages and in pre-colonial India and Africa? When did a kind of modern Western-type state appear for the first time? The problem of the origins of the state concept remains a topic for discussion and disagreement (Evans et al., 1985; Poggi, 1990).

The Weberian state

Although the definition of the concept of the state suggested by Weber is only one among many, it has proven useful for comparative research. His *Wirtschaft und Gesellschaft* comprises a systematic presentation of 'basic sociological terms' (1978: 3–62), among which is the concept of the state. After having introduced his theories of authority and of a ruling organization, starting from the elementary concept of a social action as intentional behaviour, Weber arrives at the following:

> A compulsory political organization [politischer Anstaltsbetrieb] with continuous operations will be called a 'state' insofar as its administrative staff successfully upholds the claim to the monopoly of the legitimate use of physical force in the enforcement of its order (Weber, 1978: 54).

There are a few properties mentioned here that can help us delimit a set of states: monopoly on physical force, legitimacy of a system of rules, continuous activity within a territory, obligatory membership of the citizens in a population. In whatever way one approaches the issue of a definition of the concept of the state, there are bound to be border-line cases. How many states are there now in the territory of the former USSR?

A state may also be characterized by its special mode of organization: laws, resources by means of taxation and its numerous personnel (Rose, 1984). Below, however, we will employ the concept of the Weberian state. Its strength is that it focuses on few visible insignia of the state, but actually on the monopoly of the application of legitimate physical violence within a specific territory. This is well expressed in the international criteria for the recognition of a state. It should be pointed out that it makes no commitment as to any properties of a nation, thus not mingling the two separate concepts of a state and a nation into 'nation-state'.

What is a nation-state?

It is often asserted that the most powerful community today is the 'modern nation-state'. What is, then, such a state? Let us look at Karl Deutsch's analysis in *Politics and Government* (1980), where politics is looked upon as public decision-making in terms of elections, referenda, laws, courts and administration.

Crucial in politics is government as 'the direction and self-direction of large communities of people' (Deutsch, 1980: 7). A state is the organized machinery for the making and carrying out of political decisions and for the enforcing of the laws and rules of a government. The state includes not only officials and office buildings, but also soldiers, police officers and jails.

A nation-state is a state that recognizes no higher decision-making power outside itself – a 'sovereign' state. Typical of a state is the tie to a country – a geographical area of 'material, economic, physical, and psychological independence' (Deutsch, 1980: 117). Such geographical areas may be populated by what may be designated as a 'people', that is, a group of persons with a linguistic or cultural identity. Or such an area may host two or more peoples – a multi-ethnic state, as it were. The occurrence of several ethnic or culturally distinct groups within a nation-state – sectionalism – may affect the strength of the state, as internal conflict is more probable in 'divided' states.

Deutsch underlines the dynamic aspect of states: 'their ability to steer themselves' in accordance with his cybernetic framework (Deutsch, 1963). A cybernetic perspective on the nation-state involves emphasizing goals, decision-making and implementation, information and feed-back as well as memory and coordination. The process and machinery of government is orientated towards these elements in the steering loop and the performance of polities. And power is the central derivative property in political systems, its location determining the nature of the steering system (Deutsch, 1980: 150).

Political systems such as nation-states may be centrifugal (decentralized) or centripetal (centralized) and they may be associationist or dissociationist, depending on the existence of autonomous, small self-governing groups such as local governments, labour unions, cooperatives and churches. Figure 2.1 shows a 2 × 2 table when combining these two distinctions concerning the location of power (Deutsch, 1980: 216). Here we have a set of concepts that is tied to that of the nation-state, but not all states are nation-states. Moreover, do the requirements on a modern state really imply the existence of a nation?

In the field of political sociology, Stein Rokkan, with his well-known theory of 'nation building', has examined the process of state establishment (Rokkan et al., 1970). The establishment of several modern states in Western Europe was a continuous process of institution building in countries where there was a high degree of social cohesion. Rokkan divided the nation-building process into various stages in relation to the three major courses of development since the sixteenth century: the centre versus periphery conflict, expanding the powers of central government; the state versus church conflict in the wake of the secularization process; and finally the industrial revolution, with its conflict between capital and labour.

Rokkan predicted that the process of nation building resulting in a compact state would be much more difficult a task in societies where there is social heterogeneity. Larry Diamond pinpoints, in *Democracy in Developing Countries: Africa* (1988a):

> ... the tension between the model of ethnically, linguistically, and culturally homogeneous societies that satisfy the ideal of the nation-state and the multiethnic, multilingual societies that face the difficult task of nation- or state-building in the absence of the integration ... (p. xxii)

At the same time, the vague concept of 'nation' is surrounded by myths about what constitutes a nation (Smith, 1983). Anthony Smith focuses on the crucial concept of 'national identity', which he considers 'a multi-

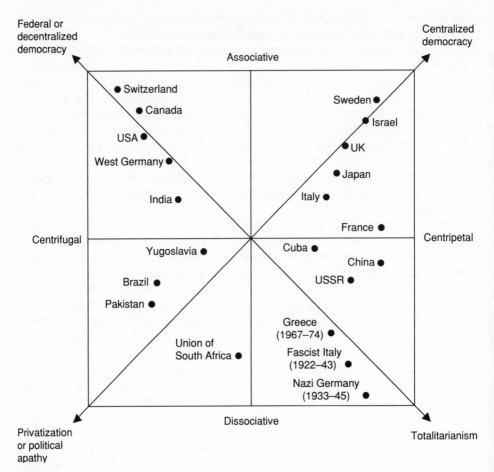

Figure 2.1 Deutsch's typology

dimensional concept', that is, a named human population that may be sharing 'an historic territory, common myths and historical memories, a mass, public culture, a common economy and common legal rights and duties for all members' (Smith A., 1991: 43).

Typical of a state is the exercise of public power over people in social groups in a predictable manner in a geographically tight space. These social groups, however, need not constitute a homogeneous society in any of the aspects that Smith lists.

Tracing the equation state = nation = people back to the rise of nationalism as a political doctrine in the nineteenth century, E. J. Hobsbawm asks: 'What is a (or the) nation?' And he answers, quite correctly, that 'no satisfactory criterion can be discovered for deciding which of the many human collectivities should be labelled in this way' (Hobsbawm, 1990: 5).

As a matter of fact, the relationship between state and groups is a complex one which renders the concept of nation-state extremely precarious. Against the nationalist principle of one nation, one state, it may be argued that its implementation may not be conducive to the foundation of compact states. Quite the contrary, nationalism may spurn human rights, as when minorities are suppressed. The principle about national self-determination may come into conflict with the principles of human rights (Pommerance, 1982; Donnelley, 1989).

The crux of the matter is that it is almost impossible to specify how much social consensus among various people in the state territory is enough to qualify a state as a nation-state. However, if 'nation-state' means a state where the citizens belong to one and the same ethnic community, then the so-called modern state is not necessarily a nation-state.

The core of the problem of the nation-state is that, when multi-ethnic states are broken up into a set of smaller nation-states, there exists no natural limit on how far the process of splitting up should go. The nation-state may not only represent the liberation of subjugated people, it may also itself foster a contempt for the rights of remaining minorities. The identification criterion of a nation is simply not clear, as both subjective and objective characteristics may be employed: a distinctive ethnicity, a culture, a historical destiny, and so on.

Because it is an open question how they are related to each other, it is vital to keep the concepts of state and nation separate. It may well be the case that the stability of the state comes under pressure if the population within the state boundaries hosts groups with different national identities. However, it is also possible that social heterogeneity, operating as a source of diversity and multiplicity, could stimulate state vitality. The impact of ethnic and religious heterogeneity on the state will be discussed in Chapter 7.

The identification of states

Standard reference books talk about 'countries of the world', the 'nations of the world' (*Encyclopedia Britannica: Book of the Year*, 1991: 746, 531) or the 'states and territories of the world' (Taylor, 1983: 273). Sometimes there are references to the 'political entities of the world' (*Encyclopedia Britannica: Book of the Year*, 1964: 533) or 'national political units' (Russett et al., 1968: 935). The variation in usage indicates that defining a state is not altogether a clear-cut process.

Various criteria may be employed in order to identify the states of the world: international recognition, membership of the United Nations, inclusion in established source books and stipulations about the size of the population or the territory. Let us use a number of criteria in order to find out how many states there are. Again, we emphasize that it is far easier

Table 2.1 United Nations member states

	1945	1950	1960	1970	1980	1990	1993
Number of members	51	60	99	127	154	159	184

Source: Europa Yearbook.

to point out the states in reality than to single out the meaning of the state concept – that is, its crucial properties.

UN membership

The United Nations was created in 1945. It has included among its membership an increasing number of states on the basis of formal recognition. But it should be pointed out that the United Nations also takes some kind of size criterion into account, because some small states, such as Nauru and Tuvalu in Oceania (each with 9,000 inhabitants), have not been accepted as member states. In addition, Switzerland is not included, and North and South Korea were not until 1991, although for different reasons.

Apart from formal recognition by other states in the world, the recognition by the United Nations is the most important hallmark of statehood that an emerging state can receive. It may almost be described as a performative act, the granting of UN membership being conducive to legitimizing a state. Table 2.1 shows the growth in the number of members of the UN since its foundation.

During the 1950s and the 1960s a large number of new states were integrated into the UN framework, which reflected the breaking up of the colonial empires – British, French, Spanish and Dutch – after the Second World War. The last state to be accepted in the 1980s was Brunei in Asia (population 250,000) in 1984.

The fall of the USSR has had the consequence that the number of member states increased considerably. In the early 1990s states from the former Soviet empire constituted a majority of the new members, namely Liechtenstein and Namibia (1990), Estonia, Latvia, Lithuania, the Democratic People's Republic of Korea, the Republic of Korea, the Marshall Islands and Micronesia (all 1991), San Marino, Armenia, Azerbaijan, Kazakhstan, Kirghizstan, Moldova, Tajikistan, Turkmenistan and Uzbekistan (all March 1992) as well as Bosnia-Hercegovina, Croatia and Slovenia (May 1992) and Georgia (July 1992). At the same time Yugoslavia was excluded and Serbia and Montenegro have not been permitted to enter in its stead. In 1993 the Czech and

Slovak republics, Andorra, Eritrea, Macedonia and Monaco all became members.

Standard reference books

There are a few internationally acknowledged reference books that may be consulted. They list the states of the world at a particular point in time, based on various criteria. One such source is the *Encyclopedia Britannica*. In the edition of 1911 there is a list in the index section, whereas later lists are entered in the various editions of the *Book of the Year*. It should be pointed out both that the 1911 list is shaky and that later volumes make no distinction between sovereign and non-sovereign states, such as the United States of America on the one hand and California on the other.

Other frequently used sources are the different editions of *The States-man's Yearbook* and the *World Handbook of Political and Social Indicators*, with its three editions. In *The Statesman's Yearbook* the table of contents lists both states (e.g., USA) and the territories of countries (e.g., Florida), which distinction is not always clear. In a similar way the *World Handbook* from 1972 and 1983 lists both states and territories. Here we also enter the classification of states made by Russett et al. in 1968, where units with a population greater than 10,000 were included. Again, both independent states and states that were parts of a confederation were incorporated.

Thus these well-known reference books give in reality one *narrow* identification and one *broad* identification of the states of the world. The first listing in *Encyclopedia Britannica* in 1911 gave 153 states; this had risen to 162 in 1965 and 175 in 1970, to reach a high of 217 in 1980 based on a broad identification. The number of 186 in 1990 is more in line with the narrow identification criterion. *The Statesman's Yearbook* offers the following series: 1925: 70/181; 1940: 71/194; 1956: 113/174; and 1991: 182/198. The *World Handbook* counts 133 states in 1964, then gives both the narrow and the broad classification for 1972: 137/199 and for 1983: 154/231. Russett et al. (1968) present one count for the twentieth century, amounting to 154/267 states.

The listing of two sets of states, on the one hand sovereign states and on the other all states, including member states, that form part of a union, is bound to create confusion. It all depends on how formal constitutional matters are matched by real-life differences between territories that are more properly described as parts of states and territories that are confederated states. For the purposes of this book, we focus on the set of so-called sovereign states, acknowledging that the concept of sovereignty has lost some of its applicability in an increasingly interdependent world (Hollis and Smith, 1990). The distinction between unitary and federal states will be discussed in Chapter 4.

Contemporary sources

For the early 1990s a list of states may be derived from the World Bank's *World Development Report*, which includes states that are members of the bank and have more than one million inhabitants alongside all the smaller states. In addition to the German *Der Fischer Welt Almanach* one may consult two French sources: *L'état du monde* and *Atlas Statistique: Encyclopedia Universalis*, which both count sovereign and dependent states. The *World Development Report* for 1991 gives the number of states that have more than one million inhabitants as 124 and the total number of states as 185. *L'état du monde* (1991) counts sovereign states as 171, whereas the *Encyclopedia Universalis* (1990) contains 165 sovereign states. The sudden process of creating new states is highlighted in *Der Fischer Welt Almanach*, which identifies 171 states in 1991 but 192 states in 1993.

One may wish to employ the distinction between a narrow and a broad definition of 'state' when conducting research into macropolitics. We focus chiefly upon so-called sovereign states, though mindful that the concept of sovereignty has little explanatory power. When we come to the institutional description, it is possible to broaden the perspective to cover semi-autonomous states that enter federal systems of government.

It seems that there is enough agreement in the various sources for counting the number of states, in the narrow sense of sovereign states, as roughly 170 in 1990. However, we follow the *World Development Report* in making a distinction between states with a population larger than one million and tiny states with a smaller population. This means that there are some 130 states from 1990 that this study will analyse. Had we included states with a population smaller than one million, the total number would have risen to 168.

The unit of analysis

If one resorts to the concept of a Weberian state, the unit of analysis in comparative politics may be identified in a straightforward manner. Some scholars employ the phrase 'the modern state', but the use of the qualification 'modern' is somewhat arbitrary. It has been claimed that the modern state entered the history of mankind around the Renaissance period and the seventeenth century (Tilly, 1975; Held et al., 1983; Hall, 1986; Anderson, 1986). However, attempts to pin down more exactly what a modern state amounted to in Western Europe are bound to meet with dissent.

It is true that there exist a large number of definitions of the 'state'. These are discussed at length in the extensive state literature, where the definition of the Weberian state is only one more or less plausible approach. However, its advantage lies in that it is easy to apply.

As we have already mentioned, the Weberian state is identified by its monopoly on the legitimate use of physical force within a specified territory. It thus combines both the power aspect and the moral implication of the state concept. When we start searching for the unit of analysis in comparative politics, the plausibility of the Weberian state concept derives from two sources, making it a better choice in a strategy for the conduct of comparative work than other candidates such as polity, government, nation or political system.

Firstly, the identification criteria are highly tangible or visible: territory, population, military and police forces, attitudes towards legitimacy. We will see in this chapter that states may vary tremendously in terms of area and population. Yet the state may be truly small or large in terms of territory, or harbour enormous or tiny populations, and still operate quite naturally as a Weberian state. There can be no talk about what is a proper size for a state, or some magic size where it functions optimally, whatever such a phrase might mean.

Secondly, the concept of the Weberian state is not only an abstract scientific notion, it actually identifies organizations that constitute a kind of reality of their own. Ongoing international politics identify the states of the world in action, meaning that the concept of the state as used by, for example, the UN constitutes a performative notion. What a state does, or what is called a 'state', is what a state actually is. International politics implies that the major actors orientate towards each other within a state centred subjective framework, which is given official sanction in various ways.

The crux of the matter is that these two criteria concerning present-day states – the conceptual criteria in the Weberian state definition and the actor-based subjective criteria in actual politics – coincide to such an extent that they designate almost the same units of analysis as the so-called states. When there is disagreement about whether a state really exists, such as in the case of Somalia today, then the critical issue is whether there is a high enough likelihood that some organization can manage to uphold a monopoly on the employment of physical force. This is the core of Weber's definition, namely that a state is a probabilistic phenomenon.

Size

Size is often considered a fundamental property of a state, as if it were a universal criterion for distinguishing between important and unimportant states. The size of a state may be measured by different indicators. States vary tremendously, whether measured by extent of territory or numbers of citizens or inhabitants. One may question whether there is actually any limit to the size of a group that wishes to organize itself as an independent state. The two properties of area and population do not co-vary perfectly, as there

Table 2.2 Size of states: area and population

	(A) States with more than 1 million	(B) All states	A as % of B
Area (sq km)	131,613,199	132,305,396	99.5
Population: 1950	2,496,992	2,501,486	99.8
1960	2,995,590	3,001,062	99.8
1970	3,652,345	3,659,073	99.8
1980	4,429,593	4,437,630	99.8
1990	5,288,215	5,298,131	99.8

Source: *Encyclopedia Britannica: Book of the Year* (1991).

are states with a fairly large population and a small area, such as the Netherlands, as well as states with a large territory and a small population, such as Australia.

Yet size may be considered important not simply because there are tremendous variations, but mainly because one may argue that the discrepancy in area or population matters for the entire fabric of the state and how it operates. There are several models of the state that try to pinpoint the effects of size.

Looking at the data on area and population for the states as of 1990, when there were still two states in Germany and the Yemen, and with the USSR included in Europe, we may outline a few major traits for the postwar period. Table 2.2 shows that almost all the people of the world live in states that have more than one million inhabitants, meaning that the number of tiny states with fewer than one million people is not large enough to make them very important. It also gives a glimpse of the rapid rise in the world population from 1950 to 1990.

It must be emphasized that state size is one thing and state importance another. The two properties may be correlated but they are not identical, analytically speaking. Yet states that have a population smaller than one million, that is, some forty states, are not the only ones to be called 'small'. In our selection of states we cover 77 per cent of all the states of the world, which contain within their borders 99.8 per cent of the world's population.

Actually, there are no natural criteria that may be used for identifying self-evident degrees of state size. Nor are there, it seems, any absolute lower bounds on state area or population. Thus in 1990 a large number of states, or 63 out of 130 (i.e., 49 per cent), have a population of more than one million but less than ten million. Which are the big and the small states in our sample?

Where are the really big states placed on the world map? And where do we

Table 2.3   Area and population of the continents, 1950–90 (in percentages)

	Area	Population				
		1950	1960	1970	1980	1990
Africa	22.7	8.8	9.1	9.7	10.9	12.3
America	29.3	13.0	13.6	13.6	13.7	13.5
Asia	21.1	55.0	55.6	57.1	58.1	58.9
Europe	20.6	22.7	21.2	19.0	16.8	14.9
Oceania	6.4	0.5	0.5	0.5	0.5	0.5

Source: *Encyclopedia Britannica: Book of the Year* (1991).

locate the really tiny states? Remembering the distinction between the two measures of size – area of state territory and number of inhabitants in state citizenship – a rough picture may be drawn with a few broad strokes.

We may expect to find several populous states in Asia, as it contains some 59 per cent of the world's population. Table 2.3 gives the data for five continents: Europe with the USSR, America, Africa, Asia and Oceania. Actually, this is the basic classification framework that will be employed for the mapping process in the descriptive sections in the early chapters of the book. One drawback when turning to an analysis of variance is that, given the criteria for selecting states employed, Oceania covers only three countries.

Asia is not the largest continent in terms of area, but it certainly comprises much of the population of the earth. We have a few gigantic states. In 1990 China estimated its population as 1,134 million people living on a territory of 9,573,000 square kilometres. India hosted 853 million people within a territory of 3,166,000 square kilometres. The third largest country in 1990 was Indonesia, with 181 million people on 1,919,000 square kilometres. Japan's 124 million inhabit a far smaller territory, 378,000 square kilometres. Far East Asia comprises a number of populous states: Pakistan with 123 million, Bangladesh with 113, Vietnam with 66, the Philippines with 61 (on 300,000 sq km), Thailand with 56, South Korea with 43 and North Korea with 23. Then comes Taiwan with 20 and Malaysia with 18 million people.

In Asia Minor there are two huge states, Turkey with 57 million people (on 780,000 sq km) and Iran with 56 million (on 1,648,000 sq km). In addition there are several states there with a population over 10 million: Iraq (18), Afghanistan (16), Saudi Arabia (14) and Syria (12).

In Oceania there is one state that is big in terms of area – Australia, with 17 million inhabitants on 7,682,000 square kilometres. In Oceania we find a number of tiny states: Fiji (population 740,000), Solomon Islands (319,000), Western Samoa (165,000), Vanatu (147,000), Tonga (96,000) and Tuvalu (9,000).

Table 2.4 Population of the continents: different estimations (in percentages)

| | (A) | | | (B) | | |
	1750	1850	1950	1750	1850	1950
Africa	13.0	8.5	8.0	13.0	8.1	8.2
America	1.9	5.1	13.3	1.6	5.0	13.7
Asia	65.2	63.4	54.9	65.8	63.9	54.2
Europe	19.6	22.8	23.3	19.2	22.7	23.2
Oceania	0.3	0.2	0.5	0.3	0.2	0.5

Sources: A = Cipolla (1965: 99); B = Woytinsky and Woytinsky (1953: 34).

The long-term developmental trends for the populations of the various continents differ, as is revealed in table 2.4. The share of the population of Africa as a percentage of the entire world population declined from about 1700 up to 1950, one cause being the transportation of a large number of slaves across the Atlantic in the eighteenth and nineteenth centuries. The historical population trend for the American continent was a different one, as at first the conquest of America resulted in a terrible reduction in the population, which was followed by a long trend of population growth. Actually, despite the immense population growth in Asia, it is the case that the relative share of the world population for Asia has declined since 1750.

The sharp rise in population growth in Africa since the Second World War has reversed this trend. Africa now hosts some 600 million people.

There are quite a few large states in Africa, although Nigeria (with 120 million people on 924,000 sq km) is the only really giant state. Egypt has 53 million inhabitants on 998,000 square kilometres, Ethiopia 50 million on 1,224,000 square kilometres, South Africa 37 million on 1,226,000 square kilometres, Sudan 28 million on 2,504,000 square kilometres, Zaïre 34 million on 753,000 square kilometres, Kenya 25 million on 583,000 square kilometres and Tanzania 24 million on 945,000 square kilometres.

There are many states in Africa that are medium-sized in terms of population, meaning they fall in between the range of larger than one million and smaller than twenty million. The very small states are not numerous: Cape Verde (population 339,000), Comoros (463,000), Equatorial Guinea (350,000), São Tomé and Príncipe (121,000) and Swaziland (770,000).

On the American continent the USA scores high on both size of population and size of territory. It has some 251 million people on 9,529,000 square kilometres. America is the largest of all the continents in terms of area and population: besides the USA it includes Canada, with its vast territory of 9,971,000 square kilometres for a population of 27 million people, and Brazil, with its huge population of 150 million people on 8,512,000 square kilometres. One should also mention Mexico, having 82 million people on an area of 1,958,000 square kilometres.

As a matter of fact, there are in addition many states with a population larger than ten million: Argentina (33), Colombia (33), Peru (22), Venezuela (20), Chile (13), Ecuador (11) and Cuba (11). At the same time several states are quite small: Antigua and Barbuda (81,000), Bahamas (253,000), Barbados (257,000), Belize (189,000), Dominica (82,000), Grenada (101,000), Guyana (756,000), St Kitts-Nevis (44,000), St Vincent (115,000) and Suriname (411,000).

It remains to look at Europe, including the then existing state of the USSR, although a very sizeable part of the country lies in Asia. Typical of the European states is the high density of their population, reflecting that their territories are not that large. The exception is the USSR, with its area of 22,400,000 square kilometres for a population of 290 million people. Other populous states are France (57 million on 544,000 sq km) and the United Kingdom (57 million on 244,000 sq km). The two now united states of Germany were quite unequal in terms of size, West Germany having 63 million people on 249,000 square kilometres and East Germany 16 million on 108,000 square kilometres.

Some nations are large in terms of population but not in terms of area. Italy has 58 million inhabitants on 301,000 square kilometres, Spain 39 million on 505,000 square kilometres and Yugoslavia (still existing as a state in 1990) 24 million on 256,000 square kilometres. Greece, with 10 million people on 132,000 square kilometres, and Portugal, with 10 million on 92,000 square kilometres, are not as dense as the Netherlands, with 15 million people on 42,000 square kilometres, or Belgium, with 10 million on 31,000 square kilometres.

Tiny states with a population of fewer than one million people may also be found in Europe: Andorra (51,000), Iceland (256,000), Liechtenstein (29,000), Luxembourg (378,000), Malta (353,000), Monaco (29,000) and San Marino (23,000).

An extensive variation in the size of the states in the world is to be found on all continents. For Europe, Africa, America, Asia and Oceania the within-continent variation is larger than the between-continent variation, with regard to both area and population.

Density

As we shall see in Chapter 7, there are theories which suggest that the size of the state is crucial for other state properties, such as state performance. However, such model claims are not implied in the Weberian state approach, as it claims only that any designation of a unit as a state requires that the territory, the citizenship and the regime be clearly identifiable.

When one speaks about state size in itself as an important dimension of the major political organization in the history of mankind or as of decisive importance for state capacity, one must remember that the two properties –

territorial size and population – do not always go together. The simple Pearson's correlations between territorial size and size of population amount to r = .50 when the large number of tiny states are included (168 states), but it is smaller, or r = .48, in our selection (129 states); if data are transformed logarithmically, then the correlation is r = .84 (168 states) and r = .58 (129 states). The implication is that there are states that are large in only one aspect of state size, as well as states that are small in only one aspect of state size. Thus, state size often refers to different things.

Actually, there is quite a staggering variation in population density measures, combining population and area. As Asia comprises almost 60 per cent of the people of the world on some 20 per cent of the area of the earth, this means that the density of the population will vary considerably on the continent. Turning to Africa, we would expect to find that population density is much lower than in Asia. However, the reverse relation between size of population and size of territory holds here, as it consists of 23 per cent of the area of the earth but hosts only 12 per cent of the world's people.

To the highly dense states belong Singapore (with 4,370 per sq km), Bangladesh (431 per sq km), and Taiwan (562 per sq km), as well as South Korea (431 per sq km). In Africa we have Mauritius (529 per sq km) and in Europe the Netherlands (357 per sq km). To the sparsely populated states belong Mongolia (1 per sq km), Namibia, Mauritania, Australia, Botswana and Libya (all with 2 per sq km) and finally Canada (3 per sq km). Whether a state with a large territory also has a huge population is entirely an open question.

As we will argue in the chapters to come, when looking at a variety of state models, it would seem more plausible to derive state stability and state performance not from state size itself but from factors in the near environment of the state, such as the nature of the economy, which would be much dependent upon its links with the international economy.

One may speculate whether the tendency towards the establishment of new states will continue into the twenty-first century. The economic conditions for state creation have improved in the sense that small territories with a population around one to three million people may become integrated in the world economy, making it possible to reach an acceptable standard of living even though the state is not self-sufficient. This means that large territories may be broken into small, compact states as a result, for example, of nationalism at the same time as the new area becomes even stronger within the international economy, as, for example, with Slovenia in the former Yugoslavia.

In the classical doctrine of state sovereignty it was often stated that self-sufficiency is a necessary condition for state stability (Levy, 1952). The strong integration processes in the international economy have had the consequence that economic self-sufficiency guaranteed by some proper state size in terms of population or territory no longer sets boundaries for state stability and performance. A state such as Singapore is almost totally non-self-sufficient, importing almost everything and exporting almost its entire GDP, but it strongly maintains its stability (although it does not perform equally well in terms of civil and political rights). Slovenia and Slovakia have successfully sought political independence, although they remain considerably economically dependent on relationships with other countries.

Conclusion

We hope we have now given a picture of what entities are referred to as the unit of analysis for comparative politics, the set of internationally accepted states, as it were. Whereas terms such as 'political system', 'nation-state' and 'polity' remain abstract and difficult to pin down, the Weberian state concept allows the articulation of truly important social systems acting and interacting with each other over the globe. The finding in this chapter is the immense increase in the number of states since the Second World War. Given the drive towards more and more states, one may ask: What are the limits to the creation of new compact states?

As we set out to describe some properties of states, it seems reasonable to focus on a proper subset of states, as it is difficult to gather information about each one. Such a sample could be drawn in various ways, but here we take the availability of data into account while at the same time selecting all the large populous countries. Actually only a handful of very tiny states has been left out. Thus the study is based on the states included in Appendix I.

Let us finally warn against the danger of speaking about states as if they were individuals. It is true that we have located a unit of analysis that may be pinned down to observable indicators such as UN recognition, territorial control and number of citizens. But the concept of a state is an abstract one. When states are described as aiming at objectives or at persistence over time, then it is only a matter of speech or a kind of anthropomorphism. States are aggregates of human behaviour, and the study of politics at the macrolevel can only refer to intentions in so far as individuals act on behalf of the state. Since the Weberian state is often called the 'European', Occidental or 'Western' if not the 'modern' state (Owen, 1992), it is legitimate to ask how it has spread all over the globe.

Since we have now identified a set of states and mapped the size of these in terms of population and area, the next step is to look into the rise and development of the states of the present-day world. What is the lifetime of states?

3

State Longevity

Introduction

The basic tenets of the modern state as it evolved from the Renaissance to the twentieth century, identified in the Weberian state conception, are impersonality and bureaucracy. The basic distinction is that between person and office or 'stato', meaning that the modern state is a set of social system mechanisms that separate the public roles from the private life styles of rulers. In *On Human Conduct* Oakeshott singles out the principles of *societas* – association by agreement – and *universitas* – legal corporation – as typical of the new state conception in the sixteenth century (Oakeshott, 1991: 201–4). The latter aspect refers to the state as the unified political authority over its citizens, whereas the former covers the state as a partnership between major social groups.

States rise and fall as if they were creatures of their own making. There has been a tradition of approaching states as biological phenomena, or organisms, as if they had a life of their own. The functionalist as well as the systems approach came close to treating the state as if it had special life processes determining its fate. In the terminology of the philosophy of science this is called 'reification', or the fallacy of misplaced concreteness. In this chapter we discuss how state age might be measured without any assumption that states are living beings.

Persistence criteria

It is true that there is often talk about states ceasing to exist, but when is a state to be declared dead or when can it be said to 'persist'? There are bound to be changes, but equating all kinds of change to a threat to state longevity will not do, as rulers may enhance the prospects of state survival by flexible adaptation. Although it cannot be approached as some kind of organism, since a state is an aggregate of human behaviour, one may speak of state age in a figurative sense.

Acknowledging that it is possible to lay down alternative criteria for how long a state has existed, it is difficult to do without some concept of state age. But how is such a concept to be arrived at, admitting that specifying a lifetime for a state involves arbitrariness? For the purpose of conducting a comparative inquiry it would be interesting to examine the longevity of states, or more specifically whether state age varies considerably. But how to measure state age?

Here, we will approach the concept of state age by focusing on the properties of the Weberian state. Recalling Weber's definition, states are distinguished by singling out the following properties: (a) a legal order for the exercise of authority or a regime; (b) territory; (c) monopoly on the use of physical violence. For the purpose of analysing state longevity we will focus on territory and the monopoly on the employment of physical force.

A major change in *two* of these Weberian properties indicates that a state has perished, namely that (b) and (c) are absent. A state is a probability phenomenon, Weber argued, as state survival increases as a function of the likelihood that (b) and (c) are maintained over time. It is undeniable though that it remains somewhat arbitrary how one labels changes in these two state properties as 'major' ones.

Turning the Weberian state around, the probability that a state will perish increases when its territory disintegrates, or when there occur sustained and successful challenges to its legal order in the form of internal violence or protest phenomena or external subjugation to foreign powers. We know already that present-day states vary considerably in terms of two such properties as territorial size and population. How do states differ in terms of age, or state longevity?

The age of states

To define the age of a state is not a simple affair. The problem of determining the birth year of the states of today is to a considerable extent a matter of convention. Should a state that has experienced profound changes, as, for example, the United Kingdom with the fall of the British Empire, be considered as of long standing, remaining somehow the same, or, having lost much of its territory, should it be counted as a new young state? There is no way to resolve this problem once and for all. As in all concept formation in the conduct of scientific enquiry, every decision concerning the characteristics of definition has its pros and cons.

Some differences in state age may be seen when one considers a few countries that are physically close to one another. Egypt appears to be the oldest existing state on the earth, having undergone a number of regimes from the Pharaohs onwards. But during the 1980s the newly founded states in Chad, Uganda and Sudan almost ceased to exist, leaving these countries in anarchy – not to mention Somalia in the early 1990s.

Let us look at the various continents and survey their state creation processes, in so far as a state existing today may be traced back into history. We begin with the old continent, Europe, and the analysis will concentrate on the predecessors to contemporary states. But how far back in time should one go?

Again, the starting-point for the enquiry into the longevity of present states of the world is the Weberian state. Being distinct from the medieval feudal state and the 'Ständerstaat', the 'modern state' referred to in sociological theory is distinguished by its very Weberian properties. States are described by Poggi in *The Development of the Modern State* (1978) in the following way:

> The modern state is perhaps best seen as a complex set of institutional arrangements for rule through the continuous and regulated activities of individuals acting as occupants of offices. The state, as the sum total of such offices, reserves to itself the business of rule of a territorially bounded society. (Poggi, 1978: 1)

The modern state originated in Europe during the Renaissance, but received its typical configuration during the eighteenth and nineteenth centuries, when its claims to sovereignty were accepted both internally and externally. A modern state may have widely different regimes, which we will return to in Chapter 4.

States are fragile. Most of the states of the world are young. Often states are created as the result of major social changes such as war, and some states succumb to the atrocities of anarchy or civil war. However, although state death and birth may occur in a rather peaceful manner, in general state transformation tends to be a violent process, as it involves clashes between groups striving for power. Moreover, states may also collapse due to an invasion from another state – a violent process of change, to say the least.

The modern state is characterized by its monopoly on the legitimate employment of force, which implies that legal control is crucial. Hans Kelsen's legal theory implies that the state and the legal order are one and the same phenomenon (Kelsen, 1945), which brings out how closely the survival of states is connected with the peaceful operation of the rule of law in societies with a specified territory. When there are difficulties in upholding the legal control over a territory, then state persistence is threatened.

Europe

It is not a straightforward task to identify the origin in time of a state. Often one mentions the year of introduction of a so-called modernized leadership. However, this criterion is associated with the introduction of political forms involving mass participation. What we are looking for here is some kind of criterion that is neutral in relation to the modernization process in the twentieth century. There are several states in the world today that have not experienced the coming of a mass political culture.

Let us start with the birth of the concept of the state. Friedrich Meinecke, in *Die Idee der Staatsräson* ([1925] 1963), argued that the concept of the state was a product of the Renaissance. The word 'stato' began to occur as a designator for the new kinds of political units that came forth in the late Middle Ages to challenge the universalist notions at that time, both the ambitions of Catholicism and the structure of feudal society.

A number of political units may be said to have been founded during the early Renaissance which have the properties that Weber singled out in his definition of the state: territorial borders, a legal order and the monopoly on the use, or the threat of use, of legitimate physical force – so-called modern states. It is arbitrary to mention a certain year as the birth date, as the process of introducing the neutral administrative machine that is typical of the modern state was a lengthy one. A few rulers may be mentioned who fought successfully for the centralization of power resources to the 'stato': Francis I in France (died 1547), Henry VIII in England (died 1547), Gustav I Vasa in Sweden (died 1560), Kristian III in Denmark (died 1559), Henry the Navigator in Portugal (died 1460) and Ferdinand and Isabella of Spain (who married in 1469, merging Catalonia with Castilia).

What differentiates these political units from other political entities at that time – for example, the Holy Roman Empire (962–1806) or the Ottoman Empire (1300–1922) – is the orientation of power towards an objective and predictable 'stato', that is, a system of administrative offices. Characteristic of the new states of the seventeenth century was the concentration of political power in an impersonal organization, the actions of which covered the entire population of the state territory in a direct relation of authority. It is hardly an accident that the modern states in Europe were the most active in extending their powers over the globe. The Weberian state is, as Weber himself claimed, capable of high levels of administrative efficiency.

The new state model of the Renaissance spread during the centuries that followed to several other countries. This is not the place to analyse the process of state formation as it developed in various parts of Europe (Tilly, 1975; Held et al., 1983; Anderson, 1986), and we will mention only a few dates which are linked with the formation of particular states: 1648 for the Netherlands and Switzerland, 1829 for Greece, 1830 for Belgium, 1861 for Italy and 1905 for Norway. The First World War changed the disposition of existing states at the end of the nineteenth century profoundly, for it resulted in the dissolution of the great empires in Europe – the Dual Monarchy in Austria-Hungary (1867–1918), the Ottoman Empire of the Turks and the Romanov Empire (1613–1917) in Russia.

The peace treaty of Versailles in 1919 spoke much about nation-states. The vague principle that each nation should also constitute a state had grown in importance during the nineteenth century with the spread of nationalist ideology. In some parts of Europe it was very important, creating a number of new states: Romania in 1881, Bulgaria in 1908, Albania in 1912, Finland in 1917, Austria, Czechoslovakia, Hungary, Poland and Yugoslavia all in 1918 as well as Ireland in 1921. The fate of Yugoslavia, however, testifies to the fact that nationalism may be a destructive force undermining the state rather than suggesting the proper criteria for state creation.

The process of state formation may comprise quite heavy changes over a long period of time. To say whether a state has really ceased to exist or has just changed dramatically is merely a matter of linguistic usage. England provides a telling example of the difficulty in specifying state identity. In 1707 Great Britain was formed, combining the country with Scotland and Wales; the creation of the British Empire meant that the sun never set over the English state; and in 1921 the United Kingdom of Great Britain and Northern Ireland was established.

The question of a German state is also perplexing. The old German-Roman empire was dissolved in 1806, leaving a number of different kinds of political entity on German soil, including the Kingdom of Prussia. In 1871 a German state was introduced as a result of the ambitions of Prussia defeating the Austrian Habsburgs in 1866 at the battle of Sadowa. However, the existence of the German state became precarious in the twentieth century after it lost two World Wars. A similar period of reshaping the map set in after the Second World War. West and East Germany were created in 1949, but in 1990 these two states were reunited in a new Germany.

Futhermore, how to classify the Russian state is a difficult task. Czarist Russia continued to expand in various directions right up until it crumbled in 1917, to be replaced by the communist state, the Union of Socialist Soviet Republics, in 1922. Russia gave up territory in the Treaty of Brest-Litovsk in 1918 which made possible the formation of the three Baltic republics, Estonia, Lithuania and Latvia, as well as Finland. In 1918 Poland declared itself an independent state, re-establishing control over territories given up to Prussia, Russia and Austria.

The outcome of the Second World War meant an increase in the amount of territory somehow controlled by the USSR. However, in a spectacular course of events in 1991 the Soviet Union was dissolved and replaced by a set of new and independent states. The majority remained in the new confederation, the Commonwealth of Independent States – Russia, Ukraine, Belarus, Azerbaijan, Moldova, Armenia, and the earlier khanates of Central Asia, Uzbekistan, Kazakhstan, Turkmenistan, Tajikistan and Kirghizstan – but Georgia and the Baltic republics, which had been annexed by the USSR in 1940, elected for complete independence. Georgia, however, entered the CIS in 1993 (Sakwa, 1993).

To sum up, a few European states date back some hundred years, but several are less than a century old. Hardly any have persisted in the strong sense that their territory for the exercise of state authority has remained unchanged for hundreds of years. The many wars in Europe have destroyed states more or less drastically.

The Occidental state model was introduced rather early in time, allowing its efficiency to be employed by the Spanish, Portuguese, French, British and Dutch states in building up huge empires that had a profound influence on the foundation of states on the other continents, as described in J. A. Hall's *Powers and Liberties: The Causes and Consequences of the Rise of the West* (1985) and E. R. Wolf's *Europe and the People without History* (1982). The superiority of the Western European states rested not only upon their military might or their economic edge in entering capitalist modes of organization, but also upon their administrative capacity in running the new 'modern' state.

The Americas

The spread of the new state from Europe to the vast American continent from 1492 onwards involved a long process of development of various modes of political domination over the colonies founded there. The first step in this process was the conquest by the European invaders of the native land of the Indians. The onslaught of the *conquistadores* crushed the major empires of the Aztecs (1325–1521) and Incas (1400–1530). As a matter of fact, the virtual extinction of the native population was appalling: the number of people was reduced from some twenty-five million to only one million, in a part of the world that had seen such an advanced culture as that of the Mayas.

After the conquest sharp political subjugation was combined with economic exploitation and religious domination; the remaining population was forced to become Catholic (Williamson, 1992). Whereas the native population was used in the mining areas in the Spanish territories, the Portuguese set up a slave economy in Brazil, importing many blacks from Africa. Besides British Honduras (Belize) in Central America and small British (Guyana), French (French Guyana, Haiti) and Dutch (Suriname) colonies, all of Latin America was Spanish or Portuguese.

It was not until some two centuries later that the new populations of the colonies resurrected their autonomy against their European governments by declaring themselves sovereign states in the wake of Spanish defeat in the Napoleonic Wars. In the case of the Spanish possessions, the four separate vice-royalties of the late colonial period split further, to produce fourteen independent states by the 1820s. Portuguese Brazil also revolted against its European power.

Once Spanish domination crumbled a number of new states were formed in Central America: Haiti in 1804, Mexico and Costa Rica in 1821, El Salvador in 1830, Guatemala, Nicaragua and Honduras in 1838, the Dominican Republic in 1844. The same development took place in South America, where Spanish rule and the Portuguese Empire were wiped out: Paraguay in 1811, Argentina in 1816, Chile in 1818, Brazil in 1822, Peru in 1824, Bolivia and Uruguay in 1825, Colombia, Equador and Venezuela in 1830.

It should be pointed out that the borders between some of the states in Latin America were changed as a result of wars in the nineteenth century. Thus Paraguay lost much territory to Brazil and Argentina in 1865. The same happened to Peru, which lost territory to Brazil and Chile. Some of the islands in the Caribbean remained under foreign rule until after the Second World War. Jamaica was founded in 1962, as were the republics of Trinidad and Tobago. Cuba became independent in 1899 as a result of the Spanish–American war.

Several European powers were involved in the colonization of North America: England, France, the Netherlands, Spain and Sweden. The French territories were large, up until the loss of Canada to England in 1763 and the sale of the Louisiana territory in 1803 to the United States. The latter became the first independent state in America (the United States of America was founded in 1776 and took a federal constitution in 1787). The USA was at that time small compared with what it eventually became after Hawaii was added in 1900 to all the other territories annexed or bought from other states during the nineteenth century. The position of the Canadian state is more ambiguous, as Canada has remained within the British Commonwealth, which means that Queen Elizabeth II is still the head of state. In 1867 the self-governing dominion of Canada was founded by an amalgamation of the English- and French-speaking parts.

One theme in state theory is the hypothesis that the Spanish and Portuguese states were radically different from the English state. Whereas the latter was suspicious of the bureaucratic aspects of the state, favouring a type of guardian state, the Latin American model emphasized proper procedures and red tape much more than efficiency or effectiveness (North, 1990). Thus the problems of economic development in Latin America would stem partly from the early introduction of a state that hampers rapid economic growth in capitalist institutions. However, one also needs to look at the way in which the independent Latin American states were assimilated into the world economy during the nineteenth century in the role as export-based economies trading raw materials against manufactures (Cammack et al., 1993).

Asia

It is not easy to identify the creation of states in Asia. The typical mode of political authority seems to have been strong personal rule, as analysed in K. A. Wittfogel's *Oriental Despotism: a Comparative Study of Total Power*

(1957) and S. N. Eisenstadt's *The Political Systems of Empires* (1963). The strong reliance on personal leadership – dynasties – may be found in China and India as well as Asia Minor. However, there were also feudal structures, as, for example, in Japan.

The process of creating European-type states took the form of a fight for independence against the European empires which dominated almost the entire continent around 1900. Only a few countries had resisted the penetration of the British, French and Dutch empires, such as Persia (Iran), formed in 1499, Afghanistan, established in 1747, Nepal, dating back to 1768, and Thailand, founded as far back as 1350. Both Japan and China have had several ancient civilizations and various systems of political domination, but Japan moved towards the creation of a modern state in 1868, abolishing the Tokugawa-Shogunat and restoring the powers of the Emperor, who moved from Kyoto to Tokyo. China developed differently, as it came under foreign rule and was torn apart by a civil war that ended in 1949.

'The great game' is what Rudyard Kipling called the struggle between the Czarist and British empires on the giant chess-board of Central Asia. The numerous independent khanates around the Caspian and Aral seas dating back to the rule of Genghis Khan (died 1227) fell one after another to Russia's southward advance. They later entered into the Soviet empire. But at the end of 1991 they re-emerged as unstable independent republics.

New states were formed after the First and Second World Wars. When the Ottoman Empire was dissolved some of its parts came under British or French rule (1918). Other parts became new states (Hourani, 1991). Thus Yemen became independent in 1918, Egypt was formed in 1922, Turkey in 1923, and Iraq and Saudi Arabia in 1932. The countries that remained under foreign rule, partly in accordance with the League of Nations under mandatory agreement, managed to achieve independent status within a few decades: Lebanon in 1944, Jordan and Syria in 1946, Oman in 1951 and Kuwait in 1961.

The violent dissolution of the French Empire after the Second World War resulted in a number of new states in Asia, the larger ones being Cambodia (1953), Laos (1954) and Vietnam (1954). The definitive end of French control in Indo-China came with their major defeat at Dien Bien Phu. The break-up of the British Empire was also a violent process, as the United Kingdom offered resistance when a number of new states declared their independence. Many of these, however, remained within the Commonwealth. Here we find India and Pakistan (founded in 1947), Burma and Sri Lanka (1948), Malaysia (1957) and Singapore (1965). Pakistan consisted of a western and an eastern part up until the formation of Bangladesh in 1971.

There were two further empires involved in Far East Asia, namely the Dutch and the Japanese. The Netherlands, who had conquered the 'spice islands' in 1602, established a colony there in 1816 and integrated the vast territory of thousands of islands in 1922. In 1949 Indonesia was founded as a republic after violent resistance from the Dutch. The Japanese domination in Korea from 1910 was ended in 1945 as a result of imperial Japan's defeat, but the country was divided into two formal states in 1948, North and South Korea.

The European state was exported to Asia in two very different forms. On the one hand, powerful states in Europe managed to subdue several of the Asian countries in the process of empire building which began in the seventeenth century and was consolidated in the late nineteenth century (Kennedy, 1987; Braudel, 1993). The weak political structures in these states, which were huge in terms of territorial area, proved no match for Great Britain, France, Portugal, Spain, the Netherlands and Germany. On the other hand, in the fight for independence from colonial powers, the actors seeking independence often had in mind the creation of states structured along the lines of the European model. Thus the dismantling of European imperialism led to the foundation of numerous states structured in accordance with the properties of the Weberian state.

The expansion of European imperialism came at a time when Oriental despotism and feudalism had started to disintegrate. This is true of both the Ottoman Empire in Asia Minor and Chinese rule in Far East Asia. China came under foreign domination after the period of its famous dynasties – Song (960–1279), Ming (1368–1644) and Manchu Qing (1644–1911) – had brought it to the forefront of civilization. It could not resist Japanese penetration in Manchuria in the 1890s and the 1930s. The introduction of a republic in 1912 was followed by anarchy and civil war between the communists and the nationalists, which ended in the foundation of communist China in 1949, leaving Taiwan as a separate state.

Likewise, the India of the Mogul dynasty (1526–1857) could not resist British inroads, in the form of the British East India Company, from the late seventeenth century to 1858. After the rebellion in 1857 India was ruled by means of a British Viceroy, collaborating with numerous semi-independent 'princely states' or maharajahs. When it became an independent sovereign state it stayed within the British Commonwealth.

Finally, one may also speak of an empire in regard to the United States' penetration of the crumbling Spanish Empire. The Monroe Declaration of 1823 had actually expressed the imperialist ambitions of the newly founded state in relation to the American continent. At the end of the nineteenth century the United States went to war in order to capture land from Spain. The Philippines had been 'discovered' by Magellan in 1521 and came under Spanish domination in 1565. With its many islands and large population, it remained under Spain until 1898, when it was ceded to the USA; it was occupied by Japan during the Second World War and became an independent state in 1946.

Oceania

The states in the region of Oceania are not old. Numerous islands were conquered by the British, Spanish and Dutch fleets, but the penetration of

Australia and New Zealand was slow as they were sparsely populated. When the Dutch arrived in Australia in 1616 there were some 300,000 Aborigines, mainly on the island of Tasmania. In 1644 New Holland was declared, with Abel Tasman claiming land, but in 1770 James Cook set up English rule by establishing New South Wales, to which British convicts were transported. The colonial nuclei of Australia's six states were in place by 1859 and in 1901 Australia was recognized as an independent commonwealth. New Zealand was made a dominion in the British Empire in 1907. Another big area in the region of Oceania is Papua New Guinea, which was actually part of three European empires: the British, the Dutch and the German. It came under the League of Nations in 1921, ruled under Australian guardianship, and in 1975 an independent state was formed. The various groups of islands in Oceania are sparsely populated. During colonial times the European powers divided the islands among themselves, but after the Second World War a large number of tiny states managed to become independent.

Africa

The initial occupation of Africa started early in the sixteenth century along the coastal areas, but it was stimulated by the gains from the massive transportation of slaves to the Americas. The extension of jurisdiction reached a completeness during the 'scramble for Africa' in the last quarter of the nineteenth century, with the division of almost the entire continent between the European powers of Great Britain, France, Germany, Portugal, Belgium and Italy. Only two countries were not drawn into colonial domination – Liberia, founded in 1847 by liberated black slaves from the United States, and Ethiopia, dating back two thousand years.

Although the British, French and Portuguese ruled by different methods, they all had a profound impact on Africa. All hitherto existing civilizations were uprooted and their economies integrated with those of their colonial masters. The purpose of exploitation and trade was mixed with missionary zeal and the rhetoric of humanitarianism (Davidson, 1989).

The major European powers were able to establish domination in the vast African territories due to their efficient systems of administration and the possibility of employing superior physical force. The road to liberation for the African population was the takeover of the colonial states established by the Europeans. These had different structures in the British, French, Belgian and Portuguese territories.

Great Britain relied on immigrants from the motherland in collaboration with the indigenous population. Thus in some British areas there were rather large minorities of white settlers who were much involved in running the colonies within a decentralized framework set by Westminster. In other parts British rule was indirect, meaning that power was exercised in terms of traditional authority structures such as African chiefdoms and kingdoms. Nigeria, for example, was ruled by Lord Lugard (died 1945).

The French model was different in that it relied more on direct rule: the colonies were administered according to the traditional prefectural system employed in France herself. Thus, although a small French population had to carry out orders from Paris, there were also elements of joint rule with the indigenous population. The Portuguese and Belgian models were different again: they relied heavily on the use of naked force (Tordoff, 1984).

By the time of the Berlin Conference in 1884–5 the map of Africa had been drawn up by the colonial powers. Little attention had been paid to her complicated system of tribes and ethnic minorities, and the territorial borders were drawn up by European rulers without any respect for cultural affinities among the Africans. This was conducive to inter-ethnic dissension, enhancing the principle of *divide et impera!*

While the German empire in Africa crumbled during the First World War, the other three empires lasted much longer. Actually, the German territories were taken over by the other colonial powers around 1915. German protectorates included Burundi, Cameroon, Rwanda, Tanganyika and Togo, which came under the control of the British, the Belgians and the French. Belgium held onto the Belgian Congo, whereas Italy was active first and foremost in Libya but also in Somalia and later in Ethiopia (1934–41). Whereas Spain dominated only Equatorial Guinea and the Spanish Sahara, Portugal ruled vast territories such as Angola and Mozambique in addition to Guinea-Bissau and São Tomé and Príncipe.

The British colonial system was formidable in terms of size, whether measured by area or by population. In Africa the British protectorates included Egypt, Libya (1942–51), Sudan, Botswana (Bechuanaland), Gambia, Ghana (Gold Coast), Kenya, Lesotho (Basutoland), Malawi (Nyasaland), Mauritius, Nigeria, Seychelles, Sierra Leone, South Africa, Swaziland, Uganda, Zambia (Northern Rhodesia) and Zimbabwe (Southern Rhodesia). In some of these colonies there were substantial white minorities occupying key positions in the administration and the economy, in particular in Southern Rhodesia and Kenya. The situation in South Africa was radically different from the beginning, as there was a substantial white minority which had arrived before the British. The Dutch settled permanently in Cape Town in 1652, and were followed by the French Huguenots.

The French Empire in Africa was not of quite the same size, but it covered a number of territories that later became independent states. The French concentrated their holdings in North and West Africa: Algeria, Tunisia, Morocco, Benin (Dahomey), Burkina Faso (Upper Volta), Central African Republic, Chad, Congo, Gabon, Guinea, Côte d'Ivoire, Mali, Mauritania and Niger. In addition they held island territories off the East African coast: Madagascar and the Comoros.

How simple it was for the European states to conquer Africa when the scramble for the continent began is well illustrated by the Belgian Congo (which eventually became the independent state of Zaïre). King Léopold II of Belgium claimed this vast territory as his personal colony in the 1870s, which met with international acceptance in 1895. It was not until 1907 that it was transformed from a personal possession into a Belgian colony.

It should be stated that in some cases there was strong opposition to European penetration, but the European powers did not have to risk great resources or personnel when subjugating African rulers, as is analysed in *African Perspectives on Colonialism* (1987) by A. Adu Boahen. The Boers put up fierce resistance against the British in the Boer Wars (1880–1, 1899–1902).

Although there have been several large African empires, notably Mali (1250–1400), Songhai of Gao (1400–1591), Ashanti (1700–1850) and Buganda (1800–1900), several African kingdoms were overwhelmed by colonial military superiority. Morever, many African political systems were badly weakened by the slave trade.

Again, the way to overcome foreign rule was to take over the administration and set up states after the European model. The process of liberation was difficult as the European colonial powers clung firmly to their colonies, resorting to violence when other means did not work. But the Second World War proved a turning-point, as the United Nations Charter encouraged 'recognition of the independence of the peoples of the world' (Brownlie, 1975: 23). Several African colonies had contributed soldiers to the Allied campaign.

Yet all the European powers tried at first to stop the independence movement by the use of force, which resulted in resistance wars in several African countries, in particular in the French and Portuguese colonies. The British Empire had already granted South Africa independence in 1910 by introducing the Union of South Africa, but in 1961 South Africa became a republic and withdrew from the Commonwealth. It controlled Namibia (South West Africa) up until 1990. Control of Egypt had been partially given up in 1922. This was followed in 1936 by a full recognition of Egypt's independence, although the British retained control of the Suez Canal until 1956. The same year Sudan became an independent republic.

The real decline of British power occurred in the 1950s, when its key colonies in Central Africa demanded independence. After the Mau Mau war in Kenya the British government decided to grant independence to these territories, at the same time offering the new states membership within the Commonwealth, which some accepted. Thus we have Ghana in 1957 and in 1960 the large state of Nigeria in Western Africa. Tanganyika followed in 1961, though a merger in 1964 with the sultanate Zanzibar resulted in the new Republic of Tanzania. Kenya was set free in 1963 and in 1964 Zambia and Malawi, a former part of the Federation of Rhodesia and Nyasaland, became independent states. Southern Rhodesia assumed independence in 1965 after Ian Smith's unilateral declaration, but Zimbabwe was granted legal independence by Britain only after a civil war in 1980.

The challenge to the French Empire in Africa was initiated in the north, where there were sizeable French minorities after the Second World War.

There were 250,000 Europeans in Tunisia, more than a million in Algeria and roughly 300,000 in Morocco. After a long period of violent clashes France gave in and acknowledged the independence of Tunisia in 1956. Similarly, Morocco became a free state after a nationalist uproar and a guerrilla war. However, the fight for independence became very bitter, bloody and protracted in Algeria, which had been ruled directly from Paris as a part of France (Morocco and Tunisia had been protectorates). Not until 1962 was the independence of the Algerian state recognized.

The break-up of colonial domination took place according to the domino effect. It was practically impossible to stop the many French colonies in West Africa from successfully claiming independence once French authority had been given up in South-East Asia and North Africa. Thus by 1960 several new states had been created in West Africa, including Guinea (1958), Togo (1960) and Cameroon (1960). In 1960 the free state of Madagascar was also recognized.

Whereas the Belgian Empire was abandoned after a short period of up-heaval in 1959–60, the Portuguese colonies had to fight a long war until the authoritarian regime in Portugal fell in 1974. Thus the former Belgian colonies of the Belgian Congo (Zaïre) and Rwanda and Burundi became independent in 1960 and 1962 respectively. Guinea-Bissau had to wait until 1974 and Angola, Mozambique, Cape Verde, and São Tomé and Príncipe until 1975.

Colonies and precolonial states

The European powers left an ineradicable mark upon their subjugated territories, not only in economical terms, having entered the colonies into their trade structure on conditions favourable to the mother state, but also from a political and administrative point of view. Whereas France relied heavily upon the Napoleonic state to govern her colonies by means of pre-fectoral principles, Britain made various distinctions in authority between its different territorial possessions.

When the British Empire was at its peak in the 1920s it controlled one-quarter of the population and area of the world. Now there are only a few British territories left – Gibraltar and Hong Kong (until 1997) besides some tiny islands in the Atlantic – and the Commonwealth organization is only a weak mechanism for collaboration between the United Kingdom and some of its former territories.

The British Empire initiated several forms of government: (1) colony or crown colony (Jamaica, Barbados, Nigeria, Sri Lanka, Falkland Islands, Bermuda, Hong Kong); (2) dominion (Canada, South Africa, Australia and New Zealand); (3) protectorate (Lesotho, Zambia, Tanzania, Egypt, Malaysia, Swaziland); (4) mandate/trusteeship (Palestine, Jordan, Iraq); and (5) condominium (Sudan).

'Dominion' refers to the legal relationship between the parent state and a self-governing colony granted the highest level of independence. Dominion was conferred on large territories with considerable white settler populations during the nineteenth century, but the formal internal and external independence of the dominion status was not fully accepted until 1931 in the Statute of Westminster. A 'protectorate' was legally subordinate to the parent state, particularly in the field of foreign affairs and sometimes in the field of defence (Roberts, 1971).

A 'condominium' was rather different in that the government of the country was controlled by two foreign powers. 'Mandate', in terms of the League of Nations framework (Class A, B and C mandates), or 'trusteeship', under the United Nations, denoted that a foreign power had been given administrative control of a country for a period of time. In comparison, the status of a 'colony' or 'crown colony' implied a stronger tie with the mother country, the territory belonging to the crown or forming an integral part of the British Commonwealth. The population in the colonies were British subjects and the colony was run by civil servants that were recognized as functionaries in the British state.

However, colonies could be granted various degrees of internal autonomy, such as Southern Rhodesia (Zimbabwe) in 1923 or India in 1909. India was a crown colony and was ruled by a Viceroy representing the British crown, whereas a colony was governed by a governor appointed by the colonial office in Westminster.

Today the British Commonwealth includes some fifty independent states, some 17 of which also accept Queen Elizabeth II as their sovereign. It is basically a mechanism for cooperation between many states which used to be parts of the British empire – with the exception of Ireland, South Africa and the Fiji islands. It is true that many states that were formerly part of the British Empire stuck to Westminster-type political institutions when their independence was granted. However, we find that there is considerable variation, as far from all of the approximately ninety countries that belonged to the empire now adhere to the Westminster model interpreted as an ideal type of government (Lijphart, 1984). Some are federal states (Canada, Australia, India), while others have presidential regimes (South Africa, Malta, Tanzania, Zambia, Zimbabwe, Kenya).

The Portuguese Empire was the last one to break up, as its two major areas, Angola and Mozambique, became independent shortly after the democratic revolution in Portugal in 1974. There has been some discussion concerning the nature of Portuguese colonial policy, in particular its often harsh methods of subjugating its colonies. Portugal used its colonies to exploit its abundance of labour. When slave labour was no longer accepted Portugal turned to legalized forced labour. There was a sharp distinction between 'indigenas' and 'assimilados', or the 95 per cent of the population who were natives and without rights versus the small percentage of the population that had adopted a Portuguese way of life. When the Portuguese colonial state was dismantled in an abrupt fashion, neither Angola nor Mozambique could benefit from a post-colonial state, as both were thrown into large-scale and protracted civil war.

State longevity

It is impossible to specify a typical state age, as the variation in terms of longevity is immense. There are old as well as young states. Some states persist for centuries whereas others come and go. A few states, where state identity has been nurtured by the experiences of several generations, are highly compact. Many states have been so recently founded that the process of building a modern state is precarious. There are even states that lack an identity to such an extent that their very survival is at stake.

States have different time-spans in the twentieth century, as new states have been created to succeed old states or empires. States may persist over centuries or they may perish after only a couple of decades. This may sound as if states had lives of their own, but they are not biological units as the organic theory of the state claimed. They are complex human organizations that have artificially created structures which may be abolished by fiat. As it is true that states may be founded by intention or dissolved by decision, we must also underline that states may have a longevity that lasts over generations.

The identity of the Weberian state involves the maintenance of a set of structures of authority regulating the use of force within a territory of roughly the same boundaries. The fundamental problem here is that there is no natural criterion that we can use to decide when a state has changed so much that its earlier identity has been lost. Since both territorial boundaries and authority structures change over time, states can be identified differently. What is taken as the starting-point of a state is a matter of convention, but it is not arbitrary. Although there are different criteria that may be used, one has to be consistent once one criterion has been selected. Thus the origin of the French state may be dated as 1944 after the Nazi occupation, or 1815 after the Napoleonic Wars, or even further back in time to 1775, 843 or 741, but then the same perspective must be employed for other states.

One must remember the distinction between the modern state, with its administrative machinery distinguishing between the public and the private, and personal rulerships, such as dynasties and feudal structures. Here we count as states only the organizations that fulfil the Weberian criteria. In order to display alternative ways of identifying the time-span of present-day states, we refer in table 3.1 to four standard source books.

First, table 3.1 shows that the identity of states may be pinned down in time in various ways. *Encyclopedia Britannica* gives years that are considerably different to the other three sources. There is agreement between Banks and Taylor and Hudson, because they employ some of the same sources.

Table 3.1 Year of state independence (averages)

	(A)	(B)	(C)	(D)
Africa	1953 (37)	1950 (40)	1889 (43)	1935 (43)
America	1846 (24)	1844 (24)	1840 (24)	1843 (24)
Asia	1920 (30)	1908 (32)	1753 (35)	1803 (34)
Oceania	1904 (2)	1904 (2)	1927 (3)	1909 (3)
Europe	1868 (25)	1828 (25)	1621 (25)	1719 (25)
E^2	.52	.46	.04	.07

Sources: A = Banks (1971); B = Taylor and Hudson (1972); C = *Encyclopedia Britannica Book of the Year* (1990); D = Derbyshire and Derbyshire (1991).

Note: The estimates differ in terms of what is regarded as the initiation of a state, Banks (1971) and Taylor and Hudson (1972) starting from 1775.

Note that the years for Asia are very different in the *Encyclopedia Britannica* and Derbyshire and Derbyshire.

Second, Europe has had a large number of independent states for a long period of time, reflecting, as we have underlined, the diffusion of the modern state model from Western Europe. On the American continent the average year of foundation dates back to the 1840s, whereas modern independent states in Oceania and Asia tended to come forth around 1900. Africa has by far the largest number of young modern states.

Third, we see from table 3.1 that state age is very short in relation to the length of time of human existence on the earth. Many states are not yet one hundred years old. Old states are dying and young ones are being institutionalized in the early 1990s. The persistence of a state cannot be taken for granted. Look, for example, at the tremendous changes in territory of the German state only during the twentieth century.

Conclusion

Although the word 'state' may be used in a variety of meanings, we focus here on what is called the 'modern' state or the 'European' state (McLennan et al., 1984). Sometimes it is also called the 'nation-state', but this expression is more confusing than clarifying. Using the concept put forward by Weber it is widely recognized that this form of state emerged in Europe as fully blown in the seventeenth century after the end of the great religious wars. What is decisive in our conceptualization is the extent to which an organization has implemented the Weberian properties of the state concept: (a) relations of authority between the rulers and those ruled in terms of a normative order, with (b) clear territorial specification of boundaries and (c) monopoly on the legitimate use of physical force in that territory.

The modern state is not necessarily a nation-state, but it may be said to be a European state, as the concept of a 'stato' dates back to around 1500 in Western Europe. The first major finding here is that there are consistently sharp geographical differences in state age. The fact that the European states were capable of subjugating large parts of the world and creating various types of domination structures in America, Asia, Oceania and Africa – colonies, dominions and protectorates – implies that there would be a geographical pattern. All the indicators on state age reflect this process of exporting the European state to other continents, first to America, then to Oceania and Asia, and finally to Africa.

State longevity is not the same as state stability. States that persist over time may be very different in terms of stability. A state may harbour different regimes and may change its constitution more or less often. Regime changes tend to be the outcome of challenges of the established state and constitutional revisions may be the formal expression of system changes. Let us move on to the analysis of constitutions and regimes.

Having recognized in Chapter 1 that the notion of stability has a prominent place in comparative politics, we must remember that it is an inherently ambiguous term that has to be handled with great care. States may display longevity, yet they may have been unstable for some periods of time. We wish to use a concept of state stability that is independent of the concept of state longevity. Thus, although the French state may be said to be very old, one cannot even claim that it has been stable during the entire post-Second World War period. A state may appear to be stable for decades only to collapse suddenly, as was the case with the Soviet Union. Or a state may remain stable, seeming to persist almost indefinitely, such as the United States. How can we employ indicators that allow the measurement of state stability and not state age as discussed in this chapter? In the next chapter we will use another property of the Weberian state – the order or regime – in order to describe state stability as something different from state age.

4

Regimes and Political Stability

Introduction

It is true that some present-day states have been in existence for a long time. Several states, however, have been founded recently. As states that persist over long periods of time may experience insecurity, it is necessary to move to an analysis of state stability. And newly founded states cannot take their existence for granted as their *raison d'être* or legitimacy may be questioned – resulting in state instability.

We have singled out state stability as one of our two basic points of reference for the understanding of comparative government. The concept of state stability is defined in relation to *one* of the properties of the Weberian state: the regime, or the legitimate order for political rule.

Political instability may be of either a short-term or a long-term nature. What starts as dissatisfaction with policies and leaders can spill over into the questioning of the legitimacy of the regime. If no workable solution concerning a new regime can be found, then the entire state may crumble. Thus political instability may be the starting-point of lengthy system transformation, which is our topic in this chapter.

In the literature, one basic aspect of state instability is the lack of regime continuity (Eckstein and Gurr, 1975; Sanders, 1981). Political regimes may fall in a country leaving the state territory intact. It has happened often in European countries, such as France, Spain and Italy, as well as in Latin America and Asia, notably Argentina and Iran.

Recognizing that the concept of state stability is ambiguous, it is vital to find one or two aspects of this concept which allow measurement. In this chapter we suggest a few ways to gauge state stability and attempt to portray a picture of its variation among various kinds of state, authoritarian as well as democratic.

The institutional foundation of states

The properties of the Weberian state imply that states have a legal order or some system of political rule that they maintain within a territory by means of the special political instruments conducive to a monopoly on the employment of physical force. Speaking of state stability we should first take into consideration the occurrence of fundamental revisions of the order, or changes in regime.

The concept of a political regime is difficult to pin down concretely, but the term refers to the fundamental elements of public law. It embodies the basic laws of the state that regulate the state organs, their powers and competences. Often these rules constrain the powers of various state bodies, channelling their activities into various functions, creating mechanisms for power sharing. Such institutions may be collected and given a formally rational structure in written constitutions. Vernon Bogdanor states:

> The concept of a constitution is closely bound up with the notion of the limitation of government by law, a source of authority higher than government and beyond its reach. (Bogdanor, 1988: 4)

It must be pointed out that countries may have constitutions that are orientated towards power diffusion or checks and balances, but at the same time the ongoing practice is straightforward authoritarianism. After all, the USSR was given a constitution in 1936, the 'Stalin constitution' that spoke of 'fundamental rights and duties of citizens' (Unger, 1981). A state that moves towards dictatorship from democracy may either dispel its constitution explicitly or simply continue with the implicit assumption that nothing has changed.

Moreover, some states have had oppressive constitutions, for example, South Africa with the apartheid system. The harsh racist regime introduced there in 1948 after the electoral victory of the Nationalist Party was based on a legal framework, including a constitution that strictly limited voting rights and an intricate system of pass laws that restricted the movement of the black population (Horowitz, 1991). Then there is the Fascist constitution that authorizes a corporatist-autocratic type of regime by means of formally written documents, such as was the case in Italy and Spain (Finer, 1988).

The regime constituting the institutional bedrock of the state cannot be identified with the written constitution. In order to describe the institutional web of a state one must look at ongoing practices and their orientation towards formally stated and actually employed rules. It is not enough to focus exclusively on some specific set of formal documents called 'constitution'. As a matter of fact, the concept of a constitution is a muddled one.

The concept of a constitution

The concept of a constitution is of help to the study of state regimes if it is employed with care. It is not all that clear what 'constitution' stands for, as explained in Geoffrey Marshall's *Constitutional Theory* (1971). A few distinctions have been emphasized in the literature (Bogdanor, 1988), which are relevant when the concept of a constitution is used for the analysis of regimes.

First, there is the separation between a written constitution and an unwritten one. However, this distinction is not really that important. Since very few countries do not have written constitutions – for example, the United Kingdom, Israel and New Zealand – this is not a very informative conceptual pair. In addition, since 'unwritten constitution' means only that there is no formally existing, concretely specified set of documents which is designated 'the constitution', it does not imply that countries that lack a constitution also lack basic institutional rules. This is very much the case in the United Kingdom, where some special documents have a sort of constitutional status Magna Carta (1215) and Habeas Corpus (1679), among others – and there is agreement as to which practices have the status of convention – as outlined, for example, in Ivor Jennings's *Cabinet* (1951) and *Parliament* (1961). To quote Vernon Bogdanor:

> If by 'constitution' we mean simply the rules, whether statutory or not, regulating the powers of government and the rights and duties of citizens, then Britain, like other civilised states, has always possessed a constitution; but clearly this was not what Tocqueville had in mind when he made his famous declaration that Britain had no constitution. (Bogdanor, 1988: 53)

When there is talk about states not having a constitution one usually has in mind not only that there is no compact document comprising fundamental state laws, but also that the regime does not fall back upon the existence of a set of fundamental laws that are different from ordinary positive law. In this meaning there is no constitution in the United Kingdom, although it has what A. V. Dicey called a 'historic constitution' (as opposed to a non-historic one; Dicey, [1885] 1924).

Second, there is a distinction between the 'formal' constitution and the 'real' constitution in use. Constitutional documents, even if so designated, are not safe indicators or true descriptions of the basic institutions of the state, because they may be obsolete to some extent or simply downright misleading. The constitution in use is a set of rules that are actually followed in state activities and which are regarded as legitimate by the key groups of power holders if not a majority of the population in the state. Here we come close to the regime concept and its important place in the state.

Now, which rules belong to the real constitution may not be easy to specify, but it is sometimes possible to use the formal written constitution as an approximation of the real regime realities. Several countries have established constitutions recently, which could minimize the distance between constitutional formalities and constitutional realities.

Thirdly, constitutional documents tend to have a special legal status. Constitutional status places the fundamental laws on a higher level than positive law or the main legal order. Sometimes such a constitutional status is protected by means of a special legal subsystem such as a constitutional court. Constitutional law may be designated special status by means of the requirement of separate decision-making procedures for constitutional change or revision. A constitution not only implies well-designed documents but may also involve a special legal status.

Finally, one may distinguish between a broad and a narrow interpretation of the constitution concept. In the *narrow* connotation, a 'constitution' means any implicitly understood and accepted rules or directives for the fundamental state activities. In the *broad* connotation, a constitution is a set of formal documents having special status above the ordinary legal order, where its institutions are safeguarded by special mechanisms such as a constitutional court or very particular rules concerning change.

The complex nature of the concept of constitution means that it is not an easy task to identify the actual operating principles or the true normative order of the state. In addition, constitutional documents have an ideological flavour, revealed in the shifting popularity of various constitutional ideas from one period to another.

Constitutional diffusion

Constitutions are not made from scratch, but stem from both international constitutional theory and the history of the individual country. One may see the effects of constitutional diffusion by looking at the date of origin of key state constitutions. Thus several of the constitutions enacted at the end of the eighteenth or the beginning of the nineteenth century expressed the principles of the division of powers according to the doctrine of John Locke as set forth in *Two Treatises on Government* (1689) or the Montesquieu model expounded in *De l'esprit des lois* (1748).

The constitutional state became politically relevant at the end of the eighteenth century. Constitutionalism was launched as a political theory about good government to be implemented by the introduction of a written constitution. The new theory of liberal constitutionalism in the nineteenth century in the synthesis by Benjamin Constant (1815) involved:

the doctrine which, in the secular age of the autonomy of politics inherent in the principles of 'national sovereignty' and 'sovereignty of the people', demanded that this kind of state should have a written Law which would set out the rights and obligations of citizens and the institutions established to make them work, with all the checks and balances required to watch over the proper functioning of state and society on behalf of the people. (Ionescu, 1988: 35–6)

The two model constitutions at that time were the American one (1787) – a constitutional republic – and the French one (1791) – a constitutional monarchy. These inspired the making of several constitutions all over the world. Constitutional monarchy was expressed in Sweden in 1809, in Spain in 1812, in Norway in 1814 and in Belgium in 1831. The American presidential system was adopted in Latin America with the exception of Brazil. Until it adopted a federal constitution in 1891 Brazil copied the 1822 Portuguese constitution, which followed the Spanish constitution of 1812.

Actually, the French and American constitutional principles remained the archetypes, because the British Westminster model was not fully developed until the mid-1850s. Then the English constitutional tradition and its peculiar contribution – parliamentarism (Bagehot, [1867] 1993) – were spread to the dominions of the emerging empire, although the crown colonies were governed from Westminster. Not only were several European states with their orientation towards constitutional monarchy given a constitution, the constitutional diffusion also reached Turkey (1876), Japan (1889), Persia (1906) and China (1912).

The doctrine of the separation of powers in combination with the prevalent notion of a 'Rechtsstaat' were embodied in the constitutional codifications around 1800. The state was looked upon as a set of branches of government: executive, legislature and judiciary. They were to be assigned separate power functions: rule application, rule-making and rule adjudication; and they should be staffed by various actors: kings or presidents, parliamentarians and judges. By such separation it was hoped that a kind of power balance would be established.

Adding the unitary – federal – dimension of the state, a large number of hybrid types were established during the nineteenth century. Strong presidential powers resulted in the Latin American context whereas the English system gravitated towards the doctrine of parliamentary sovereignty. The German and Austro-Hungarian constitutions were placed somewhere in between, underlining royal prerogatives and a strong state bureaucracy.

There have been three waves of constitutional diffusion in the twentieth century. The end of the First World War saw the introduction of new democratic constitutions which emphasized human rights, for example, the Weimar republic's constitution in 1919, those of Yugoslavia and Poland in 1921 and that of Romania in 1922. A second wave occurred after the end of the Second World War, when the term 'Sozialstaat' became as valid as 'Rechtsstaat'. Many constitutions enacted after the end of the Second World War emphasized several kinds of human rights, including positive liberties such as the right to employment. Examples are the 1949 Basic Law of the Federal Republic of Germany and the Italian constitution from 1948.

Many new constitutions rephrased or anticipated the international declarations concerning human rights, negative as well as positive, by the United Nations in 1948 and by the European Council in 1950. Freedom of speech and association are negative liberties, whereas the right to social support and employment are positive liberties. The new emphasis on positive freedom is apparent not only in new constitutions in the rich world, such as Spain (1978) and Portugal (1976/1982), but also in the Indian constitution of 1949, adding to 'fundamental rights' so-called 'directive principles of state policy' (Finer, 1988: 30). The major declarations of human rights in the eighteenth century, the Declaration of Independence in the United States (1776), the French Declaration of Human Rights (1789) and the American Bill of Rights (1791), were almost exclusively orientated towards the concept of negative freedom, underlining what governments could not do to their citizens.

A third wave of constitutionalism was set in motion by the collapse of communist regimes in Eastern Europe as well as the drive towards democracy in the Third World. Actually, the many regime changes recently may be seen as a test of constitutionalism, that is, on its power to suggest proper political institutions that would enhance state stability. Constitutional rules, whether in the broad or narrow sense mentioned above, may contribute towards predictability in state activities and operations.

The concept of a regime

The difficulties surrounding the concept of the constitution make us return to the concept of the regime. There is hardly a general definition of the concept of a political regime available in the literature. The compact edition of *The Oxford English Dictionary* (1987) talks about both 'regime' and 'regimen', tying the former together with institutions: 'Regime: 1. Regimen. 2.a. A manner, method, or system of rule or government; a system or institution having widespread influence or prevalence. b. specifically, the system of government in France before the Revolution of 1789.'

Whereas the Ancien Régime in France denoted a concrete regime in space and time described by, among others, Tocqueville (1856), it remains somewhat of an arbitrary task to identify the regimes in every country, especially stating their life-span. It would make things easier if one had recourse to a set of clear concepts of type which would allow us to classify country regimes.

When 'regime' is considered synonymous with 'regimen', then the behaviour aspects of the concept of a regime is underlined. Thus the *Oxford Dictionary*'s 'Regimen. 1. The act of governing; government, rule.' Another standard source book, the *American College Dictionary*, explicitly combines the normative and behaviour aspects: 'Regime: 1. a mode or system of rule or government. 2. a ruling or prevailing system.'

Easton made a distinction between three basic political objects: the authorities, regime and political community, which he used in his theory about political stability: the 'change of a system' means a change in one of these objects, and where all three objects change simultaneously we can consider that 'the former system has totally disappeared' (Easton, 1965a: 172).

Whereas 'political community' would be the territorial dimension of the

Weberian state, this refers only to the state members seen as a group of persons bound together by a political division of labour (Easton, 1965a: 177); 'regime' covers more properties: values, norms and structure of authority (p. 193). Regime norms specify the procedures to be used in making public decisions and implementing them; 'authorities' refer to people in ruling positions. Evidently, a crisis in the regime would hit the very institutional foundation of the state, whereas a rejection of the authorities could be resolved by appointing new leaders with or without major changes in the regime.

The problem is the connection in the concept of regime between its value and norm component on the one hand and the behaviour component on the other. How should the concept be handled when there is inconsistency between the normative content of a regime and the prevailing rule? Was there a sharp change of regime in India when Indira Gandhi ruled dictatorially in 1976–7? We need operational criteria that measure the occurrence of regime transformations or changes. To be able to speak of fundamental changes we need concepts that allow us to identify a minimum number of regime types. Political systems of rule may be classified in a number of alternative ways (Bebler and Seroka, 1990), but one neat typology is that of Weber, which, though complemented, can be used for measuring overall regime changes.

Regime typologies: Weber's system

First, to Weber, political legitimacy results from a special feeling or mode of looking upon government where the legal order or the regime is considered morally binding by the population; a government that is illegitimate cannot last very long. However, Weber underestimated how extensive physical force may be employed for political purposes. Naked power rulerships may last for quite some time, as post-Second World War events testify: East European communism, the rule of the Khmer Rouge in Cambodia, China's domination of Tibet, Saddam Hussein in Iraq, the Shah Pahlavi regimen in Iran, Pinochet in Chile, Papa Doc Duvalier in Haiti, Idi Amin in Uganda and Mengistu in Ethiopia.

Second, there is the basic division into three types of rulership: traditional rule, charismatic leadership and legal-rational authority (Weber, 1978: 215). And authority presupposes that those ruled follow the directives – commands or laws – of the rulers. A regime or a system of prescriptions may be accepted as legitimate either because it has always been accepted – traditional authority – or because the leaders are obeyed out of a special relationship of venerability – charismatic authority. Then there is the modern or legal-rational type of authority.

Third, Weber made a number of distinctions among traditional authority systems, which are applicable mainly in historical analysis. Here, we note the

Table 4.1 States with traditional rule, 1990

Country	Population (in thousands)	Rulership	Year of foundation
Bahrain	503	Reigning amir	1971
Bhutan	1,442	Monarchy (maharajah)	1947
Brunei	259	Sultanate	1984
Jordan	3,169	Kingdom	1946
Kuwait	2,143	Sheikhdom	1961
Morocco	25,113	Kingdom	1956
Nepal	18,910	Monarchy (maharajah)	1846
Oman	1,468	Sultanate	1744
Qatar	444	Sheikhdom	1971
Saudi Arabia	14,131	Monarchy	1932
Swaziland	770	Monarchy	1967
Thailand	56,217	Monarchy	1350
Tonga	96	Monarchy	1970
United Arab Emirates	1,903	Federation of sheikhs	1971

Sources: Derbyshire and Derbyshire, 1991; *Encyclopedia Britannica Book of the Year* (1991).

following types: gerontocracy, patriarchalism, patrimonialism, sultanism, estate-type domination, feudalism, medieval corporatism and absolutism (Weber, 1978: 217–301). Traditional authority systems tend to be changed by the power of charismatic leaders: 'It is written but I say unto you', in the words of the Bible. However, charismatic authority is fundamentally un-stable, as it cannot solve the successor problem. The only viable option to plebiscitary leadership, according to Weber, is the introduction of the rational-legal authority type, where power is exercised in terms of rules by office holders, who must separate their political and private roles – in other words, bureaucratic rule.

Traditional regimes

Actually, Weber had more to say about the major kinds of historical regime than he did about present-day democracy. When we turn to the experiences of regimes in the twentieth century, it is impossible not to place democracy at the forefront. Few cases of Weberian traditional authority systems now exist. The sheikh or amir and sultanate regimes in the Middle East could be classified in this way, as could the few remaining monarchies, for example, in Morocco and Thailand. However, the border-line between traditional regimes and authoritarian rule is not clear-cut, as table 4.1 shows.

Some of these absolutist regimes have taken steps to introduce constitutions that confer some aura of constitutional monarchy on the rulers. Nepal even had democratic elections in 1991. Yet a few of them, for example, Saudi Arabia, lack a constitution entirely. Several traditional regimes, however, are ruling quite small states.

There have been a few cases of sultanic rule or tyrannical leadership: Amin (Uganda), Bokassa (Central African Republic), Nguema (Equatorial Guinea), Mengistu (Ethiopia), Mobutu (Zaïre) and Eyadema (Togo) in Africa, as well as Papa Doc Duvalier (Haiti) in Central America. At the same time much traditional rule remains in the internal structures of many states, such as kinship and primary political groupings in several African countries. Local chiefs or kinship structures are publicly accepted as part of the state structure in order to increase the legitimacy of the rulers. Tradititional authorities may be organized in houses of chiefs operating as intermediaries or brokers between the central power and the local sites and receive government sanction as well as salaries. Systems of clientelism are often legitimized on the basis of tradition – neo-patrimonialism (Chazan et al., 1992).

Charismatic regimes

It is not obvious how to identify states with charismatic rule according to the Weberian conception. Who is a charismatic leader? Charisma as a basis for personal rule can occur in both democratic and non-democratic states. As examples of charismatic rule we may recognize transition regimes such as Marshal Tito's provisional government during the Second World War, or revolutionary regimes such as those of Sukarno in Indonesia, Nasser in Egypt, Fidel Castro in Cuba and Khomeini in Iran (Goldstone et al., 1991; DeFronzo, 1991).

Charismatic leadership may presage the start of revolutionary movements, as with Gandhi and his principle of 'satyagraha' or passive resistance, or Nelson Mandela as leader of the ANC. Or charisma may be employed to uphold or strengthen legal rule, as with Juan and Eva Perón. The distinction between charismatic rule and naked oppression is blurred when it comes to Lenin, Stalin, Mao Zedong, Hitler, Mussolini and Franco.

Populist leaders in trying to establish direct links with the population, derive part of their appeal from charismatic qualities. Here we may mention a few African leaders: Jerry Rawlings (Ghana), Muammar Quaddafi (Libya), Thomas Sankara (Burkina Faso) and Yoweri Museveni (Uganda). The separation between charismatic, populist and sultanic rulers is not always clear-cut; where, for example, should Kwame Nkrumah of Ghana be placed?

The border-lines between patrimonial or personalistic rule and legal-rational regimes is blurred in the Arab countries (Luciani, 1990), where the 'rentier state' rests upon both traditional rule and modern bureaucracy. In a rentier state political power focuses not on the production of goods and services in the private or public sectors, but on the allocation of funds derived from the fortuitous possession of natural resources such as oil. Both the production state and the allocation state require rational bureaucracy in Weber's sense.

Legal-rational regimes

Weber's classification is not so productive when looking at modern states. When considering the rise of the democratic type of regime since the Second World War we need an institutional typology orientated towards the understanding of the variety of democratic states. At the same time we must not forget that many states are not democracies. Thus, in addition, we need to distinguish between various kinds of dictatorship, such as totalitarian and authoritarian regimes (Linz, 1975; Ferdinand, 1991). Both the totalitarian and the authoritarian type of regime may involve non-legal exercises of power, as both kinds of rule are at times expressed in unpredictable fashion.

The military regime is a peculiar hybrid, as it involves dictatorship but often also illegitimate rulership (Bebler, 1990; Morlino, 1990). The distinction between the military junta and the one-party model of an authoritarian regime is related to the difference between right-wing and left-wing dictatorships. What distinguishes left-wing non-democratic rule is the combination of a one-party state with some kind of planned economy. Right-wing dictatorship may also make use of the one-party model, but it will more often be based on a type of military regime, as, for example, in Asia, where there have been several coups in a few countries (Chirkin, 1990; Berg-Schlosser, 1990).

Let us complement the Weberian system by looking at a few fundamental types of regimes in democracies. First, one may make a distinction between democracies that adhere to parliamentarism and executive presidentialism respectively. Second, one may speak of Westminster-type democracy and consensus-type democracy. Starting with the latter, we focus on Arend Lijphart's typology.

Lijphart's typology

A democratic regime may be the best kind when judged by state evaluation criteria such as, for example, human rights and welfare spending. But are all democracies alike? Should we make some basic distinctions in the set of democracies? In developing his consociational theory, Arend Lijphart introduced two ideal types (see table 4.2).

Whereas Lijphart earlier argued that both these sets of institutions would be conducive to state stability, he now seems to claim that, judging by stability and performance criteria, the consensus model is superior to the Westminster model (Lijphart, 1991a, 1992a).

The Lijphart model is a most general one, covering not only state institutional conditions but also properties referring to the actors in the party

Table 4.2   The Lijphart model

Westminster democracy	Consensus democracy
1) One-party and bare-majority cabinets	Executive power-sharing
2) Fusion of power and cabinet dominance	Separation of powers, formal and informal
3) Asymmetric bi-cameralism	Balanced bi-cameralism and minority representation
4) Two-party system	Multi-party system
5) One-dimensional party system	Multi-dimensional party system
6) Plurality system of elections	Proportional representation
7) Unitary and centralized territorial government	Territorial and non-territorial federalism and decentralization
8) Unwritten constitution and parliamentary sovereignty	Written constitution and minority veto

Source: Lijphart (1984).

system and in government. It raises the question: Do the concepts of West-minster and consensus democracy have empirical reality? In other words, is there as a matter of fact a strong tendency towards these two model types? Consider the following with regard to the distinction between Westminster and consensus democracy.

1) *State and executive structure*   It is not difficult to find states that are federal in nature but which tend to be run by governments who have won by only a small majority (minimum winning). Canada, Australia, India, and Germany spring to mind. And several countries which have practised grand coalitions are unitary states – for example, the Nether-lands, Finland and Lebanon.

2) *State and legislature*   It is not the case that unitary states tend towards one kind of legislative chamber format, such as mono-cameralism or asymmetrical bi-cameralism. France, Belgium, the Netherlands, Italy and Spain testify to this.

3) *Election system, party system and executive structure*   The Nordic countries, Spain, Portugal and Greece prove false the hypothesis that electoral proportionality and multi-dimensional issues promote the creation of grand coalitions.

One must remember that the Lijphart models are so-called ideal types, or extreme theoretical constructs. They are thus more tools of analysis than empirical descriptions. The Lijphart model serves as a corrective to the prevailing image that the Westminster system is *the* true or effective model for democracy in countries with a parliamentary regime (Lijphart, 1994b).

	Westminster	Consensus
Parliamentarism	I UK	II Austria
Presidentialism	III France	IV USA

Figure 4.1 Democracy, executive presidentialism and parliamentarism

It is readily seen that parliamentary states are not the only democratic regimes, and that presidential institutions also fall into the democratic category. It must be recognized, however, that many presidential regimes are non-democratic. A basic question in comparative politics is whether strong presidentialism is negatively related to stable government, at least in a democratic context (Linz, 1992; Lijphart, 1992b).

Walter Bagehot, in *The English Constitution* ([1867] 1993), gave an answer that has been considered authoritative:

> This fusion of the legislative and executive functions may, to those who have not much considered it, seem but a dry and small matter to be the latent essence and effectual secret of the English constitution; . . . That competitor is the presidential system. The characteristic of it is that the president is elected from the people by one process, and the house of representatives by another. The independence of the legislative and executive powers is the specific quality of the presidential government, just as their fusion and combination is the precise principle of cabinet government. (Bagehot, 1993: 71)

Bagehot focused on the distinction between two constitutional principles, on the one hand the principle of the balance of powers and on the other the idea of parliamentarism as power fusion. He argued that the parliamentary mode of government was superior to the presidential in terms of state performance. One needs to qualify the notion of presidentialism, however, by making a distinction between *strong* and *weak* presidentialism. In the former the president exercises true executive powers independently of the parliament, whereas in the latter there is parliamentarism, the president acting only symbolically.

The Bagehot distinction between parliamentarism and presidentialism may be combined with the Lijphart differentiation between consensus and Westminster-type democracy. Thus we have four possible regimes, not simply two as Bagehot claimed (see figure 4.1). Which type is most stable or performs best?

The United States of America comes closest to the Montesquieu model of powersharing, which lies at the heart of Lijphart's consensus model. Switzerland exemplifies limited presidentialism on account of its special executive, where the presidential post rotates in a directorate type of government. Real parliamentary systems may comprise not only states with weak presidential heads, as, for example, Germany, but also states with strong presidents, such as Finland. The problem is that it is difficult to reduce regime variations to one concise set of concepts. Moreover, real-life changes between these four democracy types must be recognized as basic in the operation of a state, such as, for example, the introduction of executive presidentialism in France in 1958 or the insertion of parliamentarism in Portugal in 1983 and Greece in 1986 (Shugart and Carey, 1992).

A combined Bagehot–Lijphart model is helpful in interpreting constitutional or basic regime changes in democratic states. What kind of typology one may start from when approaching the many states outside those fortunate ones within the OECD set will be discussed in Chapter 7. Using an augmented Weberian system of regimes we now proceed to measure the actual number of fundamental regime changes, from traditional rule to legal-rational rule, from dictatorship or right-wing or left-wing authoritarianism to democracy or back again, as well as the change between basic democracy types.

State stability

If a regime is of such basic importance to the state, then it is relevant to ask how stable regimes tend to be. One way to gauge regime longevity is to measure when the present constitution of a state was introduced. Another indicator might be the number of constitutional changes since, say, 1970. A third possibility is to look at how regimes have fluctuated over a certain period of time. Finally, one could try to measure regime duration since 1945.

Constitutional longevity

The differences between the two indices employed here with regard to constitutional longevity – the Taylor and Hudson index, referring to the situation about 1968–70, versus the *Encyclopedia Britannica* index, which deals with the position in 1990 – are not that large, but testify to the difficulties in determining regime identity by means of indicators on constitutional longevity (see table 4.3). We would expect to find that these indicators reveal considerable variation between the major continents but also within each continent. But which type of variation is actually the largest – the within- or between-continent variation?

The current constitution of a state is always of a lesser age than the state itself, meaning that regime changes tend to take place frequently. Even in Europe, with some of its old states, numerous constitutional changes have occurred. The between-group differences are smaller than the within-group differences, which means that states differ in constitutional stability within each of the continents. Most regime changes have occurred in the states in Africa, America and Asia, but, contrary to the finding in Chapter 3 with

Table 4.3 Age of present constitution and constitutional longevity

	Current constitution, 1970	Current constitution, 1990	Constitutional status: number of changes 1970–90
Africa	1959 (40)	1977 (43)	.86 (43)
America	1932 (24)	1955 (24)	.62 (24)
Asia	1954 (31)	1970 (31)	.75 (36)
Australia	1876 (2)	1909 (3)	.00 (3)
Europe	1919 (25)	1946 (24)	.48 (25)
E^2	.21	.17	.07

Sources: Taylor and Hudson (1972): *Encyclopedia Britannica Book of the Year* (1990). The number of cases is given in parentheses.

Note: Constitutional status measures the average number of major constitutional revisions in the states on the various continents.

regard to state age, the average age of present constitutions is not markedly different in the new world and the old European world.

The main finding here is that most constitutions are not very old, which means that constitutional changes are frequent. Political life is hazardous in many countries, to say the least. The present constitutions among the states of the world have mostly been adopted or changed after 1945. This applies in particular to Africa and Asia, where colonial rule received its final blow after the Second World War.

Countries where there have been no major constitutional revisions for a long time include Australia, Ireland, Mexico, the Netherlands, New Zealand, Norway, Saudi Arabia, the United Kingdom and the United States. However, this does not guarantee that the present regime is universally accepted as legitimate, which is shown in particular by the problem of national identity in Canada. Regime stability, as measured by the duration of the present constitution and the number of constitutional changes, occurs *inter alia* among the democracies in the affluent world, but not all affluent countries are characterized by regime stability. A few liberal welfare states, such as Germany, Belgium and France, have experienced major constitutional upheavals.

In several Third World countries there have been major constitutional changes rather recently: Ethiopia, Yemen, Algeria, Chad, Cambodia, South Korea, Iran, Afghanistan, Nicaragua, the Philippines, the Central African Republic and Sudan. Not many Third World countries are characterized by constitutional stability. How long will traditional rule last in patrimonial systems such as in Saudi Arabia, Oman, Qatar, the United Arab Emirates and Morocco? And how much longer will communist rule prevail in countries outside Eastern Europe, such as China, North Korea, Vietnam, Laos, Burma and Cuba? In countries afflicted by the horrors of civil war (Ethiopia, Sudan, Somalia, Angola, Mozambique, Liberia, Namibia and Lebanon) there will come new regimes – if the state of 'omnium bellum contra omnes' is to be done away with (see Appendix 4.1). The recent surge in the late 1980s and early 1990s in the foundation of new states implies of necessity the introduction of new regimes, as is the case in the former Soviet Union, Yugoslavia and the countries of Eastern Europe.

So, although states may persist for centuries, constitutions are of much briefer duration. Had we recognized the Nazi occupation of Europe as a constitutional change – it certainly was so in one sense – then the countries retaining the same regime for more than fifty years would be very small in number. At the same time, constitutions matter in a few countries with a firm belief in the legitimacy of their political regime and where the constitution or semi-constitutional practices are considered almost sacred: the United States, Norway and Switzerland.

Yet formal constitutional change and regime instability are not one and the same. Another way to measure regime stability is to focus directly on the transitions between the two major types of regime in this century, democracy versus dictatorship. This involves a number of more valid indicators, as not every constitutional change signals regime instability. Thus Denmark in 1953 and Sweden in 1974 introduced new constitutions, but they simply codified what was long accepted as legitimate through implicit practices.

Regime fluctuations

As things now stand it appears that the relevant constitutional choice or the basic regime alternatives are democracy or dictatorship. The stability of these two regime types may be singled out for special analysis. Although the number of stable democracies does not count for more than one-sixth of the total number of states, the variation over time in the stability of democratic and non-democratic regimes may be mapped. By looking at the fluctuation in indices for degree of democracy, covering all kinds of regimes scoring high or low on democratic properties, we may gain insight into regime variation in states.

There is a constant risk of the collapse of democratic institutions in some parts of the world where democracy is sought but never firmly institutionalized. Similarly, dictatorships are not stable everywhere. Table 4.4 indicates the fluctuation in democracy and dictatorship for various periods between 1945 and 1986.

The finding here is that regime reshuffling has occurred since the end of the war on all the continents, with the exception of the very stable Oceania. It is particularly pronounced in Latin America and Africa but it has also taken place in several Asian states. However, the same states do not score high on

Table 4.4 Regime fluctuations, 1945–86

	SDGU1 1970–86	SDGU2 1960–76	SDGU3 1950–66	SDGU4 1945–61
Africa	.67 (40)	1.04 (20)	.47 (6)	.52 (6)
America	1.09 (24)	1.03 (23)	.95 (22)	.92 (22)
Asia	.67 (32)	.80 (31)	.99 (27)	.98 (17)
Oceania	.00 (2)	.00 (2)	.00 (2)	.00 (2)
Europe	.48 (25)	.28 (25)	.15 (25)	.68 (23)
E^2	.05	.09	.20	.07

Note: Based on the Gurr (GU) index of democracy (1990) (see appendices 4.2 and 5.1). High scores indicate changes between democracy and dictatorship; the standard deviation (SD) expresses the fluctuation between high and low democracy scores.

regime instability all the time, as a short examination of a few spectacular transitions from democracy to dictatorship or vice versa shows.

A military coup in Bolivia in 1952 triggered a popular uprising which led Paz Estenssoro to assume the presidency, although he had failed to achieve a majority in the 1951 election. In 1964 the Barrientos coup overthrew the Paz government. A new coup in 1971 brought Hugo Banzer Suarez to power, and in 1980 there was yet one more among the some 190 military coups that have taken place in Bolivia during 154 years of independence. Regime instability is similar in Peru, where a number of coups have taken place, including the Velasco military junta (1968–75). However, there have also been attempts at democratic rule, challenged in the 1980s and early 1990s by 'Sendoro Luminoso', a Maoist guerrilla.

The events in the Dominican Republic are well known: the dictator Rafael Trujillo was assassinated in 1961, having ruled since a coup in 1930. In 1962 Juan Bosch was appointed president in free elections, only to be ousted by a coup the next year; he was later reinstated, but ousted again in 1965. The greatest attention to any coup in Latin America was no doubt paid to the overthrow by Pinochet of the democratically elected Marxist President Allende, thus in Chile in 1973, establishing a dictatorship that lasted until 1989.

In Cuba, Batista came to power by means of a coup in 1952. He was finally ousted in 1959 by Fidel Castro, who had led two previously un-successful coups, in 1953 and 1956. Also in Latin America, there was the overthrow of Juan Peron in Argentina in 1955, when the civilian government which Peron had smashed with his 1945 military coup was restored, and the Rojas regime in Colombia, introduced by a coup in 1953 and abolished in 1957 by a further coup during the ten-year period of civil war 'La Violencia', when over a quarter of a million people died. Moreover, there were coups in Guatemala (the fall of Arbentz in 1954), in Honduras (the overthrow of Diaz in 1956) and Venezuela (the short-lived military regime in 1958 under Larrazábal).

In 1952 a group of young army officers led by Gamal Nasser overthrew King Farouk in Egypt by means of a military junta. In 1953 Egypt became a republic, but Nasser did not assume a leading position, as Prime Minister, until the following year. It was not until the collapse of colonial rule that Africa started to experience a transitional wave, with regime swings back and forth. Thus in the Central African Republic military rule was introduced by Bokassa in 1962, which initiated a regimen that became all the more idiosyncratic until Bokassa was deposed in 1979. A military coup followed by a counter-coup in Nigeria in 1966 gave power to Gowon, but his rule, which involved the civil war with the Ibos between 1967 and 1970, lasted only until 1975. During the 1980s the country underwent a whole series of coups.

Actually, there have been straightforward coups in most African countries: Togo (1963), Zaïre (1965), Gabon (1967), Somalia (1969), Benin (1972), Rwanda (1973), Sudan (1985), Burkina Faso (1969, 1980), Burundi (1966, 1987), Niger (1974), Chad (1975), Ethiopia (1977), Ghana (1966, 1972, 1978) and Liberia (1980). The military forces in the newly independent states early gained an upper hand in political developments, as in Zaïre, where they helped Mobutu to power in 1965, and in Uganda, where Idi Amin overthrew Obote in 1971 (Obote returned to power after Amin's notorious regimen was crushed in 1978). A few strong, if not charismatic, leaders, such as Kaunda in Zambia, Mugabe in Zimbabwe, Kenyatta in Kenya, Nyerere in Tanzania and Banda in Malawi, chose a less violent strategy in establishing a kind of semi-dictatorship and favouring the one-party model as the mechanism for control.

Military rule was imposed in Pakistan in 1958, when General Ayub Khan seized power, as well as in 1977, when General Zia ul-Haq overthrew Ali Bhutto's democratic rule (Bhutto was executed in 1979). Several coups in Turkey since the charismatic Ataturk regime was established in 1923 have resulted in a strong military involvement in politics. The 1960 coup led to the execution of Prime Minister Menderes and that in 1980 resulted in martial law which suspended all democratic political activity until 1983.

The 1965 Indonesian military coup established a lengthy period of domination for the army, but the acting president – Sukarno – was not formally removed from office until 1967, to die under house arrest in 1971. Suharto has moved to legitimize military supremacy by semi-authoritarian rule, which has involved the wiping out of such opposition groups as the Communist Party in atrocious persecutions (1965–67). The combination of left-wing authoritarianism and military rule is to be found in Burma (Union of Myanmar) where military coups in 1962 and 1988 have paved the way for a one-party state, the 'Burmese Way to Socialism'.

The set of states which are either stable democracies or stable dictatorships

Table 4.5 Regime fluctuations, 1973–91

	SDGA1 1973–88	SDGA 1973–91
Africa	.74 (42)	.89 (42)
America	1.19 (24)	1.26 (24)
Asia	.84 (34)	.97 (32)
Oceania	.17 (3)	.17 (3)
Europe	.46 (25)	.83 (23)
E²	.14	.08

Note: Based on the Gastil et al. (1987, 1990) and Freedom House (1992) indices of democracy over time where a high score indicates regime instability, countries fluctuating between democracy and dictatorship as revealed in the standard deviations (SD) of the regime scores over time (see appendices 4.2 and 5.1).

score low as far as regime changes are concerned. Looking at the past fifteen years the picture is somewhat different, as table 4.5 indicates.

Regime instability is again pronounced in Latin America, Asia and Africa, where there have been a number of transitions from civil to military rule and even back again. Examples are Argentina, Bangladesh, Burkina Faso, Ecuador, Honduras, Bolivia, Thailand, Peru, Paraguay and Iran. At the same time the score for Europe is up sharply, which reflects the fall of the communist regimes.

One overall finding from tables 4.4 and 4.5 is that regime instability has been most conspicuous in Latin America. There is also general instability in Africa, but it reflects more the competition between more or less authoritarian civil rule on the one hand and military government on the other. Part but certainly not all of the instability in Asia mirrors the difficulties in introducing stable democracy. The within-group variation is larger than the between-group variation, which requires a search for general factors in order to account for regime stability.

Could there be political instability even though the political regime remains secure? The concept of stability in politics is ambiguous. On the one hand there are notions of long-term stability, such as regime persistence and constitutional longevity; on the other we have short-term concepts, which may be employed in the context of leadership crisis or government duration.

The question of government stability is problematic. When governments come and go frequently or when the leadership of a state is repeatedly changed, there may be talk of political instability. However, it must be remembered that political leadership that lasts too long may also indicate political instability.

Table 4.6   Long-term instability of regimes, 1945–90

	Number of regimes	Average duration (in years) (REG)
Africa	2.8 (43)	14.2 (43)
America	4.3 (24)	16.7 (24)
Asia	3.2 (36)	19.7 (35)
Oceania	1.0 (3)	37.0 (3)
Europe	2.0 (26)	30.5 (25)
E^2	.14	.23

Source: REG was arrived at by identifying the number of regimes 1945–90 (a) and estimating the number of years of independence during the same period (b), then dividing (b) by (a).

State stability: average duration of the regime

In order to arrive at a broad picture of state stability in the long-term perspective we have estimated the number of regime changes in our set of states by identifying when major events have taken place during the postwar period. Thus we have taken into consideration whether states have moved (a) from democracy to dictatorship or the other way around; (b) from civil to military rule or the other way around; (c) from one type of democratic rule to another (when the change is a major one, such as the movement from the Fourth to the Fifth Republic in France); and (d) from one kind of authoritarian system to another (for example, from a Fascist regime to a communist one). Table 4.6 comprises the data.

The pattern of long-term instability is not the same as that for short-term instability (see Chapter 9). Generally speaking, regimes last longer in Europe and Oceania than on the other three continents. They do not last long in Latin America, Asia and Africa in particular. Here we have the shift back and forth between various regimes, especially between democracy and dictatorship but also between right-wing and left-wing authoritarian rule. When we move on to enquire into the conditions for state instability, our dependent variable – state stability – will be measured by the average duration of regimes (REG). Actually, REG correlates to some extent with the two indices on regime fluctuation, meaning that it identifies the regime dimension of the stability concept (see Appendix 4.2).

Conclusion

In this chapter we have argued that the concept of state instability may be interpreted in various ways. It may be judged by the number of constitutional changes, but this measure is not quite valid due to the problems that beset the concept of a constitution. State instability may also be measured by the average duration or the number of regimes. Both these indicators seem to have more validity.

The principal finding is that state stability, measured by means of our index average duration of regime (REG), is precarious. The average length of time for a valid political regime is hardly more than fifteen to twenty years. Yet there is an interesting pattern of country variation which warrants a search for an explanation as to why state instability is so endemic in several countries.

Many countries have changed their regimes during the post-war period and some of these have experienced a cyclical pattern, moving to and fro between regimes – in particular from democracy to dictatorship and vice versa.

We have now substantiated the concept of state stability by making it richer and describing how the states of the world vary in terms of its different aspects. Let us now move on to the other fundamental state characteristic, performance.

APPENDIX 4.1 Occurrence of civil wars, 1945–93

AFRICA: Algeria, 1962–3; Angola, 1975–90; Burundi, 1972; Chad, 1979–82, 1990; Ethiopia, 1961–91; Liberia, 1990–1; Nigeria, 1967–70; Mozambique, 1978–92; Rwanda, 1956–65; Somalia, 1988–; South Africa, 1983–6; Sudan, 1955–72, 1983–92; Tanzania, 1963; Uganda, 1966, 1971–8, 1981–8; Zaïre, 1960–5, 1977–8; Zimbabwe, 1983; Sierra Leone, 1991–2.

AMERICA: Argentina, 1955, 1974–82; Bolivia, 1946, 1952; Chile, 1973–4; Colombia, 1948–58, 1978–84; Costa Rica, 1948; Cuba, 1958–9, 1961; El Salvador, 1979–92; Guatemala, 1954, 1966–74, 1982–3; Nicaragua, 1975–9, 1981–90; Paraguay, 1947; Peru, 1965, 1980–92; Uruguay, 1963–72.

ASIA: Afghanistan, 1978–92; Bangladesh, 1985; China, 1946–9, 1950–1, 1957–62, 1966–8; India, 1947–8; Indonesia, 1950, 1956–61, 1965–6; Iran, 1978–9, 1989; Iraq, 1958–9, 1961–70, 1974, 1984, 1988, 1991; Jordan, 1969–73; Cambodia, 1970–5, 1975–8, 1979–92; Laos, 1960–2, 1963–73, 1975–87; Lebanon, 1975–90; Burma (Myanmar), 1948–51, 1980, 1984–92; Pakistan, 1972–7; Philippines, 1950–2, 1972–6, 1976–92; Sri Lanka, 1971, 1983–7, 1988–92; Turkey, 1976–80; Oman, 1955–9, 1964–75; Vietnam, 1959–65, 1973–5; Yemen, 1948, 1950–2, 1962–9, 1986–.

EUROPE: Greece, 1945–9; former USSR, 1991–2; Yugoslavia, 1991–.

Source: Sullivan (1991: 34–8).

APPENDIX 4.2   Correlations between regime stability indicators

	Total	Africa	America	Asia	Europe
REG and SDGA	−.50	−.37	−.58	−.42	−.48
	(128)	(42)	(24)	(34)	(25)
REG and SDGU	−.41	−.35	−.40	−.50	−.34
	(123)	(40)	(24)	(32)	(25)
SDGA and SDGU	.78	.65	.78	.74	.93
	(122)	(40)	(24)	(31)	(25)

Note: REG = Average duration of regimes; SDGA = Standard deviation of the Gastil/Freedom House index of democracy; SDGU = Standard deviation of Gurr's index of democracy.

5

State Performance

Introduction

States are aggregates of human behaviour. We are searching for generalizations about such macropolitical units. In Chapter 4 we presented an overall picture of how stable such aggregates tend to be. In this chapter we try to give an overview of how these aggregates perform. Basically, there is a problem of responsibility in the relationship between the citizens and their state, because the rulers, although proclaiming that the state enhances the public interest, may pursue ends that are actually in their own interest.

The famous slogan from the French Revolution, 'liberté, égalité, fraternité', may be interpreted as an attempt to define the principal-agent problem in politics. Any government should pursue such principles in order to be legitimate to the population. State evaluation is a method for monitoring the activities of the state elite, holding it accountable to the population. We will discuss the principles of the French Revolution in relation to present-day data about the states of the world, evaluating state records about liberty and equality. Fraternity and its implications will be dealt with in Chapter 7. Which states perform well and which ones perform badly?

Comparative policy analysis

One should make a distriction between policy outputs or state decisions and activities, on the one hand, and policy outcomes or the social results of such decisions and activities, on the other. It is conceivable that a state may engage in a number of activities which do not reach their social goals for two entirely different reasons. Firstly, the decisions and actions of the state have the correct causal direction in terms of a set of publicly stated legitimate goals (such like égalité and liberté), but their impact is not strong enough to implement the goals; or secondly, the state operates a number of pro-

grammes which could not possibly result in the achievement of these legitimate social purposes. It makes a difference if either one of these holds. Thus
we shall look not only at the overt activities of the state but also at a set of
crucial economic and social outcomes in order to see what covert impacts the
state may have.

There is fundamentally no limit to the various state outputs or outcomes
to be included in a state evaluation enquiry. What matters is system importance or relevance, in other words, evaluation criteria that may be justified
from some normative point of view concerning what constitutes a good or a
bad state from a principal-agent framework. The crucial question is, thus,
whether the normative criteria selected are generally considered the legitimate ones to employ, for example, by the state inhabitants themselves, their
elites or the international community.

Starting from the French political trinity, in particular liberty and equality,
we focus here upon the following state outputs: (1) civil and political rights
and (2) welfare expenditures. Among the outcomes we choose the following
subset: (a) quality of life, (b) income distribution and (c) unemployment
and inflation, remembering that social outcomes are a function of many
conditions besides politics. What is the country variation in these policy
outputs and outcomes among a set of 130 states in the world (those states
with a population of more than one million in 1990)? Liberty and equality
are highly desirable human ends according to mainstream ethical theory.
What is the variation among states?

Liberté

A number of indices have been constructed in order to measure the variation
by country in the institutionalization of the rights and duties that substan-
tiate the abstract concept of freedom. The core of these indicators on liberty
is the occurrence of civil and political rights, making them at the same time
indicators of the spread of democracy around the world.

Liberty is related to democracy as a means as well as an end. In order to
qualify as government *of* the people and *by* the people a specific set of
institutions has to be introduced and maintained in a country. Democratic
institutions are of two types. First, there are the participation rules that lay
down the guidelines for the activation of the electorate in relation to referenda and national elections. Second, there are the power rules that specify
the procedures for how the political elites may compete for and exercise
power.

Democracy involves both the institutionalization of human rights of various kinds and a true probability that the power position of the ruling elite
may be contested. When indices are constructed in order to measure the
occurrence of democracy, then the central place of human rights becomes
evident. In particular some human rights are *sine qua non* for any democ-

Table 5.1 Civil and political rights (average scores)

	AVEGA	AVEGA1	AVEGU1	AVEGU2	AVEGU3	AVEGU4
Africa	2.3 (42)	2.3 (42)	2.8 (40)	3.0 (20)	4.0 (6)	4.4 (6)
America	5.9 (24)	5.8 (24)	5.6 (24)	5.4 (23)	5.3 (22)	5.1 (22)
Asia	3.4 (32)	3.3 (34)	4.0 (32)	4.2 (31)	4.3 (27)	3.8 (17)
Oceania	9.3 (3)	9.4 (3)	10.0 (2)	10.0 (2)	10.0 (2)	10.0 (2)
Europe	6.6 (23)	6.4 (25)	6.6 (25)	6.1 (25)	6.2 (25)	6.4 (23)
E^2	.36	.33	.24	.16	.11	.16

Sources: Gastil (1987, 1990a); Freedom House (1992); Gurr (1990).

Note: AVEGA denotes Gastil's index averages for 1973–91, AVEGA1 the same for 1973–88; AVEGU1 designates Gurr's index averages for 1970–86, AVEGU2 the same for 1960–76, AVEGU3 for 1950–66 and AVEGU4 for 1945–61. The scales range from 0 to 10 and order states in relation to the degree of human rights: a higher score indicates a stronger state commitment to the protection of civil and political rights. The CIVIC index referred to later is based upon AVEGA1.

racy: freedom of thought, speech and association and the freedom of the press. Other human rights, such as the principle of *habeas corpus*, are relevant for democracy in an indirect way.

Human rights indices

The concept of democratic performance is intimately connected with the concept of liberty as a set of civil and political rights (Diamond, 1992a). A number of indices have been constructed (see Bollen, 1986, 1990, 1993), in order to measure the occurrence of democracy around the world. Various democratic performance indices are listed in Appendix 5.1, which shows that they all correlate to a considerable extent.

Table 5.1 presents two indices on state performance in terms of state respect for civil and political rights for various periods ranging from 1945 to 1991. Civil or political rights (CIVIC) may be handled as a quantitative variable, allowing us to compare states of the world.

State protection for civil and political rights has hardly been visible on the two continents of Africa and Asia – in strong contrast to Oceania. Listing the few countries in Asia that currently have some kind of liberal regime (or had one, though not fully institutionalized, during the postwar period), we could single out India, Sri Lanka, Malaysia and Singapore. There is not much of human rights in Africa, as not even Liberia scores high on any of the indices, despite its historical legacy. Yet tiny Mauritius and vast Botswana constitute interesting exceptions. It remains to be seen how far the new strong demands for democratization in Africa will go in terms of a successful institutionalization of civil and political rights (Decalo, 1992).

The situation is quite different on the American continent. Here we have not only the USA and Canada, with their long democractic experiences, but also a number of countries who have protected civil and political rights, if only for specific periods of time.

In Europe the iron curtain separated the democracies in the West from the so-called people's democracies in the East from 1945 until 1989. In Greece, civil and political rights were fragile until the introduction of the new regime in 1974, following the collapse of the military regime installed in 1967. Portugal (1926–74) and Spain (1939–75) have had long experiences of authoritarian rule.

In both Portugal and Spain, civil and political coercion proved to be strong and long-lived. The Franco regime established after the civil war between 1936 and 1939 and the Salazar regime formed in 1932 did not succumb to the vacillation typical of many military regimes in Latin America. On the contrary, the Franco administration remained intact right up to the death of the Caudillo, when typically the successor problem proved impossible to solve. Portuguese dictatorship foundered on the independence wars in the Portuguese colonies in Africa.

'Latin-Americanization'

The concept of Latin-Americanization is employed in order to define a swing back and forth between liberty and coercion (in most cases military rule), characteristic of several states in Central and Latin America (O'Donnell and Schmitter, 1986). It implies not only that civil and political rights have been fragile in Argentina, Brazil, Chile and Peru, but also that civil administration is not easily maintained for longer periods of time in these countries. As spelt out in Chapter 2, the concept of the modern state was introduced in Latin America in the early nineteenth century when various countries were in rebellion towards European colonial powers. After independence there followed a period of constitutional rule during which considerable steps towards democracy were taken. Thus by 1900 some of the states in South and Central America had universal male suffrage and competitive party systems (Diamond and Linz, 1989). Table 5.2 shows a more recent picture.

'Latin-Americanization' is a label that stands for a phenomenon which still remains to be fully understood. The concept now has a wider field of application as there are several states outside Latin America whose attempts at moving towards democracy may be reversed, bringing dictatorship back in again (Przeworski, 1991). It is not really known why some states that move towards democratization fail to achieve a stable state (Weiner, 1987).

Waves of democratization and reversions

It may be that state respect for civil and political rights will grow substantially during the 1990s. It is not only the East European countries and the

Table 5.2 Democracy in Latin America

	Introduction of female suffrage[1]	Years of democracy, 1945–86[2]	Years of non-democracy, 1945–86[3]	Democratic status 1990–2[4]
Argentina	1947	7	35	D
Bolivia	1952	1	41	D
Brazil	1932	30	12	D
Chile	1949	18	24	D
Colombia	1957	33	9	D
Costa Rica	1949	42	0	D
Cuba	1934	7	35	Non-D
Dominican Republic	1942	9	33	D
Ecuador	1929	25	17	D
El Salvador	1939	18	24	D
Guatemala	1965	22	20	Semi-D
Haiti	1950	0	42	Non-D
Honduras	1955	0	42	D
Jamaica	1944	28	0	D
Mexico	1953	0	42	D
Nicaragua	1955	0	42	D
Panama	1946	11	31	D
Paraguay	1961	0	42	D
Peru	1955	30	12	Non-D
Trinidad/Tobago	1946	25	0	D
Uruguay	1932	29	13	D
Venezuela	1947	29	13	D

Sources: (1) Skidmore and Smith (1992: 64); Derbyshire and Derbyshire (1991: 123–8); (2)–(3) Gurr (1990); (4) our own classification is based on Huntington (1991).

Note: (2) States are classified as democracies if their score is 4 or higher on the Gurr democracy scale; (3) states are classified as non-democracies if their score is 3 or lower on the Gurr democracy scale.

many new states from the former giant Soviet Empire who are attempting to establish stable democratic rule (Lipset et al., 1993). There is a general trend towards democracy in Latin America and Asia, and constitutional rule may also increase in Africa, notably in South Africa. There is currently a new groundswell of democratization spreading civil and political rights all over the world. Huntington identifies the following waves: (1) 1828–1926; (2) 1943–62; (3) 1974– (Huntington, 1991: 16). If the hopes for a strong movement towards liberty materialize, then almost 50 per cent of the states of the world will institutionalize civil and political liberty. Yet there are grounds for caution in that a reverse wave might occur, as shown by the events of 1992 in Peru and Guatemala and those of 1993 in Nigeria.

Table 5.3   Stable democracies, 1960–93

	Rustow	Dahl	Wesson	Merkl
USA	x	x	x	x
Canada	x	x	x	x
Jamaica		x		x
Trinidad		x	x	
Barbados			x	
Mexico	x			
Costa Rica	x	x	x	x
Colombia	x		x	
Venezuela			x	x
Ecuador				x
Peru				x
Brazil				x
Bolivia				x
Chile	x	x		
Argentina				x
Uruguay	x	x		x
United Kingdom	x	x	x	x
Ireland	x	x	x	x
Netherlands	x	x	x	x
Belgium	x	x	x	x
Luxembourg	x	x	x	
France	x	x	x	x
Switzerland	x	x	x	x
Spain			x	x
Portugal			x	x
West Germany	x	x	x	x
Austria	x	x	x	x
Italy	x	x	x	x
Greece	x			x
Finland	x	x	x	x
Sweden	x	x	x	x
Norway	x	x	x	x
Denmark	x	x	x	x
Iceland	x	x	x	x
Turkey				x
Lebanon	x	x		
Israel	x	x	x	x
Republic of Korea				x
Japan	x	x	x	x
India	x	x		x

Table 5.3 *Continued*

	Rustow	*Dahl*	*Wesson*	*Merkl*
Sri Lanka	x			
Philippines	x	x		x
Australia	x	x	x	x
New Zealand	x	x	x	x
N	31	29	28	36

Sources: Rustow (1967); Dahl (1971); Wesson (1987); Merkl (1993).

In general there is wide agreement on which states are stable democracies; these are listed in table 5.3.

There is now a set of roughly fifty potential candidates for the title of 'stable democracy'. Some of these countries have recently introduced new democratically orientated constitutions safeguarding civil and political rights. In Africa one could mention Benin, Botswana, Congo, Côte d'Ivoire, Gabon, Mauritius, Namibia, Senegal, South Africa and Zambia (Africa Demos, 1992: 2). The transition in South Africa from the apartheid regime to a new dispensation may be seen as an extraordinary example of *negotiated democracy*, as the elections in April 1994 were preceded by years of extensive bargaining among all groups concerned. In the Americas we may have democracy in Argentina, Bolivia, Brazil, Chile, Ecuador, El Salvador, Haiti, Honduras, Nicaragua, Panama, Paraguay, Uruguay and Mexico. With regard to the Asian continent one might mention Malaysia, Mongolia, Nepal, Pakistan, the Philippines, South Korea, Singapore, Taiwan and Turkey, although developments here are slow. In Oceania the state of Papua New Guinea provides one example and, finally, in Europe there are several hopeful cases, such as Bulgaria, the Czech and Slovak Republics, Hungary, Poland, Romania, Estonia, Latvia, Lithuania, Russia, the Ukraine, Belarus and Slovenia (Huntington, 1991: 14–15).

Yet constitutional formalities are one thing and political practice another. In some of these countries, such as Malaysia and Singapore, a long-nurtured hope for democracy just fails to materialize. The prospects for democracy appear more promising in South Korea and Taiwan (Scalapino, 1993). Not even in Eastern Europe have the shadows of Latin-Americanization been removed (Agh, 1993).

Even if the prospects look bright now, things may change rapidly, for it is not likely that every attempt to introduce a new democracy will be successful. To instal and then maintain a democratic regime requires political skill and also a favourable economic and social environment. This will be discussed in Chapter 7.

Table 5.4 The size of the public sector: general government consumption as a percentage of GDP

	1955	1960	1970	1980	1985	1988
Africa	14.7	18.2	21.5	23.7	22.4	22.0
	(14)	(40)	(41)	(41)	(41)	(30)
America	13.2	14.0	14.4	15.5	17.4	16.0
	(22)	(23)	(23)	(23)	(23)	(18)
Asia	17.1	14.4	14.3	15.7	17.1	18.3
	(15)	(24)	(27)	(28)	(28)	(15)
Oceania	12.7	19.1	17.7	17.8	16.7	16.1
	(2)	(3)	(3)	(3)	(3)	(3)
Europe	15.1	14.3	13.8	15.2	15.5	15.3
	(16)	(16)	(17)	(18)	(18)	(17)
E^2	.07	.08	.18	.25	.19	.22

Source: Summers and Heston (1991).

Note: General government consists of all departments, offices, organizations and other bodies which are agents or instruments of the central, state or local government. Final consumption consists of expenditures on goods and services for public administration, defence, health and education. The number of cases is stated in parentheses.

Égalité

The public sector

When democracy is looked upon as government *for* the people, then there is the hope that government will be for the common good. Thus, besides civil war, the worst that could happen is that a state will become a warrior state, either conducting war with its neighbours or engaging in genocide. Positively, a democracy attempts to increase the general level of affluence in the country, either by supporting a welfare state or by promoting a welfare society. State performance may be measured by looking at policy outputs or outcomes (Jackman, 1993).

Equality may be enhanced by government activity, reflected in the overall size or in the composition of the public sector. States vary in the size as well as in the orientation of their public sectors towards equality in the promotion of policies such as expenditure on health and education. Table 5.4 presents an overview of government size measuring public resource allocation (with the exclusion of transfer payments). Public sector growth is a universal phenomenon.

The public sector consists of the activities of governments on various levels and with various functions. On the one hand there are the functions of the

Table 5.5 The size of the public sector: military, health and education expenditure as a percentage of GDP

	Military expenditure		Health and education expenditure	
	1960	1986	1960	1986
Africa	1.1 (26)	3.7 (42)	3.3 (38)	5.6 (41)
America	2.4 (22)	3.0 (24)	4.0 (24)	6.6 (24)
Asia	5.2 (23)	9.7 (28)	3.6 (20)	5.9 (26)
Oceania	1.9 (2)	2.1 (3)	5.1 (2)	9.8 (3)
Europe	3.9 (25)	3.4 (25)	5.8 (24)	10.0 (24)
E²	.27	.25	.28	.27

Source: United Nations Development Programme (1990).

guardian state: internal and external order; on the other there is the set of welfare state functions. The expansion of government during the postwar period is to be found in states on all the continents.

Table 5.4 measures only the allocative branch of the state, which explains why there is no relative increase in state expenditures in Europe. When data are added for the redistributive branch of government the expansion of the tax state in Western Europe is obvious (Rose, 1984, 1989).

In table 5.5 the share of military expenditure belongs to the guardian state concept, whereas the share of educational and health expenditure, including some transfer payments, constitutes part of the welfare state, promoting equality. Both types of state expenditure have risen sharply since the 1960s. Among Asian states, and to some extent among African states, the increase in military spending is very pronounced. In Europe the main trend is the relative expansion of the welfare state and a relative decline in the military budgets.

Some states allocate a considerable part of the resources of the country to military efforts. In the 1986 data the really big spenders on military items included Iraq (32 per cent), Iran (20 per cent), Israel (19 per cent), Oman (28 per cent), Saudi Arabia (23 per cent), Yemen (22 per cent), Syria (15 per cent), USSR (12 per cent), Liberia (12 per cent), Mongolia (11 per cent), North Korea (10 per cent), the United Arab Emirates (9 per cent) and the United States (7 per cent). The concentration on military spending in the Middle East in particular is enormous – almost incredible. But the fall of the Soviet Empire means a real opportunity to engage in mutual arms reduction, at least among the superpowers. It could also imply that both demand for and supply of arms will go down during the 1990s, but one must remember that the drive towards excessive military spending has many sources.

Table 5.6 General government: current receipts as a percentage of GDP

	1950	1960	1970	1980	1990
Sweden	26.2	35.0	47.0	56.7	63.9
Netherlands	33.0	33.4	44.5	55.0	49.5
Denmark	21.7	27.6	41.7	52.2	56.1
Austria	27.9	31.4	39.7	46.0	46.8
Switzerland	25.5	25.4	26.5	32.8	34.2
USA	24.0	27.5	30.3	32.8	31.9
Japan	21.9	20.7	20.7	28.0	34.6
Average OECD	25.7	28.7	35.8	43.4	45.3

Source: OECD *National Accounts* (various editions).

Note: Current receipts consist mainly of direct and indirect taxes and social security contributions paid by employers and employees. General government consists of all departments, offices, organizations and other bodies which are agents or instruments of the central, state or local public authorities.

Some states focus heavily on equality-enhancing welfare state expenditures, on programmes such as health and education. The 1986 data revealed the following countries as active in this area: Austria (11 per cent), Belgium (11 per cent), Canada (14 per cent), Denmark (13 per cent), Finland (12 per cent), France (12.5 per cent), West Germany (11 per cent), Ireland (15 per cent), the Netherlands (14 per cent), New Zealand (11 per cent), Norway (12 per cent), Saudia Arabia (14.5 per cent), Sweden (15.5 per cent) and Switzerland (12 per cent). A welfare state is not identical with a welfare society, however. Welfare societies or countries with a high standard of living may be strongly market orientated, trusting voluntary exchange mechanisms more than budget allocation in the provision of welfare services to its population.

The welfare states are those countries that to a considerable degree trust public budget-making with extensive allocative and redistributive tasks in order to guarantee their citizens a certain level of welfare. The welfare societies are those countries that rely more on the efficient functioning of markets to provide their consumers with a high standard of living. But welfare states and welfare societies are attributes of the affluent countries, mainly those in the OECD. While both kinds of state are very well off economically, they have different philosophies concerning welfare provision, one favouring generous and broadly based programmes and the other clinging to narrowly focused need-defined programmes.

Among the welfare states we find, for example, Sweden, Denmark, Austria and the Netherlands, whereas to the welfare societies belong the United States, Japan and Switzerland. The different levels in total public sector size including transfer payments in these countries are indicated in table 5.6, which focuses on total revenue data.

The public sector in the OECD countries has grown from a level of about

Table 5.7 The redistributive state: expenditure on social security benefits as a percentage of GDP, 1980

Africa (N = 11)	0.6
America (N = 19)	3.1
Asia (N = 10)	1.7
Oceania (N = 2)	10.4
Europe (N = 20)	15.5
E^2	.82

Source: United Nations Development Programme (1991).

25 per cent of GDP at the end of the Second World War to roughly 45 per cent or more in some countries in 1990, when the exceptional growth process was brought to a halt. Why is there this general growth in the 'tax state', as Joseph Schumpeter (1944) called public sector expansion in the advanced capitalist countries? Why has the public sector grown in such a different manner in various countries? Whereas the tax state has expanded from 26 per cent to 60 per cent in Sweden, the increase in Switzerland is only from 25 per cent to 34 per cent.

Both questions have to do with the distinction between a welfare state ideology and a welfare society ideology. It has been debated whether the emergence of the welfare state has its roots in the growth of an egalitarian culture (Wildavsky, 1986; Thompson, Ellis and Wildavsky, 1990) or in a revisionist socialist ideology (Esping-Andersen, 1985; Korpi, 1989). In any case, welfare states are still on the increase in the less affluent countries in the OECD whereas growth in the public sector in the more affluent countries came to a halt in the late 1980s.

A welfare state provides a number of services virtually without cost to its citizens. The allocation of education includes universal primary schooling and a variety of opportunities in the areas of secondary and higher education. Health care comprises both open and closed somatic care involving a large number of medical specialities. Social service provision consists of care for the elderly and services to a number of other clientele. In addition, a welfare state operates transfer payment programmes, the size of which is indicated in table 5.7.

In reality, a redistributive state can only be found in Europe and Oceania. Economic poverty is a definitive barrier to cash payments, as the low score for Africa indicates, although one may find attempts at public resource allocation in Third World countries that are welfare state orientated (MacPherson and Midgley, 1987). While the limits set by financial constraints cannot be bypassed in an analysis of the Third World state (Wilensky, 1975), social policies do have a history dating back to colonial times in the developing countries; these, however, tend to be directed towards urban elites.

Although the number of countries covered in table 5.7 is not extensive, it is true that states differ considerably in their effort to run equality-enhancing programmes. However, while transfer programmes are almost non-existent in the Third World, the redistributive state is huge in certain OECD countries (such as the Netherlands with 28 per cent, Belgium with 23 per cent and France with 22 per cent of GDP in 1980). This indicates a higher level of state commitment than in the Scandinavian welfare states (which, however, are larger in terms of public resource allocation).

Economic affluence is a necessary but not a sufficient condition for extensive transfer payments. In Japan, for example, cash payments amount to 12 per cent of GDP, and in Singapore they make up only about 3 per cent of GDP. Some of the welfare states in Western Europe concentrate more on transfer payments, whereas others are more active in public consumption.

Thus, in 1990, Italy's allocative branch of government (government final consumption) amounted to 17 per cent and its redistributive branch (social security transfers) involved an 18 per cent share of GDP, whereas for Sweden (27/21 per cent), Denmark (25/19 per cent) and the Federal Republic of Germany (18/16 per cent) the opposite relation held. Western Europe has only one single example of a welfare society – Switzerland (13/13 per cent) – but in the world there are several, including the United States (18/11 per cent), Australia (18/11 per cent) and New Zealand among the rich countries, and in particular Hong Kong among the newly industrializing countries, where the overall figure for the state is only about 15 per cent of GDP.

Social outcomes

Although such standard economic measures as GDP and GNP indicators elicit some details about the conditions in a country, they do need to be complemented by a set of social indicators that describe quality of life, the level of human development and the distribution of welfare in a society. What matters is how economic affluence translates into general living conditions among the population. The economic capacity of a state may be employed for various purposes, only one of which might be the reduction of mass poverty. A description of the variation by country by an index measuring the physical quality of life, human development or income distribution would inform us about the general environment of states, which after all is affected by state policy performance.

Quality of life   Quality of life is the crucial aspect of the human condition. It denotes a variety of things, such as health and sanitary conditions, communications, education, birth rates and life expectation. One indicator on quality of life is the human development index, which focuses on the deprivation of life expectancy, literacy and income for a decent standard of living (United Nations Development Programme, 1990: 13). Another relevant composite index is Morris's physical quality of life index (Morris, 1979).

Table 5.8 Quality of life

	Morris	UN
Africa	31.0 (42)	.377 (43)
America	71.6 (24)	.786 (24)
Asia	54.7 (31)	.636 (34)
Oceania	74.7 (3)	.805 (3)
Europe	91.4 (25)	.943 (25)
E^2	.69	.62

Sources: Morris (1979); United Nations Development Programme (1990).
Note: The higher the scores, the higher the quality of life.

The indices allow us to portray a picture of the sharp differences in the human predicament (see table 5.8).

The outlook in Africa and Asia is on the whole much more grim than in America, Oceania and Europe, although there are a few exceptions. The tragedy of Africa is both that the gulf between the fortunate and the unfortunate states is tremendous and that the average values for the continent are far below those of Oceania and Europe. Angola, Benin, Ethiopia, Guinea, Liberia, Niger, Sierra Leone, Somalia and Zaïre are the particularly poor states, whereas matters are brighter in Algeria and Tunisia in the North, Gabon in Central Africa and the Republic of South Africa. There is also mass poverty in Asia, notably in Bangladesh, Bhutan and Burma. Thus, India, Pakistan and Indonesia score low on the indicators, but not as low as the unfortunate countries in Africa.

The distance between poor and affluent states on the American continent is quite substantial, yet not as huge as that between the poor states of Asia and, for example, Japan, Singapore, South Korea and Hong Kong. What matters are life opportunities, and they tend to be low in countries such as Bolivia, Peru, Ecuador, Haiti and Honduras – though not as low as in Africa. The United States and Canada outdistance the other states by far, but in terms of general conditions of life Argentina, Brazil and Uruguay are closer to them than to their poorer neighbours.

To be more specific, the major finding when comparing economic indicators with general social ones is that in Europe the vast differences in economic affluence between West and East do not translate into outstandingly disparate conditions. There is an interesting curvelinear relation between economic affluence and general quality of life: very low levels of affluence result in truly miserable social conditions; as the GDP indicator ascends, however, the quality of life indicator at first rises proportionately but then evens out. Figure 5.1 shows the asymptotic nature of this relationship.

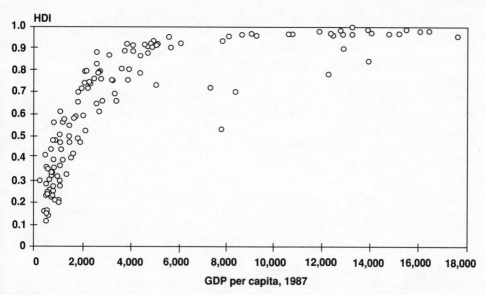

Figure 5.1   Human development index and level of economic affluence in the 1980s

Note: The human development index ranges from 0 to 1.

Distribution of income   The distribution of income is another vital element in the analysis of the human condition. The use of income distribution scores warns against any simple conclusion that increases in total economic output must result in more affluence for the entire population. At the same time rapid economic growth may be beneficial for broad masses of the population even if the income distribution remains skewed to the advantage of the rich.

How income inequality should be measured is a controversial issue in itself. Table 5.9 lists the scores of a number of indices that measure the top incomes in society. The higher the scores, the more unequal is the distribution of income. The common finding for all indices is that inequalities of income are greater in poor countries than in rich ones, whatever measure of income differentials one may employ. Note the high inequality scores for the poorest of all continents, Africa. Whether income equality was greater in the West European welfare states than in the former communist states is debatable (World Development Report, 1993).

Equality in the distribution of income is related to the level of economic affluence by means of the so-called Kuznets curve. This predicts that income inequality will rise in a process of rapid economic development, only to decline as a higher level of economic affluence has been reached. Are there significant traces of the operation of the Kuznets mechanism among states in the late 1980s after the long postwar process of economic growth in the

Table 5.9 Income inequality: income shares within the population

	HDR10 1990	HDR20 1990	EB10 1990	WH20 1983	MUS20 1979
Africa	32 (9)	52 (15)	41 (19)	58 (16)	59 (17)
America	34 (10)	54 (16)	38 (18)	55 (16)	57 (19)
Asia	32 (13)	47 (14)	35 (17)	50 (14)	49 (16)
Oceania	28 (2)	44 (2)	29 (2)	40 (2)	40 (2)
Europe	24 (14)	41 (15)	24 (21)	40 (16)	45 (14)
E^2	.39	.33	.50	.48	.34

Sources: HDR = Human Development Report (1990); EB = *Encyclopedia Britannica Book of the Year* (1990); WH = *World Handbook* (1983); MUS = Musgrave and Jarrett (1979).

Note: The indices measure the income share of the top 10 per cent or top 20 per cent of the population.

world economy? Figure 5.2 plots the relationship between income inequality (HDR20) and the level of affluence (GDP per capita, 1987).

It must be admitted that, when employed across such a large set of countries, income distribution data are beset with problems of reliability as well as validity. Yet it is clear that states with an advanced economy have greater equality of income than poor states. The implication is that in-equality of income can be accepted much more easily in rapidly growing

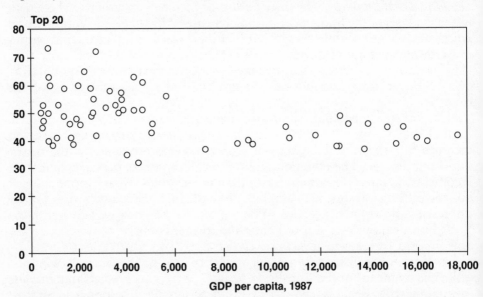

Figure 5.2 The Kuznets curve: income distribution and level of economic affluence

Note: The Top 20 index ranges from 0 to 100 per cent.

Table 5.10   Unemployment and inflation (in percentages)

| | Unemployment | | | Inflation | |
	1981	1985	1989	1965–80	1980–90
Africa	20.5 (2)	22.9 (3)	46.8 (1)	9.5 (39)	16.6 (39)
America	9.2 (13)	11.0 (15)	10.1 (16)	21.5 (23)	88.9 (23)
Asia	4.4 (9)	4.8 (9)	4.6 (9)	13.1 (20)	11.8 (22)
Oceania	5.8 (1)	6.2 (2)	6.7 (2)	9.3 (3)	7.7 (3)
Europe	7.0 (17)	9.3 (17)	8.1 (17)	8.9 (18)	14.0 (22)
E^2	.24	.22	.65	.10	.18

Sources: ILO, *Yearbook of Labour Statistics* (1991); World Bank, *World Development Report* (1992).

Note: These measures of unemployment as percentages of the workforce are not quite reliable. Too few countries present data and they are not always strictly comparable.

economies than in stagnating ones, because over time economic prosperity will even things out. The overall finding is that one of the major human values of the French Revolution – égalité – has its best chances in states with an advanced economy.

Unemployment and inflation   It is possible to broaden the outcome analysis by bringing in other factors besides the quality of life, even though one must recognize that the connection between state activities and social outcomes is often a tenuous one, in particular in Third World countries. Governments may try hard to counteract social maladies such as hyperinflation and massive unemployment, but their resources may be too few. Poor state performance may be a result of the government either doing the right things, but not vigorously enough, or simply doing the wrong things.

Yet bringing in inflation and unemployment data widens the economic and social performance analysis. Admitting that there are considerable problems in arriving at comparable data for different countries in inflation rates and unemployment, we indicate how states differ in regard to the economic environment they face. Hyperinflation and unemployment in particular enter any description of the human condition if one starts from the value of égalité. Table 5.10 shows the overall variation within and between continents.

Hyperinflation means severe economic hardship for the broad population. It has occurred first and foremost in Latin America, but also in some African countries. Inflation rates climbed to over 100 per cent in Chile between 1965 and 1980 and in Argentina, Brazil, Israel, Nicaragua, Peru, Uganda and Yugoslavia between 1980 and 1990. Massive levels of unemployment occur in Third World countries but have also appeared in Eastern Europe and Russia. Data concerning levels of employment only take into account the official economy. But a substantial unofficial economy alleviates the hardships of massive unemployment, not only in rich countries but also in non-OECD countries, such as the Republic of South Africa.

The implications of high unemployment figures for welfare reduction are not automatic. There are unofficial economies everywhere which provide alternative employment opportunities (Rose, 1989). Whereas hyperinflation occurs in Third World countries with weak economies, high levels of unemployment have begun to show up also in the rich world; almost all countries in the OECD set display higher unemployment figures for the 1980s and 1990s than for earlier decades (Madsen and Paldam, 1978; OECD, 1988; OECD, 1992).

Unemployment has reached a level even in some OECD countries which means severe hardships for a substantial portion of the population, especially the young. There is a clear long-term trend towards an increase in unemployment in the states with an advanced economy, reflecting not only a general lower rate of growth and the recession around 1990, but also weaker state performance in the sense that macroeconomic policy-making has become much more difficult.

Are there 'lucky' states?

Is life bearable in the various countries of the world? Yes, certainly in the countries that score high on both the two classical objectives of the French Revolution, liberté and égalité. Now, states may not be able to influence all the relevant performance measures: the human development index, in particular, is determined more by the overall economic situation than by politics.

The question whether states can be held responsible is a complex one. On the one hand, the attempt to codify international law implies that states are accountable for what takes place on their territory; on the other, the notion that states are responsible raises a number of problems concerning the nature of the state as an actor. Avoiding the reification of the state, it is necessary to refer to the actual leaders in a country. And they may find that their capacity to act is very small.

The problem of accountability is part of the evaluation process. There are no clear-cut answers here. Although a state might try in vain to improve on general conditions, it is also true that it may take very negative actions with regard to such key values as civil and political rights and human development. Now, what is the probability that states may perform well on all the evaluation criteria studied above? Table 5.11 shows a pattern that demands closer inspection.

The strength of the connections among the indicators is not particularly striking, but the underlying pattern is clear. First, several countries which score high in quality of life are welfare state regimes and also tend to give strong protection to civil and political rights. Second, welfare states tend to

Table 5.11   State performance indicators

	CIVIC	HDI	HED86	TOP10	INF8090
CIVIC	1.00				
HDI	.59	1.00			
	(127)				
HED86	.51	.57	1.00		
	(118)	(118)			
TOP10	−.20	−.31	−.45	1.00	
	(48)	(48)	(48)		
INF8090	−.01	.07	−.10	.34	1.00
	(108)	(109)	(105)	(47)	

Source: Tables 5.1, 5.5, 5.8, 5.9, 5.10.

Note: CIVIC = Civil and political rights; HDI = Human development index; HED86 = Health and education expenditures; TOP10 = Income inequality; INF8090 = Inflation, 1980–90.

be characterized by considerable income equality. The combination of these two findings permit us to designate those states with high performance ratings on liberty and equality as 'lucky' states.

However, at the same time there are considerable leakages among the connections. On the one hand, some states that respect civil and political rights do not score high on equality. On the other hand, some states that score high on the human development index do not protect human rights. True, there exist a large number of states that do badly on all the evaluation criteria studied here – the set of 'unlucky' states. The exception is that inflation rates hover independently of the variation in liberté and égalité, although they tend to be higher in countries with marked differences in income.

States have different degrees of freedom in relation to the alternative performance criteria. Whereas the state's political performance in terms of liberté can be affected by its leaders, the dimensions of égalité are much less under their control. This applies in particular to the human development index and inflation, where general economic factors play a major role. However, it remains true that states may take actions, including the release of hyperinflation, that seriously impair the human development potential of their population.

Conclusion

The two basic political ideals from the French Revolution could constitute the starting-point for systematic evaluation of state performance. The findings here indicate that the present states of the world differ tremendously in the extent to which they have successfully institutionalized both liberté and égalité. Here we have another great puzzle for comparative inquiry: why are some states but not others fortunate in scoring high on these two basic political values?

At the same time several states characterized by dictatorship and poverty score low on both liberté and égalité: why? Such questions bring us to the problem of causality in comparative enquiry. What factors could be employed in order to account for the variation in performance of such a macropolitical aggregate as the state? Let us first in Chapter 6 discuss the logic of explanation in comparative politics. Then we move, in Chapter 7, to test models that attempt to identify factors that condition how states perform and why some are stable but others unstable.

APPENDIX 5.1   Correlations among democratic performance indices

	Total	Africa	America	Asia	Europe
GU60 with BO60	.88	.67	.79	.85	.97
	(96)	(18)	(23)	(28)	(25)
GU65 with BO65	.83	.51	.80	.82	.97
	(114)	(35)	(24)	(28)	(25)
GA73 with GU73	.86	.68	.81	.73	.98
	(124)	(40)	(24)	(33)	(25)
GA80 with GU80	.87	.59	.87	.77	.98
	(128)	(42)	(24)	(34)	(25)
GA80 with VAD80	.82	.49	.83	.71	.94
	(128)	(42)	(24)	(34)	(25)
GA85 with GU85	.89	.67	.88	.75	.98
	(128)	(42)	(24)	(34)	(25)
GA85 with POL85	.94	.81	.89	.91	.99
	(129)	(42)	(24)	(35)	(25)
GU85 with POL85	.89	.77	.77	.78	.99
	(128)	(42)	(24)	(34)	(25)
GA86 with GU86	.91	.69	.89	.82	.98
	(128)	(42)	(24)	(34)	(25)
GA86 with HU86	.91	.65	.86	.87	.98
	(88)	(22)	(19)	(20)	(24)

	Total	Africa	America	Asia	Europe
GA88 with HAD	.94	.90	.97	.91	–
	(97)	(42)	(22)	(32)	(0)
GA88 with VAD88	.87	.72	.76	.82	.93
	(128)	(42)	(24)	(34)	(25)

Sources: Bollen (1980) for 1960 and 1965 (BO); Coppedge and Reinecke (1990) for 1985 (POL); Gastil (1990a) for 1973–88 (GA); Gurr (1990) for 1960–86 (GU); Hadenius (1992) for 1988 (HAD); Humana (1986) for 1986 (HU); Vanhanen (1990) for 1980 (VAD).

Note: It seems justified to conclude that the Gurr and the Gastil/Freedom House indices measure the same phenomena because they are reliable in terms of different time periods as well as in different sets of countries. The indexes have been arrived at in the following way: two indicators employed by Gurr, AUTOC = institutional autocracy and DEMOC = institutionalized democracy, have been combined (DEMOC minus AUTOC); two indicators reported by Gastil and Freedom House, one for political rights and one for civil liberties, have been added. In both cases the new measure has been normalized, so that a highly democratic regime has a score of 10 and a particularly undemocratic regime a score of 0.

6

The Logic of Model Building in Comparative Government

Introduction

We have now travelled half the distance to be covered in this book. Two sets of dependent variables have been derived and analysed, and it is now time to turn to the second enterprise, the attempt to deal with causality in comparative politics. The methodology of comparative politics has been much debated since the behaviouralist movement in the 1960s (Ragin, 1987; Mayer, 1989). In this chapter we will discuss some of the problems involved in looking for causal factors that account for state properties at the macrolevel in order to focus in the next three chapters on sets of conditions modelled as having an impact upon macropolitics.

We have seen in the earlier chapters that the concepts of state stability and state performance are multi-dimensional, where each subset of meanings requires its own analysis. Remembering how much variety there is in state stability and performance properties, we now proceed to the interpretation of why states are so different. Rather than concentrating on the variety, one could just as well ask why states are not all similar. What conditions, or so-called independent variables, could be conducive to the differences in stability and performance of states?

What is explanation in comparative enquiry?

Is comparative analysis basically description or does it also involve causal interpretation? Perhaps it is enough to point out conspicuous differences and similarities between how states appear in space and time? Could there be something more to the comparative enterprise, such as the explanation of patterns of cross-sectional and longitudinal variation? Any distinction between description and explanation raises serious methodological questions in general, but they have to be resolved somehow in the conduct of comparative enquiry in particular (Chilcote, 1981; Collier, 1991; Öyen, 1990).

Problems of methodology are continually raised and discussed in comparative politics. They range from fundamental issues about the nature of explanation to technical problems in econometric modelling. The consciousness of methodological problems has increased in the postwar period, initiated by the radical criticism of the traditional approach by the behaviouralists.

Behaviouralism

Behaviouralism was a reaction of the 1950s and 1960s against the dominant methods of political science and international studies (Ranney, 1962). In the 1970s the movement faded away, as what was basically sound in the new methodology had become generally accepted and what was extreme and exaggerated had met with fierce opposition (Dahl, 1961). Contested by the new institutionalism in the 1980s, the core of behavioralist methodology involved a number of elements.

1) *Formalism versus behaviour* 'Behaviour' as a key element in behaviouralism denotes what should be the basic unit of analysis in political science. To study behaviour is to look at the actions that really take place within legal frameworks and behind political ideologies. Norms or ideologies derive their relevance from their role in shaping human behaviour. To look only at the constitutional framework is not enough in the study of comparative politics.

2) *Relevance of data* Given the distinction between legal framework and patterns of behaviour, new types of information had to be sought. This implied a fundamental reorientation of political science towards the employment of more sophisticated techniques for the collection and mastering of empirical information in the form of surveys and ecological data. It also meant an emphasis on quantitative approaches to empirical information involving the use of various kinds of multivariate tools.

3) *Model building* To behaviouralists the statement of what actually takes place was not an end in itself; the analysis of single events or processes should try to establish scientific laws or statistical regularities. Political phenomena may be explained in terms of general models covering a range of diverse events. One basic aim of political science is to identify such generalizations, and whether these are lawlike or probabilistic in nature. Adam Przeworski and Henry Teune, in *The Logic of Comparative Social Inquiry* (1970), argued in favour of a nomothetical rather than an idiographical approach.

4) *Methodological balance between theory and data* Without data, behaviouralists argued, theoretical propositions would be empty. How

could we choose between competing explanations except by reference to empirical tests of data? Without the employment of data how could there be any claim to truth in the sense of correspondence to facts? On the other hand, data without theory would be blind, because empirical information has to be interpreted, and there is no limit to the amount of empirical information to be reported.

5) *Theory directs the search for data* The behaviouralist approach won a break-through within political sociology and its attempts at understanding politics by means of social forces, in particular 'cleavages' in the social structure. The emphasis on the collection of much broader data sets and the employment of new statistical techniques changed the way of conducting comparative enquiry. Behaviouralism redirected the course of political science, including comparative politics (see Heinz Eulau's *The Behavioral Persuasion in Politics* [1963]).

6) *Data confirm or falsify hypotheses* The behaviouralists underlined the mutual dependency between data and models. Hypotheses would be derived from the models to be tested against a rich set of data, preferably quantitative information (Holt and Turner, 1970). There was a firm belief in the cumulative nature of findings in comparative politics, meaning that a core body of propositions could be arrived at.

7) *Moral versus scientific argument* Behaviouralists distinguish between moral or ethical enquiry and scientific argument. Assuming that there is a gulf between statements of fact and value judgements, science would only encompass the former. In comparative analysis it was considered essential to move away from an implicit adherence to Western values that could bias the study of developing countries.

Speaking generally, it may be queried whether behaviouralism showed a strong overdose of scientism or positivism. The behaviouralist methodology overemphasized behaviour to the neglect of rules and norms, at least according to the new institutionalist approach. Institutions matter; according to James G. March and Johan P. Olsen, in *Rediscovering Institutions* (1989), the behavioralists failed to identify the role of political institutions, reducing state activities to either preferences (rational choice) or social structure (political sociology).

The new institutionalism which gained momentum during the 1980s rejects behaviouralism, suggesting that the importance of country-specific institutions is neglected and that what matters is not only behaviour but the interpretation of its meaning, containing the essence of an action. In particular, neo-institutionalism rejects the search for lawlike generalizations in comparative government.

The claims of the new institutionalism have to be evaluated critically in order to draw the correct implications for comparative research into the state. The claim that institutions matter would not be difficult to integrate within a comparative methodology had it not been for the thesis that the country-specific institutions are more or less idiosyncratic and require some kind of hermeneutic approach. The institutional dimension cannot be overlooked when comparing states across the globe, but the logic of comparative methodology requires that institutions be comparable between countries and across time. A critical question in comparative politics is whether the same institutions in different countries have the same impact upon the state. This is a problem for comparative model building, which requires some generalizations about the variety of conditions for the state.

Reductionism

The model of explanation proposed in the behavioural movement in political science during the 1960s was too ambitious for comparative politics. Searching for invariant relationships to be formulated in lawlike propositions will take us nowhere, because all that we can find are statistical relationships of various magnitudes. Acknowledging the probabilistic nature of social science knowledge, we should try to find traces of connections between variables which make sense in a causal interpretation.

In the same way as the search for laws is abortive, we have to reject monocausal interpretations. The complex nature of social systems such as the state cannot be intelligibly understood by focusing on one variable at a time. Theory forces us to consider interaction in a complex fashion. Here and there we find bits and pieces of theory that emphasize various aspects of the phenomena to be elucidated.

A basic assumption in prevailing approaches to comparative politics when the traditional approach was rejected was a hypothesis implicit in much of the work carried out within political sociology: political phenomena are substantially affected by other kinds of social phenomena, such as economic development, social stratification and cultural systems. Actually, one trend within political sociology attempted to explain the variation in political phenomena by means of ecological factors. Phenomena such as political parties or political belief-systems were to be understood against background information about social structure.

Structural properties were conceived of as determining politics in a reductionist manner: objective social conditions affect political behaviour in a direct way – what, to distinguish it from general political sociology, Sartori labels 'sociology of politics' (Sartori, 1969). To Lijphart a reductionist approach greatly overemphasized the explanatory power of social factors with regard to political phenomena (Lijphart, 1975a). Even worse, it missed a crucial property of politics, the behaviour of political elites – their capacity for adaption and innovation and their significance for the explanation of properties of political systems such as stability and conflict regulation. Besides structure we must cover institutions and actors.

One may admit that macropolitics is characterized, at least to some extent, by what Karl Mannheim interpretated as 'Situationsbestimmung'. In *Ideology and Utopia* (1936) Mannheim argued that politics simply reflects the historical situation in which action take place. However, one must question the sociological determinism involved in Mannheim's thesis. The structure of society does matter – but how much?

Deduction or induction?

Both the deductive and inductive approaches to explanatory knowledge are relevant in the interpretation of comparative politics. The deductive method proceeds from what we hope are strong theoretical hypotheses, deducing the test implications to be evaluated by means of empirical techniques. The inductive method works in the opposite direction, taking a close look at similarities and differences in the data which could be formulated as empirical hypotheses that would be potential candidates for model building or theoretical generalization.

Although the idea of inductive reasoning is controversial in the philosophy of science, comparative politics can use all possible methods for model building, remembering that they have both pros and cons. The various methods, from multivariate modelling to single-case studies (Lijphart, 1971), should be tried for whatever usefulness they may offer. As inductive conclusions are only of heuristic value, the test of models generated from observation of data has to take precedence over the derivation of test implications.

In *A System of Logic* ([1843] 1884) John Stuart Mill spelt out the canons of inductive research in a way that is still relevant, at least for the social sciences, which are less dominated by pure science or the predominance of a clear-cut paradigm in the Kuhnian sense (Kuhn, 1962). First, there is the method of agreement, second, the method of difference and, finally, the method of concomitant variation. They are all applicable in comparative politics as techniques for inventing hypotheses by looking at how variables tend to go together in various ways. However, they are not safe tools for the justification of causal hypotheses, because causality requires more than simple co-variation in the data (Cohen and Nagel, 1934).

The method of agreement argues that, if two interesting variables tend to be present in two or more cases, then there has to be some other similarity of factors between the cases – in other words, same cause, same effect. The method of difference claims that, if two variables are present in one case but absent in the other case(s), then they must be dissimilar with regard to some other factor – in other words, different effect, different cause. The method of concomitant variation looks at how increases or decreases in two variables tend to follow a pattern in some cases, meaning that they may generally vary in such a way. Finally, there is the combination or joint method of agreement and difference. It must be pointed out that these four tools are methods for reaching inductive conclusions which are only empirically plausible rather than logically valid. Or, to be more precise, they are heuristic methods for finding interesting causal guesses. The inductive inference may simply be wrong, because we make either a type 1 error, accepting a wrong hypothesis, or a type 2 error, rejecting a true hypothesis.

In modern comparative research it has been argued that the comparative method is not just any technique for comparing states, but a residual comprising what remains after the statistical techniques and the case study method have been sorted out. Thus the comparative method consists of two strategies that are applicable when a case study is impossible, that is, when there is more than one case but too few for the application of multivariate techniques (Lijphart, 1971, 1976).

On the one hand we have MSSD, the most similar systems design (Przeworski and Teune, 1970). This is a restatement of the method of difference: given that two or more countries differ substantially in the dependent variable, then if these cases are similar in all but one aspect, it is likely that this single variable is the independent variable that is the condition for their also differing in the dependent variable. On the other hand, there is MDSD, the most different systems design, which implies the method of agreement: if two or more cases are alike with regard to the dependent variable and also in one of the independent variables, then it is likely that this is the condition for the similarity between the cases in the dependent variable.

In speaking about dependent and independent variables, we search for research strategies that help us identify connections between the two. The distinction between the statistical method, the comparative method and the case study method is not clear-cut. Actually, Mill listed the method of concomitant variations alongside the methods of agreement and difference. It is similar to the statistical method, which is more powerful in testing causal guesses than the other two inductive methods, although it cannot strictly validate causal hypotheses as Mill thought.

Causality in comparative research in general, and in comparative government in particular, is always a matter of model building on the basis of available knowledge, resulting in hypotheses that need testing. There is no social science method that can identify causal links between macropolitical variables. Qualified guesses always need to be verified by looking at test implications, and it is always an open question whether the explanatory model has been correctly specified.

Much model building in comparative politics has been based on research designs where the number of cases has been small. Talking about the most similar cases strategy or the most different cases strategy is an attempt to compensate for the fact that a small number of cases is a weak basis for model building (Lijphart, 1975b). But when are two cases really similar or different? The resort to area studies, meaning that the environment of politics remains constant, does not solve the problem of causal attribution. General model building in comparative government should employ multivariate techniques.

Causality in comparative politics

The problem of causality in comparative politics remains illusory. The adherents of case studies argue that one may unravel causal interconnections by focusing in detail upon one single country. The spokesmen for the comparative method claim that an analysis of a few countries is enough to reach conclusions about how independent variables condition dependent variables. Thus, by employing the method either of agreement or difference, it would be possible to make inductive generalizations about causality (Lijphart, 1975b; Sartori, 1991).

Yet the findings arrived at from a case study or by using the comparative method are at best tentative in so far as causality is concerned. Both these methods are only heuristic devices for stating interesting causal models, but they suffer significantly from the problem of induction. Taking a Humean approach to social causation, the basic problem is how to discover whether two factors that go together in one or a few cases also co-vary when a much larger sample is drawn.

In the field of comparative politics modelling macroproperties, the concept of causality remains problematic. Although the results of case studies or the comparative methods may come close to political realities in the countries studied, the conclusions about conditions, causes and effect remain highly tentative. It is necessary to move towards comprehensive statistical modelling in order to check whether the notions about causality in macropolitics stand up when a large set of states is included in the analysis. The findings from such an approach are reported on in chapters 7 to 10.

It may be rewarding to spell out the logic of conditional analysis, because it leads one to speak about conditions rather than talking about the cause. A necessary condition (*n-condition*) for an event or state of affairs is a condition such that, if the event takes place or the state of affairs holds, then the condition will certainly be present. A sufficient condition (*s-condition*) is such that, if it is present, then the event or state of affairs will also occur. If we could identify conditions that are both necessary and sufficient, then we would have come a long way in our attempt to explain comparative politics. But often we have to be content with identifying conditions that are neither n-conditions nor s-conditions but rather conditions that contribute to the occurrence of some event or state of affairs (*c-conditions*).

Even the search for conditions that are both sufficient and necessary is too pretentious a task at the present stage of knowledge. What is currently achievable is an understanding of the pattern type of the conditions that have an impact on the state. It is not even possible to reach necessary or sufficient conditions, as we face only statistical correlations from which we may choose a set of conditions that are relevant for state properties or state events. The conduct of enquiry is based on a set of models about relationships to be evaluated by means of data that could help us identify connections (Kaplan, 1964).

We are faced with a number of statistical correlations and regression results which require interpretation in order to establish what depends on what. The language of sufficient and necessary conditions is a tool for the interpretation of various relationship estimates.

The logic of model building

To look for the conditions of the state and its different properties, such as stability and performance, one needs more than the canons of inductive reasoning. We may derive some possible explanatory variables by enquiring into mainstream modelling in comparative politics. The problem is to select the set of conditions that help us account for the occurrence of state properties. The potential set of conditions is, empirically speaking, infinite, but from a theoretical point of view we may focus on a narrow set of models comprising variables for (a) economic conditions, (b) social structure, (c) cultural factors, (d) elite behaviour and (e) institutional structure, allowing for some degree of randomness in social life. In addition, we need to look at physical conditions. Let us start from there.

There is no way to derive some final or conclusive set of independent variables for the analysis of comparative government. As the theoretical literature now stands it is necessary to search for the conditions for the stability and performance of states in the properties or variables that somehow describe the physical environment, the economy, the society and the culture, or relate to the elites or the system of rules. However, there is much space for new hypotheses as the connections unravelled thus far are neither striking nor completely understandable on theoretical grounds. What follows below is thus at best a tentative list of factors considered relevant in a number of theories about macropolitics.

Physical conditions

There is a clear emphasis in much of the literature on objective factors as the main causal sources of state properties. Plato, but more so Aristotle in his *Politics*, regarded size as a factor of crucial importance in shaping the fate of states. Actually, the size model of the state recurs from time to time, but there has been no clarification about what more specific effects size has upon state stability or state performance (Dahl and Tufte, 1973).

Geopolitical models focus on the territory of the state and its implications for state properties. It has been argued that large polities last longer, as small states more easily fall foul of a hostile environment. At the same time huge states may presuppose big problems, as there are limits to their adaptation capacity when facing a difficult environment.

When considering states whose territories are in the polar regions or consist largely of desert, the name of Montesquieu comes to mind. One

Table 6.1 Population growth: estimations and projections (in percentages)

	1965–80	1980–90	1989–2000
Africa	2.69 (43)	2.96 (43)	2.88 (43)
America	2.29 (23)	2.05 (23)	1.70 (24)
Asia	3.08 (32)	2.66 (30)	2.40 (33)
Oceania	1.83 (3)	1.63 (3)	1.47 (3)
Europe	0.67 (23)	0.39 (23)	0.30 (24)
E^2	.25	.63	.63

Source: World Bank (1992).

Table 6.2 Population growth, 1990–2025 (projections)

Country	Rank 1990	Rank 2000	Rank 2025	Population 2025 (in millions)
China	1	1	1	1597
India	2	2	2	1348
USSR (Russia)	3	3	(3)	–
USA	4	4	4	307
Indonesia	5	5	5	275
Brazil	6	6	8	237
Japan	7	10	13	128
Nigeria	8	7	6	255
Pakistan	9	8	7	240
Bangladesh	10	9	9	176
Mexico	11	11	12	142
Germany	12	13	20	78
Vietnam	13	12	14	116
Philippines	14	15	15	101
Italy	15	22	27	55
UK	16	21	26	61
France	17	20	25	63
Iran	18	14	10	166
Thailand	19	18	19	84
Turkey	20	17	16	91
Egypt	21	19	18	86
Ethiopia	22	16	11	156
Zaïre	27	24	17	89

Source: World Bank (1992).

element of his original thought in *The Spirit of the Laws* (1748) pertains to the idea that politics depends upon climate. However, his institutional theory concerning the impact of power division has better stood the test of time.

We need to look not only at population size but also at population dynamics (see table 6.1). The projections for the world population involve staggering growth rates in Africa and Asia, with an increase of more than 2 per cent a year. One can only speculate about the risk of mass famine on these two continents, which may finally vindicate the gloomy predictions of Malthus.

This immense growth in population is bound to have political implications, but whether it implies state instability or not will depend upon state performance. A few states will face severe challenges: in several countries, in particular the poor but already huge Third World nations of India, Pakistan, Bangladesh, Brazil, Mexico and Indonesia, population growth will not moderate in the next few decades (see table 6.2).

The implications of rapid changes in population have not been researched in a comprehensive and systematic manner. There will obviously be a dramatic increase in pressure on both economic resources and political legitimacy. It is estimated that the world population in 2025 will have reached as many as 8.3 billion people, before an eventual reduction in birth rates leads to a more stable position in relation to the continuing fall in mortality rates. Yet taking a Malthusian perspective on the political consequences of such phenomenal population growth, one might predict that state anarchy resulting from famine could lead to higher mortality figures in the decades to come.

Economic conditions

Economic determinism has always had its supporters. The hypotheses emphasizing economic conditions for state stability and performance (levels of affluence and the rate of economic growth) come in two forms. The first, that there is a direct link between economic factors and politics, has been promoted by Marxist or neo-Marxist scholars (Lipset, 1959), whereas the second line of reasoning, that the economic factors shape the structure of society, which then sets the boundary for politics, is represented in the so-called modernization school (Leftwich, 1990).

Economic models involve a dilemma. On the one hand, economic factors always have some relevance for politics. The allocation and redistribution of resources is at the heart of both the economic system and the polity. There is bound to be interaction between markets and the state, as the latter cannot operate without an economic basis and the former need state regulation to uphold their institutions and frame economic interaction.

Yet, on the other hand, strictly economic models tend to fail because their explanatory relevance is not enough to allow for the statement of n-conditions or s-conditions for political events. Economic factors are without exception c-conditions, which means that other factors need to be recognized, allowing for complexity. How much evidence is there for the claim that economic factors help explain state stability and state performance?

Economic factors loom large in the explanation of state properties. Not all attempts at economic modelling of state stability and state performance are victims of the temptation to consider these factors as *the* explanatory variables. Yet there are models that underline the strong causal effects of economic forces. Some scholars start from the level of affluence, predicting aspects of state stability and state performance from strictly economic indicators such as GDP per capita. Others emphasize the dynamic implications of the economy, starting from figures for economic growth. Finally, there is world systems analysis, which looks at politics as conditioned by megatrends in capitalist development, especially the position – core versus periphery – of a country in the world system (Wallerstein, 1974).

It seems reasonable to argue that state instability would follow from intolerable economic conditions. Yet the kind of economic system or the institutional framework for the economy may be just as important as overall affluence, particularly if various kinds of economic system always produce unique economic results. However, there is no such deterministic relationship between type of economic system and economic outcomes. We need to look at the sources of political instability among a broader set of economic conditions. But is it absolute or relative human misery that matters?

State instability may take different forms. It may occur in a violent or a non-violent manner. To the former belong the coup d'état and revolutions, and to the latter protest phenomena, government turnover and constitutional revision. Charles Tilly's *From Mobilization to Revolution* (1978) contains a discussion of the economic conditions for revolution which is relevant for the more general theme of state instability.

The well-known model of relative deprivation implies a different way of modelling the connection between economic conditions and state stability, as it is not focused on such aggregates as affluence or economic growth. What could be more important for regime longevity or state performance than such real-life economic parameters as poverty and hyperinflation? The relative deprivation model claims that it is not the absolute level of economic hardship that is decisive but the aspiration levels of the population. Economic change raising aspirations would be more conducive to instability than economic stagnation. Is this really true? Could not a sustained period of economic underdevelopment give rise to revolutionary movements?

In relation to the economic models, Marxist or otherwise, we wish to enquire into whether there is also some interaction between politics and economics, meaning that state properties could have an impact on the economic system. In much of the new political economy, originating in neo-Marxism or from the public choice school, economics is not considered only from the causal perspective but also from that of effect. For example, there is the question as to whether political factors have an impact on the level of affluence or the rate of growth. Thus Paul Whiteley has argued that socialist governments and strong trade union movements enhance economic growth, whereas Mancur Olson argues the other way around, pointing out the impact on economic growth of so-called institutional sclerosis, or the dominant position for strong distributional coalitions such as interest groups (Olson, 1982; Whiteley, 1986).

Economic factors are highly relevant in the famous debate 'does politics matter?'. States differ radically in terms of their programme structure, policy outputs being much larger in welfare states. Is this simply a function of affluence, as the well-known Wagner's law predicts? Or are policy outputs related to political factors such as the colour of the party of government (Castles, 1982; Schmidt, 1982; Blais et al., 1993)? Acknowledging the potential relevance of the standard GNP and GNP indicators for the understanding of crucial state properties, one may also move towards a broader set of economic factors, bringing in, for example, trade or the openness of the economy and the structure of the economic system.

Social conditions

There is also a dilemma with regard to the set of social conditions. While it cannot be denied that social factors generally have an impact on politics, it is far more difficult to identify which one in particular is actually an n-condition or s-condition for some political phenomenon. At most, it seems, social factors would be c-conditions. Scholars that emphasize social structure argue along different lines.

Some claim that homogeneity or heterogeneity matters, referring to cleavages in society based on ethnicity, religion, class or regional conflict (Rokkan et al., 1970). The political sociology models tend to be built on the explanatory principle that social forces translate into political consequences (Lipset and Rokkan, 1967; Rokkan and Urwin, 1983). Religion may matter for politics in different ways, as one may distinguish between religious heterogeneity, the type of religion that dominates a country and the extent of secularization.

Donald Horowitz argues in *Ethnic Groups in Conflict* (1985) that it is not enough to focus on aggregate measures of social fragmentation along linguistic or cultural lines. Ethnic conflicts would threaten state stability and performance more if they were centrally focused between a few major groups rather than between several groups. He states:

> In dispersed systems, the relationship between group and group is mediated by the relationship between locality and center. In centralized systems, one group confronts another directly, generally in a competitive framework. (Horowitz, 1985: 39)

Others, such as Tocqueville in *Democracy in America* (1835–40), underline the importance of the organization of social groups constituting civil society. Whereas Tocqueville focused mainly on the importance of independent and voluntary religious organizations and the contribution of local government institutions to democratic vitality and stability, the analysis of civil society may be made in a very broad fashion. Thus civil society models look at the creation of a number of different voluntary associations from the time of the introduction of modernization in society (Schmitter, 1986).

A third group would bet on the counter-argument that primary organizations are more important than secondary organizations – at least in Third World states. Thus, in Africa, ascriptive structures such as kinship tend to be more important than, for example, class allegiance in the form of unions (Chazan et al., 1992; Hyden and Bratton, 1992). However, the relevance of civil society in Third World countries should not be underestimated (Migdal, 1988).

The set of social models may be broadened, as one may wish to include such general dimensions as employment and the structure of industry. There are many theories about the impact of agriculture – its size and structure – on society in general and politics in particular – the modernization models (Levy, 1952; Apter, 1965). If it matters for state performance and state stability what the social structure of a country looks like, then we may ask how we find indicators that allow us to analyse social conditions. But since the set of such conditions is enormous we need to know how to identify the relevant social factors.

Cultural conditions

The political culture approach may be contrasted with more traditional approaches to the analysis of political ideas and orientations such as ideology, legitimacy and national character. Since these concepts do not allow the analysis of change in belief-systems, Merkl early recommends this approach as one foundation for comparative analysis in macropolitics (Merkl, 1977).

The political culture approach had ties with the functionalist movement, though it lacked its focus on system maintenance. Almond and Verba (1965) started from a few Parsonian concepts: an individual relates to politics on three grounds – interests, participation and values. And individual action on these bases depends on the cognitive map of the political system, the affective orientation towards political objects and symbols, and the evaluation of political events.

Individuals display attitudes towards (1) the political system, (2) input activities of citizens such as electoral participation, (3) output activities such as public programmes, and (4) the self as a political participant. Attitudes, whether cognitive, affective or evaluative, tend to be patterned along these lines. Thus three well-known cultural archetypes were derived – parochial, subject or participant orientations (Almond and Verba, 1965) – all of which have an impact upon state performance.

A parochial attitude is typical of a political culture where knowledge of and involvement in all aspects of the political system is low. A subject attitude occurs in political cultures where knowledge of the system is considerable but involvement is low. A participant political culture is one in which both knowledge and involvement is substantial. Almond and Verba examined data from five countries – Great Britain, West Germany, Italy, Mexico and the United States – in order to find that a participant culture occurs in a democratic polity. The importance of civic culture for developing a stable democracy has been emphasized by Inglehart (1990), while Putnam et al., in their study of modern Italy (1993), found that civic traditions were important for the achievement of acceptable institutional performance.

However, it is not possible to bypass approaches which claim that civilizations are the fundamental units in comparative research. Culture is a key concept in such an approach (Eisenstadt, 1966, 1973). And the newly emerging cultural theory launches a conceptual framework that is suitable for comparative research: hierarchical, individualistic, egalitarian and fatalistic types of cultural orientation (Thompson, Ellis and Wildavsky, 1990). Such cultural types may co-exist in societies, although there may be a tendency at various points in time for any one to become predominant.

When it comes to cultural factors, we find theories that single out specific attitudes or belief-patterns as being of great importance for politics. A set of models claims that certain cultures tend to set a general tone which orientates societies in general and politics in particular, such as, for example, Islamic fundamentalism. The well-known argument about the specific impact of Protestantic ethics (Weber, [1904] 1965) may be generalized to include the major world religions, such as Islam with its strong political message, Hinduism and Buddhism with their strong orientation towards transcendental matters, and Confucianism with its emphasis on mundane matters. It is hardly possible to refrain from political culture when conducting comparative enquiries into politics, but how are such concepts to be measured (Huntington, 1993)?

One way to try to map cultural patterns is to focus upon the structure of the most salient primary organization, the family. Entire continents display a fascinating variation in family relationships. It was argued by Harry Eckstein that democratic performance is related to the structures of authority in social systems other than the state. This is the symmetry theory, claiming that respect for civil and political rights rests upon the spread of humanitarian and egalitarian values in social systems where much of human interaction takes place – for example the family (Eckstein, 1966; Eckstein and Gurr, 1975). However, we will focus upon a cultural model that portrays the structure of the family in terms of notions about individualism and collectivism.

Political conditions: institutions or actors?

Against the variety of models which claim that the impact of economic, social and cultural factors is pronounced, if not prevalent, it is constantly argued that politics is not reducible to the economy or the social structure. Those that reject economic or sociological determinism place political factors in the centre. One may either look at the important political actors, parties or elites and their behaviour and attitudes, or one may emphasize institutional aspects, such as the constitutional rules or the hidden operational practices.

When institutions are emphasized, the historical impact of already established rules are often pointed out as the explanatory factor. However, such a historical approach to political institutions is not the only one within neo-institutionalism. One may make a distinction between a contextual and a systematic approach to the rules that structure so much of political activity. If rules are as important for politics as the new institutionalist revolution claims, whether in its sociological (March and Olsen, 1989) or economic version (Eggertsson, 1990), then institutions should make an impression on state properties and outcomes.

It is relevant to query the meaning(s) of 'institution' when the new institutionalism claims that institutions are so important in social life; however, only the implicit meaning or some of its references are hinted at. The state, the legal order and the legislature or parliamentary assembly are all mentioned as examples of political institutions; yet do not these entities consist of sets of various institutions?

No doubt the future of political institutionalism will depend on how much progress is made in identifying the theoretical and empirical meaning of 'institution'. The term denotes primarily rules or a system of rules, but sometimes its scope is widened to include technologies and cultures. In order to identify a set of institutional factors that may explain phenomena in comparative politics it is necessary to distinguish between an institution as a system of rules and the behaviour that is orientated in terms of its rules – in other words, organizations.

It is suggested that institutions comprehend a number of things, such as (1) physical structure; (2) demographic structure; (3) historical development; (4) personal networks; and (5) temporal structure (decision points in time) (Olsen, 1988: 35). However, if institutions are analysed as: (a) normative orders, (b) cognitive orders and (c) symbolic orders, then the action aspects may be referred to as 'organizations'. Institutions are primarily norms, belief-systems and symbolism. And the question is whether institutions as rules condition state activities and their outcomes.

Looking at institutions in a narrower fashion as rules, there is room for a systematic comparative enquiry into government. The state cannot, in the Weber interpretation, be described without its order, or the system of rules that make up the political institutions. The structural configuration of states has always been one of the most fascinating questions in comparative politics. Why? Because there is an implicit model about states that their institutional set-ups matter.

We must test various institutional models which claim that the alternative ways in which political institutions are framed are relevant for the understanding of state performance and state stability. The potentially relevant set of institutional factors covers the structure of the party system, the structure of the executive body and such basic principles of the state as federalism and autonomy in relation to the military.

When the focus is upon the elite, some scholars refer to the autonomous impact of elite behaviour (Schumpeter, 1944; Lijphart, 1968). The concept of a political elite has always been rather muddled. Against the elite theoreticians – Pareto, Mosca and Michels – it has been argued that there is no clear boundary between political elites and the population, in any case not in democracies (Polsby, 1963; Parry, 1969). However, Jean Blondel has shown that the number of individuals that are involved in politics at the elite level in countries all over the world tends to be small (Blondel, 1990). Crucial in democratic polities is whether there is a bias towards open competition between party elites – 'adversarial' democracy (Mansbridge, 1983) – or the making of accommodation policies between opposing camps ('Lager', 'zuilen').

It is true that the behaviour of elites matters very much in non-democratic political systems (Etzioni-Halevy, 1993), where small elite groups often engage one another in violent power struggles. Thus we expect to find that state stability is much more precarious where the political elite has a smaller basis than it does in a democracy.

In talking about political elites it is impossible to ignore the various political parties in the countries of the world. It is a basic theme in comparative politics that the phenomenon of the party is crucial in shaping national political events in the twentieth century. Again, in the 'does politics matter' literature, a number of models claim that the strength of right-wing and left-wing parties matters for policies and outcomes. Here we focus on the explanatory power of political parties and the properties of party systems for the understanding of state stability and state performance. Party systems comprise a number of important aspects, as outlined in Giovanni Sartori's *Parties and Party Systems* (1976).

Other scholars have emphasized the vital importance of elite ideologies for the operation of day-to-day politics. More specifically, elite beliefs in the legitimacy of standard operating procedures matter for the status of civil and political rights (Tingsten, 1965). The tone of politics in a country is set by the norms that elites develop towards each other. John Higley and Richard Gunther underline the contribution of elite settlements for the consolidation of a democratic regime – that democracy is based on the adherence to a set of shared norms about what it means to be in power as a government and what the role of an opposition is supposed to be (Higley and Gunther, 1992).

Framework of analysis

States can be looked upon as systems of action. They constitute one type of political system existing among other political systems, on the one hand international regimes and on the other 'parapolitical' systems, such as local and regional government, giant firms and trade unions. They operate in the midst of other kinds of social systems, such as the economy, and human collectivities, such as the family or the tribe. The environment of the state offers the boundary for political behaviour, political parties and elite activities. It consists of conditions that the state cannot change, at least not in the short term. But it also includes conditions that are less firm – the political attitudes of the population.

Often a distinction is made between objective and subjective conditions. Among the objective conditions of the state one would include a number of factors that often recur in models in comparative politics: population size, territorial size, climate and past historical experiences. The subjective conditions consist mainly of political culture or political attitudes. In one sense economic and social factors also belong to the set of objective conditions. However, the objective–subjective distinction is not easily related to the institutional conditions that lie at the heart of politics and the state, which end up somewhere in between the two.

In one sense institutional set-ups and the constitutional framework constitute an objective background for state activities, but in another sense the basic rules of the state may be changed rapidly – if, for example, concerted action is aimed at changing behaviour and attitudes. Thus we arrive at the following scheme for approaching the modelling of state properties.

I Dependent variables:

   a) State stability: regime duration
   b) State performance: civil and political rights, welfare spending, income equality, human development index and level of inflation

II Independent variables:

   c) Physical conditions: territorial size and climate
   d) Economic conditions: affluence, economic growth and the structure of the economic system
   e) Social conditions: homogeneity versus heterogeneity, industry
   f) Cultural conditions: world religions, family structure
   g) Political conditions: institutional conditions, i.e., constitutions and basic rules structuring the state
   h) Political conditions: actors, i.e., elites and political parties as well as party systems

A mix of different models is required to test state stability and state performance. Firstly, we need to test structural models which look for

	Explanatory factors		
Problems	Social forces	Institutional patterns	Actor factors
Stability	I	II	III
Performance	IV	V	VI

Figure 6.1   Framework of analysis

conditions in the environment, in particular in the economy and the social structure of society. Secondly, there is a set of institutional models which claim that the basic rules on which the state is founded are of great importance for the probability that it may persist. Finally, there are actor models which emphasize the contribution of leaders and political parties. What matters most for state stability and state performance: social structure, institutions or actors?

Below we will devote one section to each of these *sets of conditions*, asking how much they contribute to our understanding of state properties – in particular the variation in state stability and state performance. In Chapter 7 we start with models that attribute causal relevance to structural factors. Chapter 8 discusses institutional factors that are assigned causal significance, whereas Chapter 9 looks at actor-related factors. Finally, in Chapter 10 the causal relevance of the conditions from all three sets are enquired into by mixed models comprising a few conditions from each set. Chapter 11 states a few implications of the findings in Chapter 10 for the major transition question of today, namely how to move from dictatorship to democracy.

We pursue a comparative enquiry into the relation between social and economic structure on the one hand and politics on the other, testing political sociology claims about the impact of social conditions on politics. And in the tenet of neo-institutionalism we look for systematic relations between political institutions in the sense of basic rules and state outputs and state outcomes. Is stability and performance dependent on the institutional fabric of the state? Figure 6.1 shows the framework for comparative analysis.

Looking for explanatory factors, we deal first with structural models (I and IV). Is there some set of factors, such as wealth or cultural homogeneity, which is conducive to state survival or promotes special patterns of state performance? Institutional models enquiring into the implications of systems of rules have to be included (II and V). Does the type of regime matter (democracies having a longer life-span than dictatorships and military regimes or democracies producing better policy outputs and outcomes)? The explanatory analysis may be taken one step further in that we adopt actor models that ask whether people in politics really mean a difference. Do

Table 6.3 Correlations between state stability and state performance

	CIVIC	HDI	HED86	TOP10	INF8090
State stability (REG)	.53 (128)	.52 (129)	.65 (118)	−.37 (48)	−.18 (109)

Note: CIVIC = democracy index for 1973–88; HDI = human development index for the 1980s; HED86 = Health and education expenditures for the mid-1980s; TOP10 = income inequality in the 1980s; INF8090 = Inflation 1980–90; REG = Average duration of regimes between 1945 and 1990.

left-wing governments matter when we evaluate policy-making and its consequences across different countries?

The two dependent variables

Finally, we must raise the question whether and to what extent state stability and state performance are distinct dimensions. Logically speaking, a state may be stable or unstable whatever its performance records look like. However, although regimes may be based almost entirely upon repression, there are limits to how long the population will endure in a state where performance is bad. And a state that performs well would tend to be more stable than a state, for example, which did not protect civil and political rights. Thus one would expect to find some interaction between state stability scores and performance indicators (see table 6.3).

The correlations indicate that state stability and state performance are interrelated. There is a connection between regime stability and performance profile, in that it is more likely that a state with a good performance profile in terms of human rights, quality of life, welfare programmes and reasonable income equality will be stable than if it had a poor performance profile. However, the correlations are weak, meaning that other factors are causally relevant.

Focusing more specifically on the relationship between state stability, in the sense of average duration of regime, and democratic performance, as the respect for civil and political rights, we see that there is some connection. The correlations between REG and CIVIC (r = .53, N = 128) as well as between REG and AVEGU1 (r = .48, N = 123) imply that there are more stable democratic states than stable dictatorships. Figure 6.2 shows state stability (REG) or the average regime duration between 1945 and 1990–1 plotted against the CIVIC index on the institutionalization of human rights for the period 1973–88.

In the postwar period, the majority of the states of the world with a population larger than one million have been non-democratic. And most of

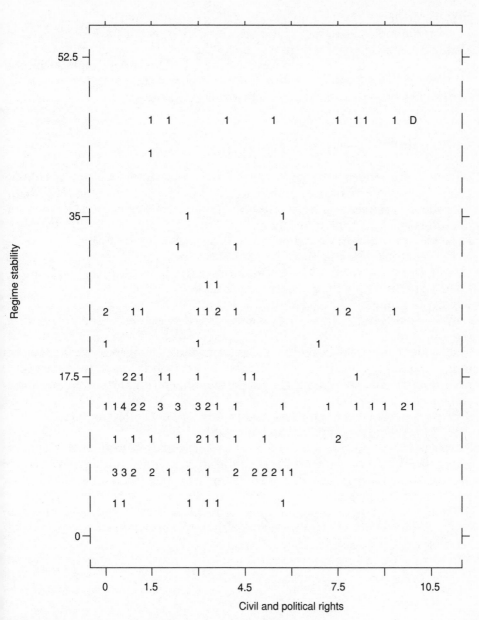

Figure 6.2   State stability versus civil and political rights
Note: For explanation of figures, see Appendix II.

these countries with a poor political performance have suffered from political instability. What complicates this simple observation is that there are states that have been stable for long periods of time and yet have managed to stem the demand for democratization. Moreover, there are also states that have attempted to introduce civil and political rights but have not been able to institutionalize a stable regime. The fact that there is interaction between state stability and state performance could be due to a common set of background factors that condition both. Perhaps state stability and state performance are to some extent dependent upon the same conditions?

Conclusion

It is difficult to identify the set of causally relevant factors within the field of comparative politics or government in a definitive way. With regard to both dependent variables – state stability and state performance – it is an open question which factors are to be included in the analysis, because there is a large variety of alternative conditions that are causally relevant.

The outcome of our methodological deliberations in this chapter is that we should focus on three sets of conditions: social, institutional and actor-related factors. We will take a pragmatic look at which of these approaches will explain more.

We will survey the variety of models offered within comparative politics, searching for hypotheses about relationships between the dependent and independent variables in terms of our framework. However, we emphasize that empirical connections are not enough, because we have to understand the causal mechanism that might play a role underlying the correlations and statistical parameters.

Selecting civil and political rights, the human development index, welfarism, income inequality and the rate of inflation between 1980 and 1990 as the key indicators on state performance, and the average duration of regimes from 1945 onwards as the indicator on state stability, we try to identify some mechanisms that account for why some states are unstable or perform less well whereas other states are stable or perform much better. Testing the strong claims made by neo-institutionalists in political science for the causal relevance of institutional models, we contrast them with structural models, in particular economic ones.

7

Structural Models

Introduction

Social determinism is a perspective that looms large in the study of comparative politics. It is argued that state stability and performance are the result of major factors in the environment of the state: social structure in general and economic factors in particular. The models that enter the structural perspective stem from the assumption that politics at the macrolevel is a function of or much influenced by large-scale social forces.

The crucial question is how much is 'much'? Stating that social forces are causally relevant to the understanding of states is very different from the claims of, for example, economic determinism and the modernization approach, which model state properties almost as a strict function of class conflicts in the development of capitalism or as totally shaped by the structural formation, from agriculture to industry. The purpose of this chapter is to discuss the open-ended question of how much impact structure has on state stability and state performance. Although we look at empirical relationships in the form of simple correlations, we raise the problem later if they can be interpreted in terms of causal mechanisms by means of model building.

Physical conditions

Very different structural conditions have been suggested in order to understand the viability of the state as well as its performance records. With regard to physical conditions there are two contradictory theories about the effects of size, one favouring small, the other large scale. The perhaps abstruse climate model argues that basic climatic conditions such as heat or frost are relevant from a causal point of view. A priori, the size hypotheses are more readily understandable than the climatic hypothesis in terms of causality.

The polis model

The idea that state properties are related to the size of the state has had many adherents in the history of political thought. Plato in his *Republic* and Aristotle in *Politics* regarded the city-state as the superior form of state. Although the Romans showed that a city-state may be transformed into a giant empire, the prevailing line of argument was to favour smallness. Cicero and Seneca as well as Machiavelli show scepticism towards the viability of large states.

There is an important version of the size argument that considers the democratic states. Thus Montesquieu, focusing on a republic, and Rousseau, dealing with popular participation, claimed that democracy could materialize only in a small state. In *The Spirit of the Laws* (1748) we have the following argument:

> In a large republic, the common good is sacrificed to a thousand consider-
> ations; it is subordinate to various exceptions; it depends on accidents. In a
> small republic, the public good is better felt, better known, lies nearer to
> each citizen; abuses are less extensive there and consequently less protected.
> (Montesquieu, [1748] 1989: 124)

Montesquieu distinguished three basic types of rule or political regime: republican, monarchical and despotic government. In a republic, as in a democracy, the people as a body have sovereign power (Montesquieu, 1989: 10); both democracies and republics may take action to secure stability. Montesquieu qualifies his argument by opening up the possibility of a medium-sized federal republic as a compromise (Montesquieu, 1989: 131). What is necessary and viable is a constitution that has the advantages of a republic and the external force of a monarchy, states Montesquieu, pointing to the republic of Holland as an example.

Rousseau, in *The Social Contract* (1762), would not engage in empirical studies in order to find the optimal size of a state, because he favoured the small state from the outset. Today he could have pointed to Luxembourg, Liechtenstein, Andorra, Singapore, Hong Kong and Bermuda as successful examples of the polis model – at least from an economic point of view (i.e., their level of affluence).

Yet these city-states are hardly representative of states in general, nor of major cities around the world. Bermuda, with its tiny population of 58,000 people and an average GNP per capita of 18,000 US dollars (*Statesman's Yearbook*), remains a British colony. The fate of Hong Kong, with its population of almost six million and high standard of living (GNP per capita = 11,490 US dollars in 1990), is difficult to predict as in 1997 British administration will come to an end and sovereignty will be transferred to communist China. In fact, the trend is away from city-states and towards megacities (Dogan and Kasarda, 1988) (see table 7.1).

Table 7.1 The growth of megacities, 1950–2000 (in millions)

	1950	1985	2000
New York	12	15	16
London	10	10	9
Shanghai	10	12	14
Tokyo/Yokohama	7	17	17
Beijing	7	9	11
Paris	6	9	9
Buenos Aires	5	11	13
Chicago	5	7	7
Moscow	5	9	10
Milan	4	7	8
Calcutta	4	11	17
Los Angeles	4	10	11
Rio de Janeiro	4	10	13
São Paulo	3	16	24
Bombay	3	10	16
Seoul	–	10	14
Delhi	–	7	13
Cairo	3	9	13
Mexico City	3	18	26
Jakarta	2	8	13
Baghdad	–	7	13
Teheran	–	7	13
Karachi	–	7	12
Istanbul	–	7	12
Dacca	–	5	11
Manila	–	7	11

Source: Dogan and Kasarda (1988: 15).

Notice in particular the prediction of a phenomenal expansion of Mexico City and São Paulo. The coming of the metropolis era, replacing the remnants of the ancient polis model, entails that local government will increase in importance at the expense of national politics. How are such megacities, several of which are larger than many of the states of the world, to be run?

After all, the entire population in several states is smaller than 10 million, whereas many cities in the Third World have passed or will pass this limit by the year 2000. By the turn of the century cities such as Bangkok (10 m), Lima (9 m), Kinshasa (9 m), Lagos (8 m), Madras (8 m) and Bangalore (8 m) will also be larger than many states, including Norway and Denmark, Ireland, the Baltic states, Slovenia and the Slovak republic. Thus, even if the city-state model was revitalized, it would not imply the creation of small compact states.

Madison: the factions model

Actually, the polis model was rejected by those who argued that greater state size brings more advantages than disadvantages. When the United States was to be formed there was a lengthy debate about the pros and cons of small and large republics. Whereas Thomas Jefferson repeated the standard argument in favour of the small state, Alexander Hamilton and in particular James Madison put forward a case for a large republic. In *The Federalist Papers*, which appeared between 1787 and 1788, Madison published his well-known article about size, factions and democracy containing the following argument for a large state:

> Hence, it clearly appears, that the same advantage which a representative republic has over a democracy, in controlling the effects of faction, is enjoyed by a large over a small republic – is enjoyed by the Union over the states composing it ... (Hamilton et al., [1787–8], 1961: 83)

What could threaten a democracy, or a republic as it was often named, was the threat of domination by special interest groups seeking favours from public legislation and budget-making – 'rent-seeking' in modern public choice terminology (Olson, 1982). Madison saw a large state as the self-correcting force against factionalism. Where there would be many factions, due to large-scale politics, the invisible hand of competition would see to it that they cancelled each other out, especially if the choice of basic institutions favoured such interest contestability (Ostrom, 1987). By implication a large or a democratic state would enhance both stability and performance. The polis model and the factions model may be integrated into a general model of the consequences of state size.

The general size model

In their *Size and Democracy* (1973) Robert Dahl and Edward Tufte break down the size model into a set of hypotheses that, in one form or another, have been propounded by other scholars in the history of political thought. If size in its various aspects (e.g., area or population) has an impact upon state stability or democratic viability, how can we account for such an impact in terms of a theory about the mechanisms which translate size into such state properties as regime stability?

The Dahl and Tufte model identifies two dimensions which are related to size and which may have an impact upon state stability or democratic viability: system capacity and citizen effectiveness (Dahl and Tufte, 1973: 24–5). State size is positively related to system capacity, which enhances democratic longevity. Citizen effectiveness is negatively related to state size, which is conducive to democratic instability. Generalizing, state stability is increased by system capacity but decreased by citizen ineffectiveness.

Table 7.2 Measures of state size

	LNPOP 1980	LNAREA 1980	LNGDP 1990
Africa	8.7 (43)	12.8 (43)	8.2 (39)
America	9.1 (24)	12.5 (24)	10.0 (22)
Asia	9.5 (35)	12.3 (35)	10.3 (25)
Oceania	8.6 (3)	13.8 (3)	10.5 (3)
Europe	9.6 (25)	12.1 (25)	11.9 (22)
E^2	.08	.04	.42

Sources: *Encyclopedia Britannica Book of the Year* (1990); World Bank, 1992.

Note: LNPOP and LNAREA are the logarithm of size data; LNGDP is the logarithm of gross domestic product data. The use of logarithms is motivated by the large variation in the data.

The Dahl and Tufte model implies that small dictatorships are more vulnerable than large ones, and that large authoritarian states are more unstable than large democracies. Furthermore, it also implies that large democracies outperform small democracies, all other things being equal. But why would mere state size matter? The polis model, the factions model and the general size model simply beg the question: are state properties really dependent on whether the state is truly small or very large?

The simple fact that we have about thirty states with a population under one million is a warning against any strong hypotheses about the implications of size on state properties. There was a clear divergence between political nationalism and economic international integration after the Second World War, meaning that tiny states need not be economically vulnerable as long as they find a place in the world economy.

Theoretically, one could argue that economic resources or position in the world economy, as suggested by Wallerstein in his world systems model (Wallerstein, 1974), would have a larger impact on both system capacity and citizen effectiveness than state size. Table 7.2 shows that state size hardly differs on the various continents. At the same time the eta-squared statistic indicates that the variation within each continent between states of various sizes is huge. On the other hand, the variation in one source of state power, economic resources as measured by the size of GDP, displays a different pattern of variation, which is closer to intuitive observations of country variations in state strength.

Although the size of a state varies tremendously, giant and tiny states are to be found on all the continents. When we come to look at the economic aspects of the state, we will see a more systematic pattern which is more relevant to the understanding of system capacity and citizen effectiveness or, in terms of our somewhat different terminology, state stability and state

Table 7.3 Distribution of states by climate

		Tropical (rainy)	Dry	Temperate (warm, rainy)	Cool
Africa	(43)	27	14	2	0
America	(24)	18	1	4	1
Asia	(36)	12	16	7	1
Oceania	(3)	1	1	1	0
Europe	(25)	0	0	17	8
E^2	.50				

Source: Shorter Oxford Economic Atlas of the World.

performance. It is true that the Dahl and Tufte model isolates efficiency and legitimacy as crucial variables for the understanding of macropolitics at the state level. But are they really critically dependent upon state size?

The climatic model

Perhaps Montesquieu is best known for his theory that climatic conditions have an impact on the state and politics. In another passage from *The Spirit of the Laws* he wrote:

> If it is true that the character of the spirit and the passions of the heart are extremely different in the various climates, *laws* should be relative to the differences in these passions and to the differences in these characters. (Montesquieu, [1748] 1989: 231)

But the climatic model is hardly taken seriously today. What Montesquieu predicted on the basis of a number of hypotheses about the impact of frost and heat on the human spirit was that there would be North–South differences in the form of industry versus laziness, equality versus slavery and freedom versus servitude (Montesquieu, 1989: Part III). Can these ideas be made sense of today? Classifying states according to a simple climatic scheme allows us to derive a state distribution that could be used for testing a modern version of the Montesquieu idea.

The climatic model suffers from the same weakness as the size model – namely, the lack of any natural mechanism that could explain why climate would make a difference on state stability and state performance. However, when combined with a model that underlines cultural factors that might be related to the actual climatic variations (for example, the type of family pattern), the Montesquieu theory seems more plausible.

Social conditions

There are several models that emphasize general social conditions, as, for example, in the modernization theme, which argued that state transformation started in society from such major structural changes as the industrial revolution or the urbanization process. One may also distinguish more specific models dealing with the consequences of particular social forces, for example, the fragmentation models stating the impact of social heterogeneity.

Autonomy of the state

Looking at models concerning social structure, it is vital to distinguish two kinds of interaction between the state and its environment. First, there is the idea of a strong relationship, where the state is determined by society, meaning that it has little autonomy in relation to social forces. The alternative approach, looking at the state as a superstructure in relation to, for example, basic economic forces, argues that the state possesses relative autonomy versus society (Nordlinger, 1981). The relative state autonomy model implies a weak relationship between state and society, where the environment has an impact on conditions for state activities, but the state is not a function of social forces (Jessop, 1982; Held, 1989). Let us look at a few deterministic models.

Modernization models

Transformation of the social structure on a grand scale and its political consequences were modelled in the modernization theme from around 1960. It was argued firstly that a major transition from agriculture to industry took place not only in the rich world but also among the poor countries. And, secondly, it was believed that this major change in social structure would have tremendous political consequences (Lerner, 1958; Deutsch, 1961). Not underestimating the importance of the modernization theme, it remains the case that there is a risk here for unwarranted generalization as well as reductionism.

The general modernization theme generated several models regarding the consequences of major social transformation for the state. Thus a frequently used agricultural model claimed that the transition from an agrarian society to an industrial one, measured by the reduction in the relative size of agricultural employment, would be accompanied by state instability and rising expectations about democracy. Table 7.4 shows the immense differences in the percentage of the population deriving their income from agriculture.

Table 7.4 Percentage of the labour force in agriculture

	Labour force, 1960	Labour force, 1988	Farm size, 1980
Africa	77.7 (43)	63.8 (43)	49.5 (42)
America	43.1 (24)	30.1 (23)	32.2 (24)
Asia	59.7 (32)	44.6 (33)	42.6 (34)
Oceania	9.6 (1)	30.6 (3)	57.7 (3)
Europe	27.6 (25)	15.0 (24)	53.0 (25)
E^2	.53	.42	.10

Sources: World Bank: Social Indicators of Development 1990 (1991); UNDP: Human Development Report (1991); Vanhanen (1990).

Note: Farm size, or the role of an independent peasantry as family owned farms, as a percentage of the total number of farms around 1980.

One finding in table 7.4 is that one should be cautious about making generalizations concerning trends in the development of agricultural structure. Evidently, a very large part of the populations of many countries in Africa and Asia are still involved in agriculture. Among Third World countries the reduction in agricultural employment has been pronounced, but in Latin America the role of the Spanish Latifundia system lingers on, and in several Asian countries the practice of share cropping is widespread. Another finding is that an independent peasantry has a stronger position in the rich world than in the developing countries.

The agricultural models emphasize either the size of the agricultural sector or the ownership structure, where the subjugation or exploitation of the peasantry results in less stability and democracy. Whether these clear differences between countries matter for politics depends on whether there is some mechanism at work that relates agricultural structure to state properties.

The agricultural model may be supplemented by an urbanization model, which views the state as significantly influenced by the transformation of a society from a sparsely populated to a densely populated structure. Table 7.5 shows the overall differences in the distribution of the population between cities and the hinterland.

Industrialization and urbanization are modelled in the modernization approach as creating the conditions for mass political participation (Allardt and Rokkan, 1970). The result of bringing the population together in large urban concentrations is that it may be mobilized into political action. Traditional rule is seriously weakened, as mass politics involves the introduction of civil and political rights and the augmentation of participation. The modernization models predict that societies with a large part of the population within the agricultural sector or in the countryside would be unstable or undemocratic, or both.

Table 7.5 Urbanization (percentage of the population living in urban areas)

		1960	1990	2000
Africa	(43)	15.4	33.1	40.1
America	(24)	45.7	63.1	68.3
Asia	(33)	29.0	45.9	50.9
Oceania	(3)	53.3	61.7	63.7
Europe	(24)	53.5	68.6	72.3
E^2		.41	.34	.31

Source: World Bank: *World Development Report* (1992).

Fragmentation models

When the importance of social conditions is emphasized, there is often a focus on 'cleavages'. The concept of a cleavage refers to the alignment of the population around social dimensions which are conducive to conflict, manifestly or in a latent fashion (Rae and Taylor, 1970). Social or cultural fragmentation occurs when strong social groups are organized against one another. Typical cleavage bases include class, religion and ethnicity. And the fragmentation models claim that the extension and intensity of cleavages have a strong impact upon the state, in particular its stability.

To the French Revolutionaries, a desirable state was not only a republic where liberty and equality ruled; they also required fraternity. In the history of normative political principles, the emphasis on fraternité has not stood up as well as the requirements for liberté and égalité, but the concept plays a major role in political sociology.

Before we try to map the occurrence of fraternity in the world, we must briefly pin down its double meaning in political discourse. The compact edition of *The Oxford English Dictionary* contains the following entries on 'fraternity':

> 1. The relation of a brother or of brothers; brotherhood. 2. The state or quality of being fraternal. 3. A family of brothers. 4. A body or order of men organized for religious or devout purposes. 5. A body of men associated by some tie or common interest; a company or guild. 6. A body of men of the same class, occupation, etc.

Translated into a political context, fraternity would stand for a shared feeling or consciousness about some common purpose to be pursued at the level of government. What the requirement of fraternity excludes is the predicament of a political body where citizens are either indifferent towards one another – political apathy or alienation – or where citizens are in severe conflict with one another about the ends and means of the political community, as, for example, in civil war.

Fraternity as a political ideal would amount to something like brotherhood in a republic. *The Oxford English Dictionary* mentions as one of the key meanings of 'brotherhood': 'Fellowship; community of feeling uniting man and man; also concretely those united in such fellowship'. Yet what unites men and women may be entirely different sorts of things. On the one hand there is the notion of universal fellowship, and on the other there is national fellowship – or simply nationalism. A political community may focus on what unites its members, their national identity making them different from other men. Or a political community may be orientated towards universal principles that could unite all men, as, for example, human rights and international cooperation broadly conceived.

These two interpretations of brotherhood clash violently. National identity could become the basis for large-scale state atrocities towards so-called internal enemies, that is, groups with a different ethnic identity. And it may trigger external wars aiming at the dominination of one fraternity by another. Although nationalism may be the source of community among men and women, generating solidarity and achievements, it may also be harmful, giving rise to nationalist ferment and aggressive behaviour.

To some, fraternité denotes a universal brotherhood independent of state boundaries, whereas to others it stands for national unity. The developments of the French Revolution reveal this ambiguity. The process of 'Napoleonization' implied that the idea of brotherhood could serve as the basis for the building of a French empire, offsetting in its turn the emergence of the search for the *Volk* (in the terminology of Johann Gottfried Herder) by other countries:

> ... it is indeed true that modern nationalism is a product of the French revolution and as a concept was born out of the failure of the revolution's universalism. (Szporlouk, 1988: 81)

However, nationalist theory has also harboured a 'soft' thesis, claiming that national identification amounts to popular sovereignty that fosters humanity, respect and cooperation between nation states (see Meinecke's *Weltbürgertum und Nationalstaat* [1908]).

The fragmentation model claims that a stable state could not possibly be one where there is strong dissent among major social groups concerning the direction of the political community. Social heterogeneity along cleavages could topple both liberty and equality in a political body. Among various social cleavages such as ethnicity, religion and class, the fragmentation models underline especially ethnic but also religious fragmentation.

Several models pinpoint the political implications of certain kinds of phenomena labelled in different ways: 'ethnic politics', 'race', 'tribal politics', 'nationalism', 'language communities', 'cultural pluralism' (van den Berghe, 1981; Horowitz, 1985; Thompson, 1989; Kellas, 1991; Smith,

Table 7.6 Ethnic and religious homogeneity versus heterogeneity

	ELF	DOM1	DOM2	DOM3	RF
Africa	.61 (43)	51 (41)	51 (43)	51 (42)	.48 (43)
America	.37 (24)	86 (24)	66 (24)	71 (24)	.22 (24)
Asia	.41 (28)	77 (33)	73 (35)	74 (34)	.16 (35)
Oceania	.33 (3)	84 (3)	83 (3)	90 (3)	.49 (3)
Europe	.24 (25)	84 (25)	83 (25)	84 (25)	.32 (25)
E^2	.26	.32	.25	.26	.32

Sources: ELF = ethno-linguistic fractionalization: Taylor and Hudson (1972), Barrett (1982); DOM1 = percentage of dominating ethno-linguistic group in a country: Rustow (1967); DOM2 = Barrett (1982); DOM3 = Vanhanen (1990); RF = religious fractionalization: Barrett (1982).

1992; Gurr, 1993). Here we focus upon the state in deeply divided societies. These models suggest that state stability and state performance would be low in countries where there is both extensive and intensive religious and ethnic dissent, either open or tacit.

The level of fraternity varies from one country to another according to the two cleavages of ethnicity and religion. It can be measured in two different ways, either directly or indirectly – either surveying attitudes or by looking at the probability that two randomly selected individuals belong to the same ethnic or religious group. Table 7.6 presents data using the second kind of indicator.

The ethnicity fragmentation index – ELF – is a composite of two such indices, one for the 1960s and the other for the 1970s. It is unlikely that the fragmentation scores would have changed rapidly over the last decades if they have not increased in political relevance. The ethnic fragmentation index is scaled in the opposite way to the ethnic domination index, which measures the proportion of the population that belongs to the dominating language group. The religious fragmentation index – RF – is scaled like the ELF index: higher scores imply more fragmentation or the probability that two randomly selected persons belong to different religious groups.

On average, ethnic fragmentation tends to be high in Africa, somewhat lower in America, and generally low in Europe and Oceania. In Asia the average score on ethnic homogeneity is rather high, as 77 per cent of the population typically speak the dominating language. Religious fragmentation is calculated on the basis of the relative proportion of Protestants, Roman Catholics, Muslims and members of other religions. High religious fragmentation scores are to be found mainly in Africa but also in Europe and Oceania. In terms of religious structure, most Asian countries tend to be homogeneous.

Since the within-group differences are larger than the between-group differences, it is worth while identifying countries that score highly on these

Table 7.7 Ethnic fragmentation

Afghanistan	.63	Malaysia	.71
Angola	.80	Mali	.82
Belgium	.55	Morocco	.53
Benin	.75	Mozambique	.75
Bolivia	.70	Namibia	.78
Botswana	.51	Nepal	.69
Burkina Faso	.72	Niger	.74
Cameroon	.86	Nigeria	.88
Canada	.76	Pakistan	.63
Central African Republic	.74	Peru	.63
Chad	.80	Philippines	.79
Congo	.69	Senegal	.77
Côte d'Ivoire	.87	Sierra Leone	.78
Ecuador	.60	South Africa	.68
Ethiopia	.70	Sudan	.72
Gabon	.76	Switzerland	.56
Ghana	.72	Tanzania	.95
Guatemala	.58	Togo	.72
Guinea	.70	Trinidad	.61
India	.90	Uganda	.92
Indonesia	.77	USSR	.68
Iran	.76	Venezuela	.54
Jordan	.52	Yugoslavia	.77
Kenya	.86	Zambia	.79
Laos	.61	Zaïre	.80
Liberia	.86	Zimbabwe	.53
Malawi	.65		

Sources: Taylor and Hudson (1972); Barrett (1982).

Note: Ethnic fragmentation index >.55.

two fragmentation indices, since their level of fraternity may face severe difficulties (see table 7.7).

A few countries score very high on the ethnic fragmentation index – Uganda, Tanzania, India, Kenya and Nigeria. One might add that the territorial aspect in the pattern of ethnic fragmentation in a country could have political implications. Thus there is a risk that, when ethnically distinct populations are mixed in several parts of a country, an explosive situation could result (as in the former Yugoslavia, where the Serbs, Croats and Muslims constitute considerable minorities within Croatia and Bosnia Hercegovina). Yet in Horowitz's theory of ethnic conflict there are more dimensions than simply the occurrence of different groups with varying ethnic identities, such as ranked or hierarchical and unranked ethnic systems

Table 7.8 Religious fragmentation

Angola	.49	Lesotho	.61
Australia	.57	Liberia	.64
Benin	.53	Madagascar	.64
Botswana	.54	Malawi	.73
Bulgaria	.52	Malaysia	.55
Burkina Faso	.59	Mauritius	.62
Cameroon	.73	Mozambique	.62
Canada	.57	Netherlands	.61
Central African Republic	.63	Papua New Guinea	.51
Chad	.70	Rwanda	.64
Côte d'Ivoire	.67	Sierra Leone	.57
Cuba	.50	South Africa	.48
Ethiopia	.61	Tanzania	.73
East Germany	.53	Togo	.64
West Germany	.56	Trinidad	.70
Hungary	.54	Uganda	.66
Indonesia	.59	United States	.55
Kenya	.69	Uruguay	.49
Lebanon	.51	USSR	.59

Source: Barrett (1982).

Note: Religious fragmentation index >.45.

(Horowitz, 1985: 22). One may note that, although Somalia scores very low on the ethnic fragmentation index (.09), its state collapsed as a result of clan conflicts.

Table 7.8 lists a number of countries that score highly on the religious fragmentation index. They are generally not the same ones as those that score highly on the ethnicity index.

Religious fragmentation in countries such as Togo, Malawi, Kenya, Ethiopia and Tanzania is high. Some very large states have to accommodate large-scale ethnic *and* religious cleavages: Indonesia, the former USSR, South Africa and Malaysia. The fact that most of these countries have had great difficulties in maintaining some sort of state shows that fraternité may be very difficult to arrive at in countries with extensive and intensive ethnic or religious fragmentation. But does ethnic or religious fragmentation in itself reduce state stability and state performance?

Do ethnic or religious fragmentation constitute the major challenges to political unity? All the major kinds of cleavages – ethnicity, religion and class – are aggregate forces that have a tremendous impact upon the state. But here we concentrate in particular upon the stability and performance on the macrolevel of politics. Can the claims of the fragmentation models be confirmed when we take a broad perspective on the state?

Table 7.9 Protestantism and Islam (as a percentage of the total population)

	Protestantism	Islam
Africa	18.5 (43)	34.2 (43)
America	11.8 (24)	0.5 (24)
Asia	1.8 (35)	44.4 (35)
Oceania	64.5 (3)	0.0 (3)
Europe	27.3 (25)	2.6 (25)
E^2	.24	.27

Source: Barrett (1982).

Cultural conditions

Among the cultural models of politics we find ideas about the role of religion. What is at stake here is a few hypotheses that single out Protestantism (or Calvinism) or an Islamic culture as being of crucial importance (Huntington, 1993). As a matter of fact, it has been claimed that world religious systems have opposite consequences: whereas the Protestantic ethic is supportive of democracy, the Islamic ethos inhibits democracy. Our question is: how important are these two major religious belief-systems for state stability and performance? Let us first look at how these religions are represented in the world today (see table 7.9).

If Calvinism implies thrift, as Max Weber assumed, then we may expect that affluence is higher in Oceania and Europe than elsewhere. If an Islamic culture involves religious devotion, then we may generally expect less secularization in Asia and Africa. The Protestantism model might claim that its Calvinist spirit is conducive to democracy, whereas the Islamic model could imply that Islamic fundamentalism prohibits the institutionalization of liberty and political rights.

It remains to say something about the family structure models. A few family models have been formulated (Todd, 1983) which try to classify a country variation in family structure according to two conceptual pairs: liberty versus authority and equality versus inequality. Here we employ a scale that ranks the various family patterns according to how much freedom there is to leave the family and how unequally the family inheritance is divided (see table 7.10). Each state is identified as having one major predominating family structure.

The model behind Todd's classificatory scheme is that low scores indicate both freedom and inequality, meaning that one child inherits all, which favours mobility and economic development, whereas high scores indicate the opposite – namely, an obedience to family authority but equality in

Table 7.10   States with different family structures

		(1)	(2)	(3)	(4)	(5)	(6)	(7)	(8)
Africa	(43)	–	1	–	1	1	–	7	33
America	(24)	2	–	–	4	17	1	–	–
Asia	(36)	–	10	5	–	–	5	15	–
Oceania	(3)	2	1	–	–	–	–	–	–
Europe	(25)	3	–	9	7	–	6	–	–

Source: Based on Todd (1983).

Note: Todd's classification orders eight different family systems. A higher score stands for greater collectivism: (1) absolute nuclear family; (2) anomic family; (3) authoritarian family; (4) egalitarian nuclear family; (5) anomic and egalitarian nuclear family; (6) exogamous community family; (7) endogamous community family; (8) African family system.

inheritance. There are clear differences between the African family structure and that in Oceania and Europe. The variation in type of family patterns may be translated as a cultural dimension, where the Todd scores measure the extent of individualism in culture (Thompson, Ellis and Wildavsky, 1990).

A theory about the social consequences of these different family structures could underline the implications of individualism in the form of private property rights. Immobile family structures are conducive to ambiguous property structures that would create conflict and reduce efficiency in economic transactions. Individualism could enhance rapid economic development that in turn might enhance state stability and performance – if economic efficiency matters for these state aspects.

The cultural models focusing upon religion or family structures do not allow a straightforward interpretation of the causal mechanism at work. However, aggregate level relationships could be accounted for by means of microlevel theory about human motivation, the place of individualism and the implications of private property rights. Still another macrocultural indicator is the size of a white settler population, the theoretical interpretation of which is also not evident. It could tap a tradition or strength of Western cultural values in general (Inglehart, 1990; Putnam et al., 1993). However, this is not a very precise concept, as a large white settler population in, for example, Africa has not meant more racial equality.

Economic conditions

One does not have to adhere to economic determinism to start searching for economic models of the state. A distinction may be made between two kinds of economic model of political stability and performance: the economic

Table 7.11 Level of affluence (in US dollars, assuming constant prices)

| | GDP/capita | | | | | GNP/ |
	1950	1960	1970	1980	1985	capita, 1989
Africa	684	589	734	850	866	776 (N = 42)
America	1,949	2,295	3,046	3,607	3,410	3,093 (N = 23)
Asia	704	1,232	2,067	3,525	3,794	4,251 (N = 28)
Oceania	4,431	3,920	5,201	5,747	6,075	9,107 (N = 3)
Europe	2,554	3,703	5,424	7,202	7,714	12,541 (N = 22)
E^2	.39	.52	.51	.45	.48	.42

Sources: Summers and Heston (1988); World Bank, *World Development Report* (1991).

Note: The number of cases for GDP varies: Africa from 9 in 1950 to 41 in 1985; America from 18 to 23; Asia from 12 to 27; Oceania from 2 to 3.

systems model and the general affluence model. One may argue that state properties are related to a particular type of economic system, or claim that it is not the system itself but the level of affluence or rate of growth of affluence that conditions state stability and performance.

The affluence model

Harold Wilensky argued in *The Welfare State and Equality: Structural and Ideological Roots of Public Expenditures* (1975) that economic factors are of crucial importance for politics, in particular for state performance. A higher level of affluence results in more public spending, since the supply of, as well as the demand for, public policies increases with more abundant resources. Wilensky's model is a modern version of Wagner's law (Borcherding, 1977; Wildavsky, 1986), which implies that more affluent societies will engage in welfare spending which poorer societies cannot afford. But how much can state performance be accounted for by economic factors? Which important economic factors are also relevant to state stability?

The level of economic affluence may be measured in various ways. Table 7.11 presents both gross domestic product and gross national product on a per capita basis from 1950 to 1989.

The 1989 data (*World Development Report*, 1991) show that there are certainly poor states and rich states, as well as a number of states in between. In Europe the rich states are all situated in the West, in particular in the North alongside super-rich Switzerland (29,880) and affluent Austria (17,300). The economic well-being of the East European countries is very difficult to tap in a precise way; most probably their GNP has been over-estimated for a long period of time. The large discrepancies between Norway

(22,290), Sweden (21,570), Denmark (20,450), West Germany (20,440) and the Netherlands (15,920) on the one hand, and Poland (1,790), Czechoslovakia (3,450) and Hungary (2,590), on the other, are probably not over-estimated. The data for the early 1990s will show that these differences have become even more marked, as the system change away from a command economy has resulted in considerable losses in output.

Similarly, the economic division between South-West Europe and South-East Europe is a clear-cut one, and the distance will grow even wider. Yugoslavia (2,920), Romania (1,720) and Bulgaria (2,320) cannot expect to catch up with Portugal (4,250), Spain (9,330), Italy (15,120) and Greece (5,350). The same observation applies to the countries of the former USSR. The question here is how much real affluence will be reduced in the process of economic system transformation.

On the American continent there is the clear-cut economic north–south divide. The United States (20,910) and Canada (19,030) have a standard of living that is several times higher than that in the Latin American states: Uruguay (2,620), Brazil (2,540), Argentina (2,160), Venezuela (2,450) and Chile (1,770) being among the better-off countries and Peru (1,010), Colombia (1,200), Paraguay (1,030) and Bolivia (620) among the less well off. In Central America there are states doing fairly well, such as Mexico (2,010) and Costa Rica (1,780), but also states that are not doing so well, such as Honduras (900) and Haiti (360).

Extreme poverty characterizes the states on the African continent. Only a few countries in the North, plus Gabon (2,960) and South Africa (2,470), are exceptions. Thus Egypt (640), Algeria (2,230), Morocco (880) and Tunisia (1,260) are in a different league from Niger (290), Kenya (360), Tanzania (130), Malawi (180), Zambia (390) and Zaïre (260). In several states economic conditions are extremely harsh, in particular in countries that have experienced long civil wars.

In Asia there are both poor and very rich countries. The oil exporting countries are affluent, some of them more than others. Saudi Arabia (6,020), Oman (5,220) and the United Arab Emirates (18,430) have standards of living comparable with those in the OECD countries, whereas conditions in Iran (3,200) are closer to those in several Third World countries – although certainly not the poor states.

In South-East Asia, besides Japan, the so-called Baby Tigers have shown that the gap between rich and poor countries may be closed in a relatively short period of time (Balassa, 1991). The level of affluence in Japan (23,810) as well as that in the newly industrializing countries – Singapore (10,450), South Korea (4,400) and Hong Kong (10,350) – may be compared with levels in several West European states. The contrast to the predicament of the huge Asian states – China (350), India (340), Pakistan (370), Bangladesh (180), Thailand (1,220) and Indonesia (500) – is stark, but Asian poverty is not quite as bad as African poverty.

In Oceania, Australia (14,360) and New Zealand (12,070) belong to the

Table 7.12 Average annual rates of economic growth (in percentages)

	1950–60	1970–81	1965–89
Africa	1.51 (29)	.58 (42)	.86 (37)
America	2.04 (18)	1.98 (23)	1.17 (22)
Asia	2.82 (16)	3.01 (28)	2.84 (19)
Oceania	.85 (2)	.60 (3)	.90 (3)
Europe	3.66 (16)	2.74 (18)	2.68 (16)
E^2	.14	.13	.16

Source: World Bank, 1983: annual growth in GDP per capita 1950–60, 1970–81; World Bank, 1991: annual growth in GNP per capita 1965–89.

rich set of OECD countries, whereas Papua New Guinea (890) is part of the Third World. Typical of Australia and New Zealand is not that they are rich countries but that their level of affluence has grown at such a slow rate. Could the average rate of economic growth be a factor when accounting for state properties?

The growth model

According to another economic model, the dynamism in the economy matters for politics. Acknowledging that the rate of growth may hover in a random fashion from one year to another, it is maintained that the long-term differences in average growth rates are of crucial importance. Slow processes of economic decline may result in state instability or a reduction in state performance. The relative deprivation model implies that political change would be most intense during periods of social change, as, for example, during rapid increases or decreases in affluence. Thus the prospects of a move towards democracy would be substantially higher in periods of economic growth (Olson, 1963).

More generally, rapid social change could account for state events or developments. External shocks such as war or social upheaval call for state responses which have an impact upon its stability and performance – the displacement model (Peacock and Wiseman, 1961). Table 7.12 contains the growth rate data.

Rapid economic change on a long-term basis has occurred in Asia and Europe. It is true that yearly growth rates in national economies fluctuate considerably as a response to short-term conditions, but economic growth rate measures averaged out for a number of years are telling indicators on sustainable dynamic economic processes in a country. The substantial long-term growth rates for the two continents of Europe and Asia are all the more impressive as they cover an immense variation between countries with truly dynamic economies and states where the economy is more sluggish.

The dismal development on the African continent is apparent in the data. The performance of Oceania is not much better, whereas the American data conceal both strong economic expansion as well as economic retardation. The countries with high average rates of economic growth between 1965 and 1989 were Botswana (8.5), South Korea (7.0), Singapore (7.0), China (5.7), Lesotho (5.0), Switzerland (4.6), Indonesia (4.4), Japan (4.3), Thailand (4.2), Egypt (4.2), Malaysia (4.0), Canada (4.0), Burundi (3.6), Tunisia (3.3) and Italy (3.0). Yet, noting the high average growth rates in Yugoslavia (3.2), one cannot draw any conclusions about automatic effects of growth on state stability and performance.

In contrast the countries whose economies changed slowly, or even negatively, during the same period were Kuwait (-4.0), Libya (-3.0), Uganda (-2.8), Niger (-2.4), Zaïre (-2.0), Zambia (-2.0), Madagascar (-1.9), Ghana (-1.5), Jamaica (-1.3), Chad (-1.2), Venezuela (-1.0), Senegal (-0.7), Mauritania (-0.5), Peru (-0.2), Tanzania (-0.1) and Argentina (-0.1) (World Bank, 1991).

It is difficult to narrow down the exact meaning of a process of long-term economic growth, but it sets a tone for the conduct of life within a state that affects all spheres of existence. The level of affluence may be more important than the rate of change in the economy, but a sustainable growth rate of about 3 to 5 per cent per year affects the standard of living within a decade significantly. Just as a poor country with strong economic growth can progress in the direction of the rich countries, so can a rich country tumble downwards. The developments in South-East Asia and their counter-examples in Latin America testify to the fuzzy border-line between rich and poor countries.

The level of affluence as well as the rate of change in the economy is of interest for understanding state properties. It is not difficult to model state stability or state performance with regard to the level of either. However, other relevant economic factors may also be identified.

The openness of the economy

The impex model claims that the economic interaction between nations is important (Cameron, 1978). The openness of the economy can influence the state along several lines of development. The original Cameron model argued that, the higher the impex measure (imports plus exports as a percentage of GDP), the higher the level of state activities in the form of welfare performance – the state compensating for the uncertainty stemming from the world economy.

It seems as if the extent of openness in an economy depends on how large

Table 7.13 The openness of the economy

	1980	*1985*
Africa	44.4 (38)	24.5 (39)
America	32.8 (23)	23.8 (23)
Asia	45.7 (22)	31.9 (22)
Oceania	49.1 (3)	38.8 (3)
Europe	85.1 (18)	58.2 (18)
E^2	.24	.27

Source: Summers and Heston (1991).

a nation is in terms of population. The larger the nation the less openness there is, indicating that we may expect to find openness among the smaller European democracies (see table 7.13).

The data indicate a general reduction in the openness of the economies of the world, but the country differences remain pertinent. Thus Europe scores high, as expected, despite the fact that the communist countries are entered here. The low figure for Asia fails to bring out the existence of a number of so-called NICs (newly industrialized countries) and NECs (newly exporting countries), which score very high on the impex index. The extent to which an economy is characterized by openness may have an impact on state stability in either of two ways: it could mean more resources, which would enhance state stability, or it could signify disorder, as the state is opened up to foreign or alien influence.

Dependency models

The openness of the economy model could be developed by including other aspects that determine the place of a country in the international economy. Typical of post war economic developments has been an almost phenomenal increase in world trade. Has this benefited all states equally? What are the implications of growing interdependencies on the state and politics?

Theoretically, one could argue that a country's position in the world economy, as suggested by Wallerstein in his world systems model, would have a large impact on both its overall affluence and its rate of economic growth. Table 7.14 shows that a few economic dimensions – core position in the world economy, indebtedness and debt–service ratio – reveal sizeable differences between the states on the various continents. The world systems models evolving out of the dependency approach seem to capture more regarding state strength than the pure physical models presented earlier. We include not only an index on centre versus periphery placement but also two crucial measures on direct external dependency, that is, the debt burden

Table 7.14 Economic position within the world economy

	COREP 1989	Debt/GNP in % 1990	Debt/Export in % 1990
Africa	.02 (42)	112.7 (36)	20.8 (38)
America	.29 (24)	70.6 (20)	22.5 (21)
Asia	.11 (35)	61.8 (17)	18.0 (18)
Oceania	1.00 (3)	83.9 (1)	36.0 (1)
Europe	1.32 (25)	40.9 (7)	14.5 (7)
E^2	.54	.14	.05

Sources: Terlouw (1989); World Bank (1992).

Note: COREP measures the position in the world economy, a higher score meaning closer to the core. Debt data do not cover the OECD.

as a percentage of gross domestic product and as a percentage of total exports.

Looking at the aspects of economic interaction from various angles related to international trade and the expanding world economy, there emerges a systematic pattern. The strategic position of Europe appears clearly when classifying states according to periphery, semi-periphery and core. The centre-periphery model (Shils, 1975), launched almost simultaneously as the dependency framework, rebuked the modernization models (Frank, 1967; Szentes, 1983). Scholars have called attention to the fact that several highly indebted countries are suffering considerable negative consequences not only economically but also politically (Singer and Sharma, 1989; George, 1992).

Yet, while in no way denying the general politics of dependency and debt, we must make a systematic test of the models that predict specific effects upon the state from its position in the world economy or its economic ties as debtor with creditor countries. Several states in Africa and Latin America are almost swamped by debt. Is this why these states also tend to be unstable?

Economic systems models

Just as one may widen the economic approach from simple GNP per capita models to trade or debt dependencies, one may focus on the overall system of economic institutions in a country. Institutional questions have been emphasized in neo-institutionalist economics (Williamson, 1985; Coase, 1988) pertaining to the classical problem in political economy of the state versus the market (Hayek, 1935).

Predicting that the economic system of capitalism comprises the seeds of its own destruction, Karl Marx formulated an economic model of state instability or revolution that has played a large role in social science theory

(Bell, 1976). Admitting that there are problems in interpreting the exact shape of Marx's model, it does warrant a search for the sources of state instability in the economic system. Is capitalism conducive to state instability? Or are the major forms of economic system systematically related to state performance, for example, in such a form that some of Marx's predictions turned out to be wrong, and that civil and political liberties are in fact to be found in capitalist systems?

Any description of an economic system would have to include a statement of how the market, property institutions and public systems for budget allocation and redistribution are combined in different countries. The analysis may recognize: (1) the organization of decision-making: centralization and decentralization; (2) the provision of information and coordination: market or plan; (3) property rights: private, cooperative and public; and (4) the incentive system: moral or material (Monthias, 1976; Gregory and Stuart, 1989).

A distinction has often been drawn between capitalism, market socialism and planned socialism, but can we actually speak of existing market socialist regimes? Gastil's framework, presented in *Freedom in the World* (1987), is a more refined one:

1 Capitalist: a high degree of economic freedom and relatively little market intervention by the state
2 Mixed capitalist: an activist state with income redistribution, market intervention and regulation, although the size of direct budget allocation of resources is not that large
3 Capitalist-statist: substantial state intervention in markets and large public sectors, although the state remains committed to the institutions of private property
4 Mixed socialist: some economic freedom, private property and individual initiative within the framework of a socialist economy
5 Socialist: basically a command economy with little economic freedom, private property or individual initiative.

Gastil classified a large number of countries within these categories as the situation appeared around 1980 (see Appendix 7.1).

All classification systems are open ended, and Gastil's placement of some countries may be disputed. How, for example, does one make a clear distinction between mixed socialist and pure socialist systems? Should China not belong to the latter and Tanzania and Algeria enter the former set? Then the collection of mixed capitalist states seems too large, as it includes countries that should be classified as either capitalist-statist – Uruguay and Singapore – or mixed socialist – Egypt, Sudan, Nicaragua and Tunisia.

The Gastil index is complemented by other indices that determine the structure of economic institutions in a country. Vanhanen's index of concentration of economic power measures the degree to which economic resources – public, private or foreign – are controlled by a few (Vanhanen, 1990). Two more indices establish the status of market economy institutions, that by

Table 7.15   Economic system indices

	Vanhanen	Gastil	Wright	Pourgerami
Africa	83.7 (42)	1.7 (43)	3.0 (40)	1.8 (30)
America	69.2 (24)	1.1 (24)	2.6 (22)	2.1 (23)
Asia	76.6 (34)	2.0 (35)	3.2 (32)	2.1 (18)
Oceania	43.3 (3)	.0 (3)	1.3 (3)	3.0 (2)
Europe	56.0 (25)	1.8 (25)	2.6 (25)	2.5 (19)
E^2	.27	.08	.10	.26

Sources: Vanhanen (1990); Gastil (1987); Wright (1982); Pourgerami (1988).

Note: Higher scores mean a greater concentration of economic resources in general; the scale for economic freedom (Wright) and status of markets (Pourgerami) goes from high to low.

Wright distinguishing between high (1), medium-high (2), medium (3), low-medium (4) and low (5) economic freedom (Wright, 1982), and Pourgerami's between capitalist (0), mixed capitalist (1), capitalist-statist (2), mixed socialist (3) and socialist (4) economic systems (Pourgerami, 1988).

It is not difficult to find models which claim that a concentration of economic power has a negative impact upon state stability and performance. However, it has to be pointed out that economic resources may be concentrated in different ways. Centralization of economic power may occur in either socialist or capitalist-statist economies, where resources are concentrated in the public sector or so-called *parastatals*, but also in market-orientated societies, where vast resources are concentrated in multi-national companies.

Several questions concerning the conditions of a state's economic system spring to mind. Is decentralized capitalism a necessary or sufficient condition for state stability? Why has the communist system failed – because of its reliance on an inefficient planned economy or as a result of its general lack of political legitimacy, as argued by Clark and Wildavsky (1990)? Another crucial question is whether affluence and economic institutions have the same impact upon state performance, perhaps reinforcing each other?

Friedrich von Hayek stated a clear case for decentralized capitalism in *The Road to Serfdom* (1944), where he argued that any kind of state planning would threaten freedom in a democracy. One difficulty with Hayek's libertarian position is that it ignores the large differences between two forms of capitalism. It is vital to note the gulf between decentralized capitalism on the one hand and state capitalism on the other, because this makes an impact on how to model the relationship between economic system properties and the state. We will also refer to the first type of politico-economic regime as 'the market economy' in order to avoid the negative connotations of the word 'capitalism'. A strong argument for the implications of economic growth in the typical institutions of the market economy has been stated by Oliver Williamson (1985).

A diametrically opposed argument has been stated by Charles E. Lindblom in *Politics and Markets* (1977). Here a model is presented to the effect that state interference in the economy in the form of planning and welfare spending increases democracy. Favouring not only the welfare state, with its large public sector, but also perhaps idealist schemes for market socialism, Lindblom launches an attack on decentralized capitalism as biased in favour of big capital.

Whereas Hayek and Lindblom try to establish a relationship between economic system and state performance, Gunnar Myrdal links state stability with a planned economy. He claims that economic development can only be forthcoming where the state is strong and stable, that is, when it is bolstered by a socialist economy of some sort. In *Asian Drama* (1968) he explains the difference between the weakness of India and the strength of China by focusing on state stability and the strategy for economic development.

Model testing

We have identified a number of models which claim that social conditions are important for understanding the state. Could they offer insights into why state stability and state performance differ from one country to another? Modelling the sources of state stability and state performance with regard to social conditions is a challenge to our knowledge about complexity in politics. Political outcomes depend upon so many factors that states can hardly be a simple function of their physical and social environments.

The value of the social models when formulating an explanatory argument in comparative politics is their contribution at the intermediate stages. By testing all too simple models about relationships between social factors and the state, the stage is set for the construction of more complicated models that include the relevant social models. In a way it is necessary to establish some negative results first, doing away with any deterministic models such as that treating economic factors.

One way to check if social conditions are relevant is to look at simple correlations (see table 7.16). What one might realistically hope for is to find a few significant relationships that could be employed for more refined analysis in combined models.

Several striking findings may be noted in Table 7.16, as a number of correlations are strong enough to warrant the construction of more complex models integrating some of the social factors. The first major positive finding is that the relevance of economic factors is strongly confirmed: what matters most obviously for both stability and performance is the level of affluence.

Table 7.16 Relevance of social conditions

	State stability REG	CIVIC	HDI	State performance HED86	TOP10	INF8090
LNPOP	−.01	.11	.17	−.18	−.06	.06
LNAREA	−.05	−.13	−.12	−.05	.08	.12
CLIMATE	.48	.25	.53	.48	−.61	−.11
AGRI88	−.51	−.59	−.88	−.56	.39	−.04
FARMSIZE	.23	.40	−.08	.20	−.37	−.17
UR196	.53	.56	.79	.49	−.31	.13
ELF	1.24	−.23	−.47	−.34	.47	.12
RF	−.06	−.09	−.21	−.06	−.06	−.16
PROT	.35	.39	.18	.34	−.34	−.14
ISLAM	−.11	−.35	−.36	−.12	.07	−.15
FAM	−.42	−.59	−.66	−.37	.25	−.02
WHITESET	.49	.47	.67	.54	−.58	−.00
LNGNP	.64	.68	.85	.71	−.45	−.08
EG6589	.29	.27	.41	.21	.09	−.15
OPEN80	.58	.30	.32	.60	−.39	−.20
COREP	.58	.64	.64	.59	−.55	−.08
DEBT/GDP	−.02	−.28	−.33	.12	.00	−.01
DEBT/EXP	−.03	.14	.03	−.06	−.20	.07
ECOSYS	−.24	−.58	−.12	−.17	−.05	.08
ECONCON	−.57	−.88	−.55	−.52	.33	.04

Source: Tables 7.2, 7.3, 7.4, 7.5, 7.6, 7.9, 7.10, 7.11, 7.12, 7.13, 7.14, 7.15.

Note: For explanation, see Appendix 10.1, variables and measures.

The impact of other economic factors, such as the openness of the economy and the type of economic system, should also be analysed. And one has to try to estimate the differential impact of each one of these different economic indicators while holding the others constant.

Second, the data show that Islamic domination has little impact on state stability but tends to be combined with poor state performance. It confirms the theory that the weak institutionalization of a separation between church and state, sacred and secular in typically Islamic states makes the transition to democracy a difficult process, although a few Muslim states (such as Turkey, Malaysia and Senegal) have attempted a sort of semi-democracy (Korany, 1990).

Third, there is confirmation for the climate and the family structure models. The correlations here are so pronounced that these factors have to be looked into. Even though there is no obvious causal mechanism at work here, these findings require more interpretation.

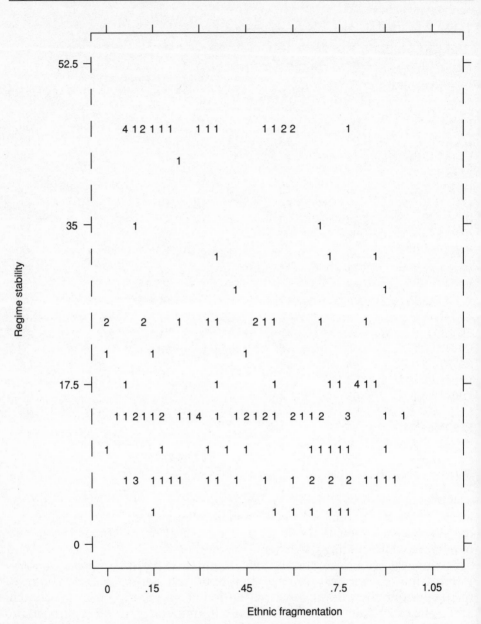

Figure 7.1 Ethnic fragmentation and regime stability

Fourth, the major negative finding is that the social fragmentation models display such poor correlations. If there is indeed such weak interaction between ethnic or religious heterogeneity and state properties, this is a very important if not astonishing finding in relation to the accepted beliefs about ethnic and religious fragmentation always resulting in state stability and performance. Let us look at this a little more closely. Figure 7.1 displays the relationship between ethnic fragmentation and regime stability.

The hypothesis that ethnic fragmentation leads to state instability predicts a negative correlation between the variables in figure 7.1. The finding is that the relationship is negative, $r = -.24$ ($N = 129$), but it is far too weak to support the hypothesis. There are too many unstable countries that are ethnically homogeneous. And not all states that are ethnically fragmented are unstable. Ethnic fragmentation is not a sufficient condition for state stability, nor is it a necessary condition for state instability. The only conclusion one may draw from figure 7.1 is that ethnic fragmentation may be a contributory condition to state instability. The crucial question is: what other conditions matter? Figure 7.2 shows the relationship between ethnic fragmentation and civic and political rights.

Again, we have a negative correlation, $r = -.23$ ($N = 127$), but it is not as strong as is claimed in the fragmentation models (Jalali and Lipset, 1993). There are simply too many countries which score low on state performance (CIVIC) that are not ethnically heterogeneous.

A set of correlations is one thing and causal connections another. We may observe that several stable states performing well are placed in cold climates and have a substantial population with a Protestant creed, but we may certainly not conclude that there is causality at work. When simple correlations tend to be high, there is always the possibility that the causality involved may be reversed, for example, state stability and performance impacting upon economic factors. Besides, other forces may be at work, making the independent variables only intervening ones. Thus we need to attempt causal modelling. However, first we will search for other potentially relevant factors among the institutional and actor-related sets of conditions.

As the analysis proceeds in the following chapters we shall need to take into account the implication of such economic factors as affluence, as they seem to affect the state considerably. In relation to the general impact of affluence on all state dimensions investigated here, the model of the relative autonomy of the state receives straightforward confirmation. The other economic factors – extent of concentration of economic resources, degree of openness in the economy and position in the world economy – are also of great potential relevance. Evidently, the relationship between the economy in a wide sense and the state is such that the latter may at the very best have some degree of freedom, but it does not float freely in relation to the economy.

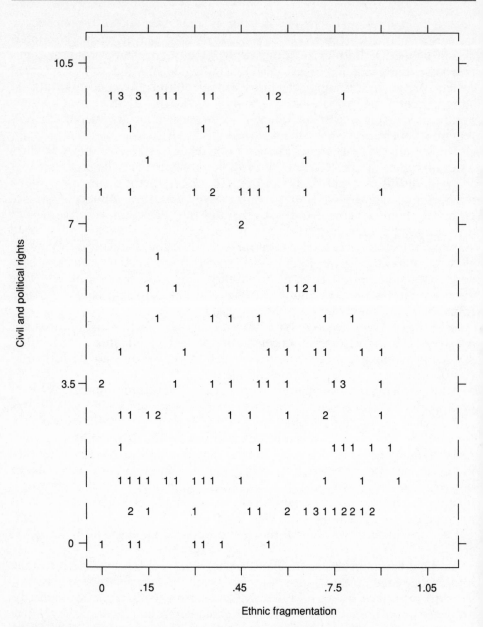

Figure 7.2 Ethnic fragmentation and civil and political rights

Conclusion

The fact that some states are more unstable or perform less well than other could be a function of the environment. The set of theories concerning structure may be divided into four subsets: physical, economic, social and cultural conditions. In constructing models about the properties of such an aggregate of human behaviour as the state there is always a tendency towards determinism. Structural determinism raises the question of what could be done to ameliorate state behaviour if long-term physical, social, economic or cultural factors were of utmost decisive importance?

One major finding here is the absence of determinism in all the correlations reported on, which means that hopes for better state outputs and outcomes in the short term are not altogether in vain. At the same time, state stability and performance do not occur in a structural vacuum. The other major finding is that economic factors in a wide sense must be taken into account when modelling these state properties. Now, given that the relationship between structure and the state involves elements of indeterminism, we must ask: could institutions matter with regard to state stability and performance?

Appendix 7.1 Gastil's economic system classification around 1980.

Capitalist: USA, Canada, Dominican Republic, El Salvador, Costa Rica, Colombia, Ecuador, Chile, Ireland, Belgium, Luxembourg, Switzerland, Spain, West Germany, Iceland, Liberia, Cameroon, Kenya, Malawi, Jordan, South Korea, Japan, Thailand, Malaysia, Australia, New Zealand, Haiti, Barbados, Guatemala, Honduras, Cyprus, Niger, Côte d'Ivoire, Sierra Leone, Gabon, Chad, Lebanon and Nepal.

Mixed capitalist: Uruguay, United Kingdom, Netherlands, France, Portugal, Austria, Greece, Finland, Sweden, Norway, Denmark, Senegal, Tunisia, Israel, Singapore, Nicaragua, Guinea, Burundi, Sudan and Egypt.

Capitalist-statist: Mexico, Panama, Venezuela, Peru, Brazil, Bolivia, Paraguay, Argentina, Italy, Ghana, Nigeria, Zaïre, South Africa, Morocco, Iran, Turkey, India, Pakistan, Sri Lanka, Philippines, Indonesia, Jamaica, Trinidad, Mauritania, Central African Republic, Uganda, Saudia Arabia and Taiwan.

Mixed socialist: Yugoslavia, Zambia, Madagascar, Guyana, Mali, Burkina Faso, Togo, Congo, Rwanda, Somalia, Libya, Syria, China and Burma.

Socialist: East Germany, Hungary, Soviet Union, Bulgaria, Romania, Czechoslovakia, Tanzania, Ethiopia, Algeria, Iraq, Albania, Benin, Angola, Mozambique, Afghanistan, Mongolia, North Korea, Cambodia, Laos and Cuba

(*Source*: Gastil, 1987).

8

Institutional Models

Introduction

What besides broad social conditions might account for the properties of the basic aggregation unit in macropolitics, the state? In this chapter we search for traces of the impact of institutional conditions for the substantial variation among states. In the traditional approach to comparative politics political institutions had a central place. The state institutions had a value in themselves, because particular institutions were regarded as intrinsically good (that is, those of the major Western powers such as the United States and the United Kingdom).

The reorientation of comparative politics around 1960 meant that the extrinsic merits of political institutions began to be researched. Having found in Chapter 7 that economic conditions are important for state properties, we ask in this chapter whether there are institutional models that can claim to explain country differences in state stability and state performance.

Political institutions

The basic problem of how political institutions impact upon state outputs and social outcomes has become highly relevant in comparative politics. In discussing the importance of political institutions as a determinant of public policy in relation to other conditions, economic or cultural (Wildavsky, 1986), the literature has identified a number of factors (Tarschys, 1975; Ashford, 1978; Dye and Gray, 1980).

The science of comparative government is replete with observations about institutions – how they vary from one country to another and how they cluster into the institutional patterns that we label in various ways, such as 'democracy', 'presidentialism', and so forth. In case studies, the institutional description may do justice to all the paraphernalia of nuances that characterize one state uniquely. However, for the conduct of comparative analysis of states, such an idiographic approach will not do.

It may be true, as the new institutionalism argues, that the country-specific configurations of political institutions lie at the heart of the state; it could also be correct in its assertion that each state has its own very special set of institutions that determine much of its political life. An interpretative methodology such as hermeneutics may be the most adequate research strategy when approaching the state.

Yet whatever emphasis is put upon the unique institutional context for state outputs and outcomes, in the last resort we have to rely upon some type of nomothetical methodology if we are going to specify the importance of various institutions. Political institutions have to be compared in order to identify which states have similar or dissimilar organizations. Which institutional concepts are the most valid ones in a comparative research strategy?

Defining which institutional concepts are truly cross-cultural is one of the difficulties when looking at the institutional conditions of the state. The other equally complex problem is to find indicators that will allow us to put forward institutional conditions alongside other kinds of condition (for example, the social and cultural factors that we found relevant in Chapter 7). Rather than attempting to describe the complex state institutional web in each single country, therefore, it may be more profitable to seek for general concepts that may be employed in comparative modelling of the state.

Political institutions may be interesting on account of their intrinsic value or because of their effects on outcomes. Since we wish to focus on the latter instrumental aspect, we need to introduce a few general categories for the analysis of institutional patterns; these could not possibly be as rich in the required nuances if we were to look at political institutions merely for their extrinsic value. What, then, is the overall picture concerning the impact of institutions on state stability and performance?

Governance models

In the history of political thought we find numerous suggestions that various institutional properties have an impact. We have here a set of models that take us to the very heart of political science. Let us introduce a number of distinctions between political institutions, starting from the most general and moving towards more specific ones. The rules that define the most basic conditions for politics regulate the relationship between the citizens and their elites. Can we derive institutional models from the extensive discussion of democracy and its various modes (Held, 1987; Sartori, 1987)? And what are the rules for interaction between various elites? Let us look at various frameworks that model institutions for political participation and representation, and then proceed to other state models.

Dahl's model

In *Polyarchy* (1971) Robert A. Dahl presented a theory of democracy by defining polyarchy in the following way:

> Polyarchies, then, may be thought of as relatively (but incompletely) democratized regimes, or, to put it in another way, polyarchies are regimes that have been substantially popularized and liberalized, that is, highly inclusive and extensively open to public contestation. (Dahl, 1971: 8)

Dahl distinguished two fundamental institutional dimensions of the state: degree of public contestation and degree of participation. When both dimensions are low we have closed hegemonies; a low degree of public contestation and a high degree of participation implies inclusive hegemonies; a high degree of public contestation and a low degree of participation characterizes competitive oligarchies; whereas a high degree of public contestation and a high degree of participation are typical of democracies.

To Dahl a democracy is the ideal type of state (Dahl, 1956; 1989), but it is not strictly feasible in the world today. The closest one could get, realistically speaking, is a polyarchy. The crucial question is what difference do the institutions of polyarchy make? The everyday lives of citizens are considerably affected by state stability and state performance. So what is the contribution of contestation and participation to state stability and performance?

Crucial for the extent to which democracy has been institutionalized, Dahl would argue, is the combination of a high level of participation and a large degree of contestation. The nature of the party system is the clue to the level of contestation, and the extent to which contestation is permitted in the public institutions of a country is crucial for the logic of politics in that country. Several models point out that competition is as important in politics as in markets. In Joseph Schumpeter's model of democracy the institutional conditions for opposition are considered more important than participation (1944).

Even if we accept Dahl's claim that democracy can never be fully realized, we may still be eager to find out whether democratic institutions such as they exist in polyarchies promote state stability and performance. Both of Dahl's theoretical dimensions – participation and contestation – may be measured by a number of institutional indicators. Now, are participatory institutions (such as various types of referenda) more important than representative institutions (such as party government)?

Mill's model

The theory that democratic institutions, if adequately established, contribute towards state stability can be found among several scholars (Sartori, 1987).

A classical argument in favour of such decision-making mechanisms as conducive to state stability was formulated by John Stuart Mill in his *Considerations on Representative Government* (1862). Mill stated that the notion of democracy as providing institutions for true popular participation was non-implementable in large states, but that party government offered a realistic approximation.

Majority decision-making in a system of representative institutions based on proportionality would enhance political stability if the internal and external environment of the society were favourable. But are the institutions of *adversarial* democracy always conducive to stability? We need to distinguish between different institutions, as there exist other kinds which are also conducive to state stability and which show a performance record typical of democratic regimes.

The critiques of Mill's representative and majoritarian model claim that other kinds of institutions are to be preferred because they enhance both state stability and state performance (Pateman, 1970; Lively, 1975; Mansbridge, 1983). On the one hand it is argued, according to Rousseau's political thought, that participation is more essential than representation; on the other it is claimed that, even if one favours representative institutions, one need not endorse the simple majority system (Dunn, 1992).

Calhoun's model

There is a long-standing tradition of democratic thought based on the virtues of majority voting in different bodies that requires a qualified majority interpretation. 'Real' democracy, it is stated, depends on more than plurality or simple majority, as was argued by Madison (Dahl, 1956).

A succinct argument concerning the necessity of the so-called concurrent majority was elaborated by the South Carolina senator John C. Calhoun in *A Disquisition on Government* (1853). Although Calhoun's argument was set forth in a particular situation where he stubbornly defended the vested interests of the American South, including slavery and a confederate interpretation of the constitution, there is an interesting idea, similar to that proposed by Madison, of institutions that guarantee the rights of minorities.

Calhoun suggested that the historical cases of Rome, Poland and the Iroquois Confederacy in precolonial America showed the practicality of a special type of negative power that protected the interests of certain groups against being swamped by others. He stated:

> It is this negative power, the power of preventing or arresting the action of the government, be it called by what term it may – veto, interposition, nullification, check, or balance of power – which, in fact, forms the constitution. They are all but different names for the negative power. In all its forms, and under all its names, it results from the concurrent majority. (Calhoun, [1853] 1953: 28)

Calhoun saw the operation of the *concurrent* majority institution in the capacity of the tribunes of the plebs to veto a proposal under discussion in the Roman Senate, in the infamous principle of *liberum veto* in the Polish Diet during the seventeenth and eighteenth centuries and also in the strategic power game between the three estates in English government before the firm establishment of parliamentarianism: the King, Lords and Commons.

However, Calhoun was first and foremost interested in the application of his principle to the basic problem of defining the state in a federal or confederal context. Just as the six nations in the Iroquois Confederacy – Mohawks, Oneidas, Cayugas, Senecas, Onandagas and Tuscororas – were only sovereign when acting together on the basis of unanimous opinion, Calhoun claimed the Southern States had the same legal status within the union. He saw basically two types of government: constitutional government versus absolute government, the two having different guiding principles of compromise and force (Calhoun, [1853] 1953: 29).

The idea of stable government as dependent upon institutions that enhance consensus may be developed along alternative routes. The best developed model of consensus politics today is the model of consociationalism, to which we now turn.

Althusius' model

The term 'consociationalism' was launched by Arend Lijphart in 1968 as a theoretical expression for a set of mechanisms that are conducive to state stability and a good performance record (Lijphart, 1968). Lijphart's model was not a novel idea. The key term dates back to Johannes Althusius' 'consociatio', or the pact or association, as the explicit form for creating state institutions. In his book *Systematic Analysis of Politics* (1610), Althusius argued from a contract theoretical point of view that any state is made up of various social groups in society which lend their consent to government. The association constitutes the political body and it needs to be continuously reinforced by consensus building.

Whereas scholars adhering to the idea of majority political institutions emphasized the concept of stable government as a zero sum game where the plurality winner takes all in a competitive setting in which cross-cutting cleavages have a centripetal force (Lipset, 1959; Riker, 1982), consociationalists claimed that stable government required an entirely different institutional framework, at least in divided societies searching for Madison's checks and balances (McRae, 1974; Lijphart, 1977).

A standard definition of 'consociational' democracy would have to underline the occurrence of segmented pluralism, meaning that a society with deep-seated ethnic or religious fragmentation, frequently of a mutually reinforcing type, would be characterized by strong conflicts between groups. Government by elite cartels is designed in order to turn a democracy with a fragmented political culture into a stable democracy (Lijphart, 1974:

79). The concept of concordant democracy was developed by Gerhard Lehmbruch (1979) to denote a strategy of conflict management by cooperation and agreement among the different elites, similar to the way in which corporatist institutions function, rather than by competition and majority decision. The consociational model has been broadened to become a more general model – the consensus model – which was discussed in Chapter 4.

Where Schumpeter emphasizes elite competition (Schumpeter, 1944), the consociational model underlines elite cooperation. Where Downs focuses on the decisive placement of the median voter (Downs, 1957), consociationalism concentrates on the significance of the politics of accommodation among substantial but isolated groups with a high potential for conflict. Finally, William Riker's prediction that minimum-sized government would constitute the backbone of stable government (Riker, 1962) is criticized in favour of oversized coalitions, including grand coalitions.

Let us now move on to map some of the variety of institutions in the states of the world today. There is a rather substantial body of classificatory schemes for the institutional analysis of macropolitical aspects as surveyed in *Contemporary Political Systems: Classifications and Typologies*, edited by Bebler and Seroka (1990). However, we bring up only those classifications that are related to the governance models mentioned above.

Participatory and representative institutions

Participation may be monitored by means of an indicator on general election turnout, but it is not all that revealing when it comes to the basic political institutions of a country. States that show high participation figures may only allow one party to put up candidates and states with rules that allow contestation may have low turnout figures. Two other institutional indicators catch more of the variation in fundamental political rules, namely the shape of the party system and the size of the largest party. Both elections and party systems are structured by institutional rules (see table 8.1).

The data concerning turnout levels reflects the occurrence of dictatorships in Africa, America and Asia, but the high figure for Europe cannot be taken as evidence of democratic institutions, because election participation used to be high also in communist systems – voting being a public duty of the citizens. Party system institutions really do allow us to categorize the states of the world. The crucial distinction is between one-party states and states where the rules acknowledge the existence of more than one party.

Two kinds of one-party system may be distinguished. One type is characterized by the domination of the state over the party, whereas in the other type the party is in control of the state. For examples of the first kind we should turn to Latin America and Africa, whereas the other type was practised in communist states, in Eastern Europe as well as in the Third

Table 8.1 Participation and contestation

	Turnout	Party system	Size of largest party in voter support (as a percentage)
Africa	29.2 (34)	.07 (43)	89.2(34)
America	32.4 (23)	.33 (24)	57.5 (23)
Asia	34.5 (27)	.09 (35)	73.5 (26)
Oceania	50.8 (24)	1.00 (3)	40.9 (3)
Europe	60.0 (25)	.76 (25)	59.7 (25)
E^2	.36	.41	.26

Sources: Vanhanen (1990); Sullivan (1991).

Note: Turnout: average proportion of the population participating in national elections; party system: 1 = multi-party system, 0 = one-party system; size of largest party: average proportion voting for the largest party.

World. Cammack, Pool and Tordoff make the following comment about parties in Latin America, Africa, Asia Minor and East and South-East Asia:

> All four areas have in common, then, a close identification of successful parties with the state. Success in such conditions goes along with both a lack of autonomy, and a weakening of the prospects for open competition for power. It is therefore the closeness of party and state which accounts most satisfactorily for the failure of competitive liberal democracy to develop out of existing party systems in the Third World. It also accounts for the fact that change tends to come (if at all) in violent or at least unconstitutional ways. (Cammack et al., 1993: 129)

In a one-party system, where the result of any attempt to organize parties that might contest the position of the only party allowed is severe punishment, something about the quality of that party is indicated. Under state domination the party is typically only an appendix of the state and its rulers.

In Africa there were multi-party systems operating at the dawn of colonial rule and during the first stage of independence. But African political parties have been in decline since independence, as in most states they have been run down in favour of the burgeoning state machine. In Latin America there has been the same dominance of the state. Many of the political parties there were founded as ruling parties after the creation of a regime. And previously formed parties have faced great difficulties in maintaining their freedom when regimes swing from one kind to another. In Latin America there are only a few examples of a large and long-lived political party, notably the Mexican Institutional Revolutionary Party and the Colorado Party in Paraguay (Randall, 1987).

Table 8.2 Parliaments and government coalitions

	Parliamentary systems	Unicameralism	Coalition governments
Africa	.02 (43)	.67 (43)	.09 (43)
America	.13 (24)	.25 (24)	.33 (33)
Asia	.19 (36)	.51 (35)	.14 (35)
Oceania	1.00 (3)	.67 (3)	1.33 (3)
Europe	.48 (25)	.36 (25)	1.36 (25)
E^2	.26	.46	.10

Source: Sullivan (1991).

Note: Parliamentary systems: 1 = parliamentarism, 0 = non-parliamentarism; unicameralism: 1 = unicameral, 0 = non-unicameral; coalition government: 2 = multi-party coalitions, 1 = one-party majority government, 0 = non-democratic types of government.

The new wave of democratization in Africa has implied that political parties are once again looked upon with enthusiasm rather than suspicion. This means that constitutions, such as that in Zambia where the one-party regime was given constitutional status between 1973 and 1975, have to be revised. Whereas party government has become the typical mode of day-to-day politics in Western Europe, it has failed in the Third World up till now because of the close identification of parties with the state.

Even in countries where there has been democracy for a number of years, such as Costa Rica, Colombia and Venezuela, this has been more of an elitist and conservative type than true competitive party government. The National Party in Singapore is a good example of a party which found it difficult to give up its dominant position, even when the circumstances for party survival in the case of electoral defeat must be considered favourable.

It is interesting to look for more minute institutional distinctions among the set of democratic states in order to grasp that democracies are by no means all of the same kind from an institutional point of view. Some of these distinctions are also relevant when taking a broader approach in comparative politics. Non-democratic states also have executives and legislative assemblies, which may be structured in various ways. Table 8.2 shows some of the institutional alternatives.

It appears that after all the variation between the continents in terms of more detailed institutional properties is very much tied up with the basic distinction between democracy and dictatorship. In Africa we find very few parliamentary systems and little in the way of coalition or single majority governments. The typical African form of rule is the one-party state, whether of a leftist or rightist nature.

Oceania, with its three states boasting Westminster-type regimes, scores in completely the opposite manner. The data for Europe reflect the now abolished communist regimes, meaning that we may expect quite a different pattern in Eastern Europe in the future. As we look at single states these institutional characteristics become both more informative and relevant from a causal point of view.

The prevalence of parliamentarism among the democracies is apparent: only the United States and Switzerland fall outside this category, and France, Finland and Poland are border-line cases. At the same time, parliamentary systems may vary considerably in terms of other state properties, such as unicameralism and bicameralism, especially in federal states.

Emphasizing special institutions that enhance compromise and consensus, not adversarial competition (Lijphart, 1977: 5), consociationalism models show stability and performance as dependent on a few which increase minority influence and territorial or functional autonomy. Among these are grand coalitions, mutual veto and proportionality in the translation of votes into seats on the one hand, and federalism or special rights for language groups on the other (Lijphart, 1977: 25–52).

Countries that are stable and show good state performance as a result of consociational devices are Austria, Switzerland and the Netherlands. But one must also take a look at a few spectacular failures, such as Lebanon, Yugoslavia and Sri Lanka; Belgium falls somewhere in between the two categories. Finally, one may mention the Indian federal structure, where the borders between the member states follow the territorial location of several of India's many different language groups.

Presidentialism

Another basic institutional property of the state is the type of executive it employs for immediate government purposes. The basic distinction is between parliamentary and presidential systems, although we have to recognize various subtypes. At the same time this distinction is not exhaustive. Other types of executive occur, such as monarchies, military juntas and communist politburos. Several of the states with a formal monarchy have parliamentary executives, and military as well as communist regimes tend to be headed by presidents. The distinction between parliamentary and presidential executives therefore has to be complemented by other categories (Shugart and Carey, 1992; Mainwaring, 1993; Stepan and Skach, 1993; Valenzuela, 1993).

The classification of presidential systems cannot be based entirely on constitutional formalities, because parliamentarism may be practised within a presidential state. Presidentialism, if it implies a real type of rulership, must be defined in such a way that it does not overlap with the occurrence of parliamentary executives. There is one really difficult case to categorize, and that is Switzerland. Its government is the Bundesrat or Federal Council, consisting of seven members, elected from seven different cantons for four years of office by both chambers of the Swiss Parliament, the Ständerat or

Table 8.3 States with presidential rule, 1990–1

Limited presidentialism	Unlimited presidentialism
Afghanistan	Algeria
Argentina	Angola
Bangladesh	Benin
Bolivia	Burma
Botswana	Cameroon
Brazil	Chad
Bulgaria	Congo
Chile	Ethiopia
Colombia	Gabon
Costa Rica	Indonesia
Côte d'Ivoire	Iran
Czechoslovakia	Iraq
Dominican Republic	Kenya
Ecuador	Libya
Egypt	Madagascar
El Salvador	Malawi
Finland	Mali
France	Senegal
Guatemala	Sierra Leone
Honduras	Somalia
Hungary	Syria
Lebanon	Tanzania
Liberia	Togo
Mexico	Yemen
Mongolia	Zaïre
Mozambique	
Namibia	
Nicaragua	
Pakistan	
Panama	
Peru	
Philippines	
Poland	
Portugal	
Romania	
South Africa	
South Korea	
Sri Lanka	
Switzerland	
Taiwan	

Table 8.3 *Continued*

Limited presidentialism	Unlimited presidentialism
Tunisia	
Turkey	
Uganda	
Uruguay	
USA	
Venezuela	
Zambia	
Zimbabwe	

Source: Derbyshire and Derbyshire (1991: 59–72).

Council of States and the Nationalrat or National Council. The Federal Council cannot dissolve Parliament and cannot be removed by means of a vote of no-confidence. The seven members of the Federal Council act as ministers heading each one of the seven administrative departments of the Swiss republic. The Swiss Parliament also elects one of the members of the Council as the President of the Confederation for only one calendar year. A similar scheme was employed during the 1950s in Uruguay.

Whereas presidentialism implies a republic, parliamentary executives can exist in both a republic and a monarchy, as long as the latter does not amount to personal rule by the monarch. Listing the countries with real presidentialism, we rely on a classification of limited and unlimited presidential executives (Derbyshire and Derbyshire, 1991). The distinction between limited and unlimited presidentialism refers roughly to constitutional and unconstitutional presidential states (see table 8.3).

The identification of presidential executives in table 8.3 is not exhaustive since states with communist and military executives can also embrace real presidential powers. The earlier communist regimes in Eastern Europe had presidents, as does China today. The dividing line between presidential states and military regimes also remains blurred in some instances.

Federalism

The words 'federation' and 'federal political system' have no standard definition, as there has been much discussion as to what the actual characteristics of federal states are (Riker, 1964, 1975). One tradition cites devolution of power as typical of federalism, in contrast to the centralization of power in unitary states (Ostrom, 1991). Another tradition underlines the manner in which federal states tend to be created, that is, by means of some kind of covenant between states to become sub-states in the new federation (Kriek et

Table 8.4 Federal states: population and sub-states, 1990

Country	Population (millions)	Number of states or provinces
Argentina	33	22 provinces
Australia	17	6 states
Austria	8	9 Länder
Brazil	150	23 provinces
Canada	27	10 provinces
Germany	78	18 Länder
India	853	25 states
Malaysia	18	11 states
Mexico	82	31 states
Nigeria	120	21 states
Pakistan	123	6 provinces
Russia	147	21 republics
Switzerland	7	26 cantons
United Arab Emirates	2	7 sheikdoms
United States	251	50 states
Venezuela	20	20 states

Sources: *Statesman's Yearbook* (1989–90); *Encyclopedia Britannica Book of the Year* (1991).

Note: The United Arab Emirates include the former Trucial States Abu Dhabi, Dubai, Sharjah, Ajman, Umm al Qaiwain, Ras al Khaimah and Fujairah.

al., 1992). Here, we discuss whether federal states could be more stable and display a better performance record than unitary states.

If we begin by observing that such federal states as the Soviet Union, with its fifteen union republics, Yugoslavia, with its six republics and two autonomous regions, and Czechoslovakia, with its two republics, did not endure, we must also recall that these states were created from above. A look at other examples of federal states in the world indicates that state stability is a property of federal political systems, especially when they were formed by a process from below (see table 8.4) (Burgess and Gagnon, 1993).

We observe that the federal state framework is not used as frequently as the unitary framework, the number of federal states being quite small considering the total number of states. Yet we must also note that the set of federal states hosts a large proportion of the population of the world, or some 1,900 million people. At the same time it holds equally true that not all large states have a federal framework. The unitary framework is present in China, Indonesia, Japan and several large European countries, such as the United Kingdom and France (Forsyth, 1989).

Some huge states employ the federal framework, such as Russia (with 17 million square kilometres), Canada (with 10), the USA (with 9.5), Brazil (with 8.5), Australia (with 7.7), India (with 3.2) and Argentina (with 2.8). However, federalism is not only appropriate in states with vast territories, because it is also considered viable in states with extremely small territories, for example the Comoros (470,000 people on 2,000 sq km) and St Kitts-Nevis (40,000 inhabitants on 200 sq km). In addition, the unitary framework is found in China (with 9.6 million sq km) and the Republic of South Africa (1.2 million sq km), and there are federal states with small populations, including the United Arab Emirates and Austria and Switzerland (Forsyth, 1989).

At the same time it must be pointed out that a formally federalist framework is not the same as real power decentralization. Some federal systems are quite centralized, for example, Austria and Mexico. Unitary states may display decentralization as well, in particular if local government possesses considerable discretion (Page, 1991). Actually, it is not easy to pin down what federalism stands for except in a formal constitutional sense.

First and foremost, federal states are those states that call themselves such. Characteristic of federalism is the existence of government elected from below, at the regional level, but such devolution of state power occurs not only in quasi-federal unitary states, such as Spain and Italy, but also in traditionally centralist France, where the process of devolution in the 1980s has undermined government from above, or the Napoleonic state.

A rather intriguing problem in federalist theory is the delineation of the member states. How many sub-states should there be and how large should each one be? What constitutes a viable member state in a federal dispensation? Often the federal structure reflects less rational criteria than various historical factors, meaning that member states may differ tremendously in size, both in territory and in population (Elazar, 1972, 1984, 1991).

Secondly, one frequently used indicator on state decentralization is the division of the allocation of funds within the public sector between central and local levels of government. Measuring the proportion of central government final consumption in relation to overall general government final consumption, there is some truth in the claim that federal states tend to score lower than unitary states. Although federalism exists in various shades, we focus here primarily on whether such institutions matter for state stability and state performance. The distribution of power between the federal government and the various sub-states cannot be predicted only on the number of member states. Swiss federalism is weak, several functions having been devolved to the many small cantons, whereas the federal government in the United States is strong, although the number of member states is even larger. German federalism, with a smaller number of member states, is strong, while Canadian federalism, with a few large member states, is weaker. Here the province of Quebec has asked for special territorial autonomy, or what is referred to either as 'home rule', for example, in the cases of Greenland and Åland, in the unitary states of Denmark and Finland respectively, or as 'asymmetrical federalism'.

Confederalism and international regimes

What matters is the underlying idea of the state, that is, whether it derives somehow from a confederalist notion of the state as consisting of member states (as, for example, in the former Czechoslovakia, with its two parts, the Czech lands and Slovakia). The members of a federal union are considered the constituent parts of the state which have rights that need to be protected within a constitutional framework, often including a special court of appeal. The dividing line between federal and confederal states is related to the rights of the member states to relinquish the obligations of the union contract.

The formal confederal framework is hardly used at all. Actually, one of the most conspicuous examples of this mode of organizing the state is what replaced the Union of Socialist Soviet Republics in 1991: the Commonwealth of Independent States (CIS). One may also call the British Commonwealth a confederation, but here is the border-line where so few common functions between the member states exist that the concept of a Weberian state becomes inapplicable. In 1993 Belgium changed its constitutional status from a unitary to a federal state. The growth of international regimes is apparent in public international law (Forsyth, 1981; Brownlie, 1990).

The increase in the visibility and power of international organizations that has taken place during the postwar period may be interpreted as a real form of confederalism, particularly with regard to the European Community or European Union, the Western European Union and the Conference on Security and Cooperation in Europe. The growth of international regimes is very much characteristic of the postwar developments challenging the sovereignty of the national state (Krasner, 1982; Keohane, 1984; Bennett, 1988).

One should not neglect the many international regimes (Archer, 1992) when trying to account for state stability and performance. Membership of international economic or political organizations may not only recognize the position of a state, it is also conducive to both stability and performance. However, in comparative politics the existence and impact of international regimes are hardly ever included in model building.

The international system has two different types of effect on the state. Firstly, there is the formal impact, such as membership criteria; not all kinds of state are accepted to enter international communities. For example, the requirement of human rights has grown stronger in the 1980s and early 1990s (this applies to the United Nations and the Council of Europe). Secondly, membership of international organizations opens up the possibility of receiving a number of benefits, such as economic aid and military protection. A number of regimes have been created in order to manage aspects of trade and commerce in the international world economy: the GATT framework, the Organization for Economic Cooperation and Development (OECD), the European Community, free trade zones in North America (NAFTA) and South-East Asia (ASEAN) as well as the former

Table 8.5 Authoritarian institutions

	Type of regime	*Military government*
Africa	3.2 (43)	.63 (43)
America	2.1 (24)	.58 (24)
Asia	3.2 (36)	.49 (35)
Oceania	1.0 (3)	.00 (3)
Europe	2.2 (25)	.00 (25)
E^2	.16	.23

Sources: Derbyshire and Derbyshire (1991); Sullivan (1991).

Note: Type of regime: parliamentarism = 1; limited presidentialism = 2; unlimited presidentialism = 3; communist state = 4; military regime = 5; traditional regime = 6; experience of military government = 1, no experience = 0.

COMECON agreement. NATO and the Western European Union are examples of an international military association (Bennett, 1988).

The difficult problem of how to enter state membership in international organizations into models of state stability and state performance remains unresolved. One would have to take into account a variety of international regimes, such as IGOs (international governmental organizations), INGOs (international non-governmental organizations) and BINGOs (business international non-governmental organizations), the number of which has proliferated since the Second World War.

Authoritarian institutions

Dictatorships come in different shades. The more authoritarian the regime, the harsher it is, and the more totalitarian, the more society is penetrated. One may argue that authoritarianism reached its peak in communist states or in unconstitutional systems with a Fascist orientation. However, at the same time such states attempted to legitimize their power by invoking the interests of the people. Their populist orientation contrasts starkly with the exclusiveness typical of military and traditional regimes.

Actually, the concept of an authoritarian state is a complex one which can be unpacked in different ways. To the distinction between totalitarian and traditional regimes one may add a number of institutional hybrids, such as civil regimes versus military regimes and any combination of civil-military authoritarian regimes (Morlino, 1990: 98). The distribution of authoritarian institutions on the continents is mapped in two general indices in table 8.5.

Whereas the military junta is a non-European phenomenon (with the exception of Greece between 1967 and 1973), dictatorship is certainly not unknown on the European continent, although its attractiveness is at its lowest in the early 1990s. Several regimes in Africa and in Central and South America have been military ones, which makes us predict that state instability will be high on these continents. Dictatorships have been the prevailing regime type in Asia, reflecting the historical commitment to despotism on the Oriental continent. Yet military juntas have been able to usurp power for some periods of time, most often in South Korea, Pakistan, Indonesia, Burma and the Fertile Crescent.

The military regime model

Military regimes are transient regimens. The crux of the matter is the successor problem. The military establishment often seizes power for the accomplishment of some specific purpose that is relevant only for a certain period of time. After a few years the usurpation of power has to find a new cause or the military regime has to be dismantled. The logic of a military government is thus that it must sooner or later falter, as there can be no legitimate successor but a non-military regime.

Thus one may give a few examples of transitional military regimes, giving the date of the most recent coup as well as that of the actual or hoped-for return to civilian rule: Afghanistan, 1992/1993, Burkina Faso, 1987/1991, Burundi, 1987/1992, Central African Republic, 1981, Chile, 1973/1989, Equatorial Guinea, 1979, Ghana, 1981/1993, Guinea, 1984, Haiti, 1991, Lesotho, 1986/1993, Mauritania, 1984, Niger, 1974, Nigeria, 1985/1993, Panama, 1968/1989, Paraguay, 1954/1989, Rwanda, 1973 and Sudan, 1989 (Derbyshire and Derbyshire, 1991: 60–1).

Bebler emphasizes that the military regime model has occurred in the Third World. Actually, it may appear in different forms:

> Empirical studies on contemporary military regimes have conclusively shown that under this heading we deal in fact with various configurations and shades of military-civilian, military-police-civilian, and civilian-military (under the military's tutelage) coalitions. (Bebler, 1990: 263)

Military regimes have prevailed in Africa since around 1965, in the Near East since the interwar years, in South-East Asia from 1945, and in Latin America and Eastern and Southern Europe in various periods of time during the twentieth century. Yet with some notable exceptions, such as the Stroessner dictatorship in Paraguay and Suharto's rule in Indonesia, not too many military regimes have survived more than five to ten years. But military juntas are not often dismantled in favour of democratic regimes. Some military rulers attempt to prolong their power by introducing presidential administration, thus legitimizing their dictatorship. Civil war may be the result, as events in Nigeria, Uganda and Zaïre have shown.

One should distinguish between military entrance into politics, military rule and military outcomes (Finer, 1976; Nordlinger, 1977). What is the motivation that drives the military to attempt to play a political role has been debated: personal motives, reformist zeal, preservation of the status quo, revolutionary goals (Finer, 1988; Janowitz, 1964). Although several military takeovers have been made on the grounds that the prevailing order was threatened, it is also true that there have been reformist military coups, such as in Egypt (1952), Iraq (1958), Syria (1963) and Libya (1969) (Cammack et al., 1993).

The occurrence of a military takeover reflects how the boundary lines between the political leaders and the military are institutionalized. Typical of Latin America and Africa is that the separation between politics and the military is weak. Only a few countries in Africa have not experienced military rule: Botswana, Gabon, Côte d'Ivoire, Senegal, Kenya, Tanzania, Malawi and Tunisia. Similarly, only a few countries on the other continents have avoided some form of military regime, such as India, Sri Lanka, Malaysia and Singapore in Asia, and Mexico, Costa Rica, Colombia, Guyana and several Caribbean states in Latin America. As Bebler points out: 'Civilian-dominated systems have clear sway also among the industrially most developed countries, among the countries with strongest military establishments, and among nuclear powers' (Bebler, 1990: 271).

The military has not only intervened in politics several times in many countries, it also attempts to preserve its influence after giving up its rule. Thus the exit of military juntas is often based upon agreements that protect the military in various ways, including the judicial examination of crimes committed by them when in power.

The communist model

Socialist one-party rule is an example of the combination of civil bureaucracy and dictatorial control, whereas right-wing authoritarian control often takes the form of a military regime. At the same time it should be stressed that communist rule may take the form of military intervention, such as in Poland under Jaruzelski, and that right-wing authoritarian rule may be based upon one-party domination.

Although it was known that communist states faced increasingly difficult problems, the system collapse in several countries around 1989 came as a surprise, in particular on account of its non-violent nature. One may argue that the communist state did not disappear as a result of political tensions expressed in the organization of explicit resistance towards the regime, but because of ever-growing economic and ecological problems.

Be that as it may, the communist state appeared to be stable, if not performing very well. Now we know that, besides poor performance with regard to policy outputs and outcomes, there was from around 1975 an increasingly severe stability problem. At that time the communist economies started to decline, first in Poland and then in the rest of Eastern Europe.

An analysis of the special features of communist institutions would take us into the history of state regimes, which is much too broad a theme for this volume. The political institutions of the Leninist state were very much tied up with the economic institutions of the Stalinist planned economy. An immense concentration of political and economic power in the hands of a small elite protected by the double hierarchical institutions of both the Soviet state and the communist party could not guarantee state stability.

Communist regimes were not all alike. In some states there were participatory elements which mitigated the harsh features in others. The communist states in the Third World were different from those in what was called 'the Second World'. Here the separation between the party and the military was drawn differently: in some the party remained the power centre, whereas in others the military was decisive for regime continuation.

The collapse of the communist regimes in Eastern Europe resulted from a combination of legitimacy deficit and economic inefficiency, the one factor reinforcing the other (Clark and Wildavsky, 1990; Banac, 1992). It was possible to mobilize citizen approval for the communist ideals at an early stage and during the Second World War, but the more distant the accomplishment of the promises became, especially economic ones, the less support could be evinced for the party and the regime.

Institutional consolidation or sclerosis?

The process of institutionalization received much attention during the 1980s in the wake of the new institutionalism (March and Olsen, 1989). One trend has been to focus in more detail on country-specific contexts of political institutions. Rather than asking what, if any, are the differential impacts of various special institutions, an alternative is to look at the length of time of institutionalization as the crucial factor.

Two models of institutional evolution have been launched. The first, the consolidation model, argues that the length of time of uninterrupted institution building is of positive significance for the state, enhancing both state stability and state performance (Huntington, 1965). There is a particular starting-point in time when a modernizing political leadership is introduced which also coincides with the overall process of social and economic transformation.

The second model implies a less positive attitude to institution building, arguing that the longer the period of time since the introduction of a set of modern state institutions, the more institutional sclerosis there will be (Olson, 1982). And institutional sclerosis could be significant for the state, as it could enhance the power of special interest groups (trade unions, employers' associations), which may threaten not only economic performance but also the stability of the state.

These concepts of consolidation and sclerosis are highly theoretical ones.

Table 8.6 Institutional development

	Date of modernizing leadership (SCLER1)	Starting-point for social and economic transformation (SCLER2)
Africa	1952 (43)	1957 (6)
America	1876 (24)	1928 (12)
Asia	1930 (33)	1944 (19)
Oceania	1867 (3)	1904 (2)
Europe	1828 (25)	1894 (25)
E^2	.62	.50

Source: Black (1966).

They do not single out the introduction of democratic institutions as the starting-point of the modern institutional state, but rather the consolidation of modernizing leadership or the beginning of the process of economic and social transformation away from agriculture and towards industry. How are such vague concepts to be measured? Table 8.6 suggests two approaches.

One gains the interesting impression from these data that political modernization predates economic and social modernization on all continents (this is also the gist of Black's model). The time differences simply reflect the choice of a measuring rod. The basic premise of the institutional models is to represent the length of time since the introduction of a modern leadership as conducive to state maturity – meaning more stability, democracy and welfare services. The crucial difference in table 8.6 is between Africa and Asia and the other continents, because very new states are found only in the former. The consolidation model predicts that states will be more stable and perform better, the more time has passed for consolidation – leaving us with a warning about any hopes for improvement in Africa in particular. However, the institutional sclerosis model predicts that this is not necessarily so, as states that have been longer established, such as those in Latin America, could suffer from institutional decay.

The relevance of institutional conditions

Political institutions may be important for two reasons, their intrinsic value and their extrinsic value. Here, we focus on the latter, searching for any clues as to the impact of political institutions on state stability and performance. Table 8.7 contains the simple correlations.

Table 8.7   Institutional relationships

	State stability	State performance				
	REG	CIVIC	HDI	HED86	TOP10	INF8090
TURNOUT	.29	.27	.49	.34	−.58	−.00
SCLER1	−.50	−.59	−.71	−.45	.42	−.07
SCLER2	−.53	−.52	−.61	−.58	.45	.21
PARLSYS	−.22	−.66	−.44	−.32	.08	−.10
PARLAM	.47	.67	.44	.43	−.32	−.16
MULTIPA	.49	.78	.58	.56	−.47	−.16
PASIZE	−.41	−.83	−.57	−.39	.24	−.10
UNICAM	−.13	−.17	−.25	−.09	−.02	−.08
FEDERAL	.17	.28	.26	.12	.25	.08
MILITGOV	−.56	−.41	−.49	−.49	.30	.25
GOVCOAL	.52	.74	.54	.56	−.57	−.16

Source: Tables 8.1, 8.2, 8.3, 8.4, 8.5, 8.6.

Note: For explanation, see Appendix 10.1, Variables and measures.

A number of findings stand out here. First, institutional longevity is associated with state stability and good state performance, confirming the consolidation model. It remains to establish whether there really is some causal mechanism at operation here. Older states may be expected to be characterized more by regime duration than younger states, but it is not equally obvious that the former would tend to display better policy outputs and outcomes than the latter. Is there an underlying causal mechanism explaining why the date of state consolidation is important?

Second, states where elites that come to dominate both state and society through the domination of the largest party tend not only to have a bad performance record but also to be unstable. Third, a number of basic institutional features are related to state stability. Clearly, military governments tend to be highly unstable. But the level of interdependence between more minute institutional distinctions and stability is not clear, because regimes with institutions that invite contestation and opposition can be unstable and regimes that prohibit such mechanisms may prove stable, at least for some length of time.

Fourth, the performance indicators correlate significantly with institutional properties. A number of relationships here are rather strong, for example, that between institutional sclerosis, the type of party system and the governmental system on the one hand and a good performance record on the other.

Conclusion

In this chapter we report on a number of findings which support the hypotheses that the framing of political institutions has an impact upon state stability and state performance. There is ample support for a number of models that emphasize the positive contribution of open and pluralistic institutions, and also for those underlining the length of time of institution building. However, these simple relationships cannot be taken as evidence of causal mechanisms. We need to look at another set of factors, focusing first on the actors in political life and then moving on to test models that combine various elements.

Yet the findings in the correlations between institutions and state performance are that the relationships are as might be expected. However, they are not that strong, meaning that we should try to add other factors to the institutional ones, for example, social conditions. By themselves, the correlations are not strong enough to arrive at the neo-institutionalist theory that institutions are of utmost causal importance. It is necessary both to look at how institutional and social factors interact in relation to the state, and to include actor-related factors.

9

Actor Models

Introduction

States as aggregate units of human behaviour are conditioned, as we have seen, both by social forces, such as economic affluence and cultural belief-systems, and by overarching institutions, such as military governments versus parliamentary regimes. But where does the personal element enter in politics?

People may matter in politics in several ways. Distinctions may be made such as that between charismatic rule versus mass involvement, the influence of political parties versus organized interests, and right-wing activism versus left-wing movements. In particular, the relevance with respect to state performance of actors with a distinct political ideology has been much debated. This chapter also discusses the lifetime of politicians, as all leaders come and go but some stay longer than others. The domination of a state by a single individual is obviously more marked when that leader survives for decades.

Degrees of freedom

Political institutions matter, but they do not explain everything. Rules if adequately institutionalized structure activities, but in politics there is always the individual person or special collectivities taking action or refraining from taking action. Perhaps the twentieth century has witnessed the strength of the personal element to an extent never previously matched. How is it possible to understand the Nazi state without Adolf Hitler, the communist state without Joseph Stalin, the Egyptian events without Nasser, Iraqi politics without Saddam Hussein and Argentina without the Perons?

What is the scope for political actors in relation to the state, its stability and performance? It depends upon the implications of social structure and institutions. As long as social, economic and institutional conditions do not determine state stability and performance there will always be room to take action which either enhances or undermines state stability.

Although states are aggregate of behaviour and cannot, so to speak, act as if they were individuals, political actors, in a group or individually, may function on behalf of the state and embark on a course of events that determines its direction. While Weber's concept underlines the impersonal and bureaucratic aspects of the state, it remains true that Weber was very much aware of the power of single persons, in particular charismatic leaders, to change the course of events (Weber, 1978).

However, even at a more mundane level of analysis, one cannot bypass the fact that politicians have some degree of freedom in relation to social forces and institutional set-up. Clearly, the goals of leaders may play a role in state performance, both for policy-making and outcomes. The stability of the state may be enhanced or endangered by specific actions. This chapter discusses various alternative ways of modelling the impact of key actors upon the state on the basis of the concept of degree of freedom. Structural and institutional determinism seem as odd as strict personal indeterminism. Often single political actors have no great influence, because social or institutional factors constrain individual action. The amount of freedom for individuals acting on their own or in organized groups such as political parties, governments or cliques depends on the circumstances.

Charisma

Some politicians direct their states in a charismatic fashion if they reach positions of leadership, or if they carry revolutionary momentum, undermine existing state structures. In spite of the fact that politics involves millions of people, individuals, such as Nelson Mandela, Lech Walesa and Corazón Aquino, may bring down an entire system of rule (apartheid, communist Poland and Marcos's Philippines, respectively) or, like Ruhollah Khomeini, identify a whole new concept of the state (modern Muslim rule) (Goldstone et al., 1991).

State persistence may be promoted by the employment of shrewd tactics and strategies on the part of traditional rulers, such as King Hassan II of Morocco and King Hussein of Jordan. Established systems of rule may be undermined by such actors as Kemal Atatürk, Fidel Castro and Mahatma Gandhi engaging in proper action at a suitable time in the right circumstances.

The tragedy of politics is that, if disastrous opportunities are presented to persons with ruthless determination and fervent zeal, single actors can have a fatal impact upon state performance, bringing about catastrophe affecting millions of people. The impact of the individual personalities of Pol Pot in the Khmer Rouge movement, Ceauşescu in communist Romania and Idi

Amin in Uganda cannot be ignored by referring only to social forces or institutions.

Although there has been a lengthy but inconclusive debate about what is most important – structure or actors, social forces or intentional behaviour – the student of comparative politics must clearly recognize the role of actors in macropolitics. The variety of political parties is just as important. The basic theme of 'does politics matter' is as relevant for the state as for local government policy-making (Sharpe and Newton, 1984).

It is impossible to remove the personal element from such heavily bureaucratized organizations as the state. Opportunism may be employed to bolster state stability, but it may also be conducive to instability. Since individuals' tactics and strategies may turn out differently, the omnipresence of personal factors in politics at all levels of government adds uncertainty and complexity to the understanding of the operations and outcomes of formal organizations. What is the life-span of political leaders?

Leaders and leadership duration

When governments come and go frequently or when the leader of a state is frequently replaced, there is talk of short-term political instability. However, it must be remembered that leadership that lasts too long may also indicate instability. What is the normal period of a government? When do leadership changes become so frequent that they indicate instability?

By measuring the duration of executive leadership for the period 1945 to 1987, an overall picture of the life-span of leaders may be obtained (see table 9.1). The indicators calculate (a) the number of executive leaders, (b) the average number of executive leaders and (c) the average duration of leadership. One might expect that short-term political instability would be high in countries where there is considerable regime instability, as described in Chapter 4. Interestingly, table 9.1 indicates that this is not so.

Table 9.1 indicates that short-term political instability does not correspond with the measures on state stability reported on in Chapter 4. As a matter of fact, the average duration of leadership is shorter in democratic Europe and Oceania than in non-democratic Asia and Africa. This is very different from the variation in regime stability, whose main feature is exactly the opposite.

The three measures on executive stability co-vary to a considerable degree. Executive instability is to be found among two different types of regime – democratic countries with numerous changes in government (Belgium, Finland, France, Greece, Italy, Switzerland and Uruguay) and non-democratic countries with several military coups (Argentina, Bolivia). The indicators have high scores for countries with stable authoritarian regimes such as Côte d'Ivoire, North Korea, Malawi, the United Arab Emirates, Zambia and Zimbabwe. Thus there is tension between short-term and long-term political

Table 9.1 Leadership duration, 1945–87

	Number of leaders (LEAD)	Average number of leaders (AVELEAD)	Average duration of leadership (years) (AVEDURA)
Africa	3.6 (42)	1.2 (42)	10.7 (42)
America	12.3 (24)	3.0 (24)	4.6 (24)
Asia	6.1 (35)	1.7 (35)	11.3 (35)
Oceania	7.7 (3)	2.4 (3)	4.3 (3)
Europe	12.6 (25)	3.1 (25)	7.8 (25)
E^2	.29	.24	.13

Source: Based upon data from Bienen and van de Walle (1991).

Note: LEAD = number of political leaders during the postwar era; AVELEAD = a normalized average score which takes into account the year of establishment of the state; AVEDURA = average duration of leadership in years since 1945.

stability. Several democratic states tend to have stable regimes but they also have leaders that change frequently.

The finding is in agreement with the distinction between two basic mechanisms for the removal of political leaders. One of these is the classical shift between majority government and the opposition or the coming and going of coalition governments, as in Western Europe (Laver and Schofield, 1990; Budge and Keman, 1990). The second may be revolutionary, as with the coup d'état in states where the political authorities are disposed of in an unpredictable and often violent manner. Although the coup d'état mechanism is employed first and foremost by right-wing military juntas, it may also be used by left-wing Marxist groups, as occurred in the model October Revolution in 1917. The institutions or rules of the game in democracies imply that leaders do change within certain intervals of time, whereas dictatorships place hardly any formal limit on the time-span of rulers.

Once the length of time that political leaders have at their disposal has been established, the next question is what is the relevance of ideology for political leaders? The concept of ideology sorts the political elites in various countries into more or less coherent subsets in terms of values and attitudes. Does ideology matter for state stability and performance? One would expect to find relationships between the various performance indicators and party ideology. The analysis of political leaders takes into account their belief-systems and their basic orientations to state and society.

Orientations of political actors

The left–right distinction is not the only relevant way to sort political actors into various sets, but its universal applicability cannot be doubted. It crops up whenever political parties start to organize and engage in activities.

As already argued in Chapter 8, every analysis of state stability and performance has to recognize political parties as an important variable. Party systems, the national configuration of individual political parties, may be looked upon as one of the main links between government and society. Political parties can be seen as the formal organizations for expressing the cleavages in the social structure, acting more or less freely as the vehicles for social movements. Representative government would be inconceivable without the existence of party systems, but their influence is not confined to democratic states. The political party plays a crucial role in that it expresses the ideological continuum from the extreme right to the extreme left.

Political parties constitute mechanisms for the mobilization of social opinions and what such opinions offer candidates in the formation of governments. Sartori writes:

> But when the society at large becomes politicized, the traffic rules that plug the society into the state, and vice versa, are established by the way in which a party system becomes structured. At this point, parties become channeling agencies and the party system becomes the system of political canalization of the society. (Sartori, 1976: 41)

Sartori moved beyond the institutional analysis of party systems in terms of rules for the legitimate acceptance of number of parties – one-party system, two-party system or multi-party system (Duverger, 1954) – to propose a typology underlining the ideological distance between the parties in the system – that is, polarization.

The Sartori typology focuses on both polarization and fragmentation in the party system, questioning the chances of survival of polarized polities. A party system involving centrifugal drives, irresponsible opposition and unfair competition would hardly be conducive to state stability and performance (Sartori, 1976: 140).

Sartori also underlines the central role of so-called anti-system parties in shaping the party system: 'Accordingly, a party can be defined as being anti-system whenever it undermines the legitimacy of the regime it opposes' (Sartori, 1976: 133). He recognizes communist and Fascist parties as anti-system parties, and his model shows that democracies having strong communist and/or Fascist parties are characterized by political instability. The model seems to be valid for classical examples of state instability, such as the Weimar Republic (1918–33), France during the Fourth Republic (1946–58) and Italy in the 1970s. At the same time one may point out that the political

Table 9.2 Actor orientations in states, circa 1985

	Regime orientation (NEWPOL)	Centre-right support (RIGHT1)	Centre-left support (LEFT1)
Africa	.14 (43)	31.1 (10)	11.8 (10)
America	−.02 (24)	32.3 (21)	27.7 (21)
Asia	.01 (36)	29.6 (14)	9.5 (14)
Oceania	−.33 (3)	16.6 (3)	37.5 (3)
Europe	−.40 (25)	31.6 (16)	40.4 (16)
E^2	.07	.01	.22

Source: Encyclopedia Britannica Book of the Year (1990).

Note: Regime orientation: −1 = left-wing authoritarian; −.5 = left-wing orientated; 0 = indifferent; .5 = right-wing orientated; 1 = right-wing authoritarian. Centre-right support: excluding authoritarian right-wing parties. Centre-left support: excluding authoritarian left-wing parties.

crisis in Italy in the 1990s reflects more the vagaries arising when elites cling to power for too long, resulting in *lottizzazione*, or clientelism, if not out-right corruption.

Yet the distinction between the right-wing and the left-wing anti-system party may be employed in a more general search for the role of actor orientations with regard to state stability and performance, whether in democratic or non-democratic countries. The standard scale of the ideological spectrum, from left-wing to right-wing extremism, with the moderate democratic parties in the centre, could be employed to map the orientation of the parties in the states of the world (see table 9.2).

A most interesting finding is that, on the whole, support for the right is stronger in Africa and Asia than in Europe and Oceania. It must be admitted, though, that the strong position of various left-wing political parties in the data in table 9.2 refers to political geography before the collapse of East-European communism in 1990–1. A left-wing ideology may be strong in two ways: either there is a left-wing authoritarian regime or the combined strength of centre-left parties in democratic states is substantial. Does left-wing strength in either form matter for state stability and state performance?

At the same time there is the finding that the eta-squared values are low in table 9.2, showing that the ideological orientation of the chief actors in state politics varies more within each continent than between the continents. This reflects exactly the map of political geography before the collapse of communism, when there were Marxist regimes both in Europe and on the other continents. Of course, the strong position of the left in Europe also reflects the existence of well-established socialist movements outside the communist systems.

Actually, table 9.2 and its indicators cover two different types of actor orientation: it takes into account both hegemonic and competitive ideologies. In non-democratic countries the tendency of the regime may be either to right or to left. First, there are the left-wing authoritarian regimes (those with scores -1), which included during the 1980s countries such as Afghanistan, Albania, Algeria, Angola, Benin, Bulgaria, Burkina Faso, Cambodia, China, Congo, Cuba, Czechoslovakia, Ethiopia, East Germany, Hungary, Iraq, North Korea, Mongolia, Mozambique, Burma, Poland, Somalia, Syria, Tanzania, the USSR, Vietnam, Yemen (Aden) and Yugoslavia.

Second, there are the right-wing authoritarian states (score: $+1$), which, circa 1985 were mainly in Africa and Asia: Burundi, Cameroon, the Central African Republic, Chad, Chile, Guinea, Indonesia, Iran, Jordan, Kenya, Kuwait, Malawi, Mali, Mauritania, Nepal, Niger, Nigeria, Oman, Paraguay, Rwanda, Saudi Arabia, Sierra Leone, Sudan, Togo, the United Arab Emirates, Yemen (Sana) and Zaïre.

The actors in these two sets of authoritarian states should be sharply differentiated from the set of actors which belong to rightist or leftist ideologies in competitive polities. On the other hand, a number of states score $-.5$, meaning that they include a number of strong social democratic movements, some of which are outside Western Europe: Australia, Austria, Belgium, Costa Rica, Denmark, the Dominican Republic, Ecuador, Finland, France, West Germany, Greece, Israel, Italy, Jamaica, South Korea, New Zealand, Nicaragua, Norway, Peru, Portugal, Spain, Sweden and Venezuela.

This set of states should be clearly separated from the countries where the score is $+.5$, indicating strong rightist parties. Here we find actors in the following countries: Canada, Egypt, El Salvador, Honduras, Japan, Liberia, Mexico, Morocco, Singapore, South Africa, Sri Lanka, Turkey and the United Kingdom.

The indicator on centre-right and centre-left support covers only non-authoritarian states. The data support the finding that rightist ideologies have attracted party actors more in Asia, Africa and America whereas leftist ideologies have been more successful in Europe – that is, up until 1990.

When searching for the state output or outcome impacts of these broad actor orientations, one should remember that all the states differ in a number of other relevant aspects, such as economy, culture and institutional set-up. Even if we were to find correlations between orientation and state stability and performance, all findings would have to be tested by means of models that combine these types of factor.

The extent of polarization between leading political actors may not be as important as the sheer size of one set of actors in a country, namely those that belong to the single largest party. If a party manages to become dominant at the polls with considerably more support than a simple majority, then this elite faces a situation that is fundamentally different from one where there is a balance between contesting groups. A predominant elite could achieve such a position either in competitive elections or in one-party states.

The position of a set of political orientations may also be indicated by the occurrence of domination on the part of one elite group. Such a position may be measured by means of widespread support for one single political party, whether right or left – see Chapter 8. When a political party receives more than 50 per cent of the electoral votes, then the actors belonging to the major party in the country will sit safely in power. Yet such data on party actors reflect a great deal of the basic institutional framework in the various states on the five continents. In Africa the one-party state model is the most favoured. The high average scores for the largest party being considerably over 50 per cent in Asia, America and Europe express the occurrence of dictatorships in several states. Had we looked at the most recent elections, in around 1990, the scores would have been significantly lower on all continents as a result of the widespread manifestation of transition politics in the so-called third wave democratization process, which will be analysed in Chapter 11.

Status of trade unions

A number of indicators may be employed to measure the position of actors with a leftist orientation. As Manfred Schmidt has emphasized, the power of the left in a society is not only a matter of the political position of socialist and communist parties; of equal importance is the access to power of the trade union movement, which is partly a function of its organizational density (Schmidt, 1982). Here we include, besides data for trade union membership, information about whether states allow collective action, or if there is considerable constraint on the operation of trade unions – an institutional factor. It is not only right-wing authoritarian states which attempt to control trade union activities; left-wing governments are also hesitant to allow unions to operate freely. Several authoritarian states have tried to boost membership in order to employ the unions as vehicles for regime goals. We cannot therefore expect trade union density to go together with freedom of collective action (see table 9.3).

Freedom of collective action tends to be accepted only in democratic states. However, this does not mean that trade unions have many members only in such states. Quite the contrary, there are unions with heavy membership in some non-democratic states and weak union movements in a few democratic states. In several African and Asian countries the trade unions are almost non-existent, in particular where there are right-wing authoritarian regimes. On the other hand, the communist states tended to report excessively high membership figures, even though there was no freedom of collective action.

Table 9.3   Trade unions in the 1980s

	Membership density	Trade union institution
Africa	29.0 (37)	.21 (43)
America	22.7 (23)	.63 (24)
Asia	24.8 (19)	.20 (35)
Oceania	44.3 (3)	1.00 (3)
Europe	64.1 (25)	.64 (25)
E^2	.31	.20

Source: Sullivan (1991).

Note: Membership density: estimates of proportion of employees being members of trade unions; trade union institution: 1 = freedom of collective action, 0 = no freedom of collective action.

Does right versus left matter?

A set of well-known models focuses on the impact of politics on state performance. Thus it has been argued that the political power of parties of the right is a decisive negative determinant of the size of the welfare state (Castles, 1978; 1982; Whiteley, 1980). A different argument is that the strength of the position of parties of the left is conducive to welfare spending and equality (Schmidt, 1982).

There are a number of hypotheses about the implications of actor orientations, some referring to leftist governments, others to trade union power or, more generally, to the power division between the left and the right in society. The search for the consequences of the political organization of right versus left includes not only the determinants of public spending but also outcomes such as economic growth.

Paul Whiteley, in *Political Control of the Macroeconomy* (1986), argues that left-wing governments care greatly about economic performance, in particular welfarism and economic growth. The strong emphasis on employment results in high growth in social democratic regimes. The Olson counter model is that a strong position for the left in government implies more income redistribution, which drives down economic performance due to its negative impact on incentives (Olson, 1982). Do actors, or more specifically their orientations, also matter for state stability and state performance?

Authoritarian regimes, whether of the right or left, emphasize state stability, as both are vulnerable to demands for democratic change. It is difficult to tell generally which type of regime tends to be more stable. Before 1989 the typical communist left-wing authoritarian regime appeared capable of rejecting many demands for change. Right-wing authoritarian regimes, on the other hand, seemed to be shaky, as they came and went in Latin American and Asian countries. This is all history now that left-wing dictators

Table 9.4 Relevance of actor models

| | State stability REG | State performance | | | | |
		CIVIC	HDI	HED86	TOP10	INF8090
AVELEAD	.13	.52	.35	.19	−.13	.16
POLORI	.12	.14	−.20	−.15	.26	−.03
NEWPOL	.12	.10	−.23	−.19	.26	−.09
RIGHT1	.01	.10	.12	−.02	−.12	−.07
RIGHT2	.04	−.03	−.26	−.20	.08	−.10
LEFT1	.24	.43	.46	.33	−.29	.08
LEFT2	−.11	−.23	.13	.17	−.37	.01
UNION	.33	.78	.42	.33	−.24	.07
TRADEUD	.24	−.05	.27	.28	−.47	.01

Source: Tables 9.1, 9.2 and 9.3.

Note: For explanation, see Appendix 10.1, Variables and measures.

have been wiped out all over the world and the prospects for those remaining are hardly sound – as, for example, in Cuba and China.

Right-wing authoritarian rulers have been no less conspicuous than left-wing dictators. At the same time, their future relevance does not appear to be negligible. Key political actors, in particular the military, may continue to deliberate upon on the pros and cons of a right-wing dictatorship.

Douglas Hibbs states in *The American Political Economy* (1987) that centre-right government focuses upon inflation, expressing a preference for low inflation even if it is combined with considerable unemployment. When we look at table 9.4, which reports on correlations for actor orientations models, it is important to remember that the impact of parties may be cancelled out by strong social or institutional conditions.

There are some major findings in table 9.4. First, state stability is not affected by the ideology of its leaders. State stability has sources other than party ideology, meaning that both right-wing and left-wing regimes may be stable or unstable. Second, a theory that claims a prominent role for actors in relation to state performance is more promising. Third, although the statistics are not as pronounced here as when we looked at social and institutional conditions, there are conclusions worth underlining. That there is no correlation between right-wing versus left-wing authoritarian rule and state stability is interesting, as it means that both sets of actors face difficult-ies. The strength of the left in government or the strength of the trade unions in society is to some extent correlated with welfare state expenditures, as predicted in Castles' and Schmidt's models. The strong interrelationship between freedom of trade unions and lack of civil and political rights is also not difficult to account for, but this finding corroborates more the institutional findings from Chapter 8. After all, the legal status of trade unions is, strictly speaking, a true institutional factor. More relevant is the observation that a high density of trade unions goes together with less income inequality.

With regard to state performance, state or market, or the left set of actors versus the right set of actors becomes of decisive importance only when public policy-making moves beyond the minimal provision of public goods. However, this opportunity of choice would become real only when nations have been modernized to such an extent that the state has large revenues. Economic development opens up the possibility of extensive public policy-making, meaning that we have to move to models that combine various factors in order to understand the significance of political orientations when economic or institutional factors are held constant.

As nations modernize, resources become available for civilian public expenditure. Whether this possibility becomes a reality in terms of a large welfare state involves a real choice or a resolution based on political ideology. As nations modernize their economy and social structure as well as institutionalize their public bodies, they face the basic choice between public resource allocation and market operations as the mechanism for apportioning scarce resources to semi-public or private goods. And politics seems to matter for the way that choice is resolved. This applies in particular in relation to non-military expenditures, which in advanced economies refer mainly to semi-public or private goods.

With regard to state stability, an interesting finding is that the position of the trade unions is more important than the strength of the left or the right in terms of the composition and ideological orientation of the government. Both the legal acknowledgement and the actual strength of trade unions in terms of membership tend to enhance state stability. This result needs to be tested in models that introduce other factors as well, in particular economic factors.

Conclusion

What is the true extent of freedom in macropolitics? If politicians have much scope for choosing policies, then we would expect to find that the ideological inclination of right versus left is of considerable importance. However, if background factors carry some weight, then the ideological composition of the elites, whether in democracies or non-democracies, would not be significant in shaping state stability and performance.

One major finding in this chapter is that the measures of short-term political instability do not co-vary with the indicators on long-term instability, interpreted first and foremost in Chapter 4 as regime instability.

Another set of interesting results reported on here indicates that the ideological orientations of leaders cannot be neglected, in particular with regard to state performance. Welfare state spending and income equality tends to be related to left-wing strength in government or in society, at least to some extent. It is important to include measures on the power and position of trade union actors when modelling state stability and performance.

Thirdly, there is the finding that the eventual degree of freedom for the individual actors matters little for regime duration. Thus state stability is not influenced by the presence of left-wing or right-wing authoritarianism. On the other hand, freedom of collective action tends to go together with state stability, but it reflects more the institutional web of government than the personal element in macropolitics. Could these traces of interaction be ascertained as causal relationships? Let us move on to test the combined models.

10

Legitimacy and Efficiency

Introduction

Taking a broad approach to the understanding of why states differ so considerably in terms of stability and performance, we ask if there are any general factors that might help us account for macropolitics. Are there conditions that have such an impact on the state that we are justified in designating them 'causes'? Can we formulate causal generalizations about the conditions for state stability and performance?

In this chapter we take a true Humean approach to the problem of causality in comparative politics, asking if the models introduced earlier are corroborated when multivariate techniques are employed. The regression technique allows us to look at the interaction between the three sets of key factors – to be referred to as condition sets – singled out in the analysis of independent variables in Chapters 7, 8 and 9: environmental, institutional and actor-related factors.

We have found traces of interaction – correlations – between a variety of conditions and state properties. Actually, once we start searching for causal models in comparative government, we find several, some stressing factors that operate within society: physical, social, economic and cultural variables. Other models underline the impact of institutional factors. Finally, there are the actor models, emphasizing the contribution of political parties and leaders. Looking at simple correlations between independent and dependent variables, there is considerable support for structural, institutional and actor-orientated models. But we need a theory that could clarify how various conditions underlined in different models interact in a causal structure. Legitimacy and efficiency, we suggest, are crucial links between the state and society.

Legitimacy and efficiency constitute the connections between the dependent and the independent variables in the framework of analysis outlined in chapters 1 and 6. These two factors would make sense of the findings in the explanatory analyses in chapters 7 to 9, because they offer the intermediate links that transfer the impact of the three condition sets onto state stability and state performance. The economic factors are especially important for state efficiency or capacity being conducive to stability and performance. The institutional factors influence in particular state legitimacy which impacts upon both stability and performance.

Conditions and causes

Thus far, we have identified both the dependent and the independent variables in the analysis. It is now time to take the final step to enquire into the causal relevance of models that combine the effects of several independent variables on the two dependent variables.

We focus on two state properties that are commonly considered interesting and relevant: state stability and state performance. It may be questioned whether state stability could be considered an ultimate goal. As with any organization, the operation of the state has results which may or may not be beneficial to their principals, that is, broader citizen groups in the population in relation to the state. Given the power resources that a state may command, the orientation of its decisions and activities is of crucial importance for the welfare of the population. Actually, states have different performance profiles. There are some which score high on basic evaluation criteria, such as liberty, equality and quality of life, and some whose performance is poor.

One may enquire into the extent to which states tend to be stable over time without any hidden bias in favour of the status quo. In a sense stability comes before performance, as states must be viable before they become responsible for an ambitious set of programmes that enhance liberty and equality. At the same time stability in no way implies performance, because there are states that maintain their power by repression, which as long as it is efficient may compensate for a lack of legitimacy.

Yet one cannot talk of a natural tendency for states to maintain themselves. States are aggregates of human behaviour, and their properties, such as regime longevity, result from the infinite number of individual actions and their unintended outcomes. Given a certain degree of freedom, single actors or collectivities with a common objective may enhance or reduce state stability. States only have intentions, interests and objectives in so far as there are persons acting on behalf of the state who propagate these wishes. Here, we ask if there are any general conditions that have an impact on the stability of the state.

The two key characteristics looked at here are measured by a choice of the following set of indicators: (A) state stability: average regime duration (REG); (B) state performance: civil and political rights (CIVIC), welfare expenditures (HED86) and income inequality (TOP 10). We found little support for the explanation of average inflation rates in the models derived from the literature. In Chapter 11 we take up the human development index again.

State stability is measured by looking at the average duration of regimes since 1945. State performance includes variables that have a bearing on the classical political values of liberty and equality. Thus we look at the institutionalization of civil and political rights, welfare expenditure and the extent of inequality in income distribution.

The findings from the empirical analysis on simple correlations between various background variables can only suggest where to look for causes. The simple correlation scores indicate merely that there is some kind of interaction between the independent and the dependent variable. Besides the possibility that the interaction is spurious, meaning that some other variable accounts for the interaction, we must interpret the empirical associations in such a way that they make sense from a theoretical point of view.

Now, we ask what is the significance of all the factors analysed in Chapters 7, 8 and 9 when they are combined in regression analyses – that is, at models which combine different independent variables. There is bound to be interaction among the independent variables, so we need to be aware of this in setting up our controls for the impact of some independent variables on the others. We examine regression models that are composed of social, institutional or actor-related factors in order to allow us to analyse the differential impact of various factors that may be interrelated.

The concept of causality is important in comparative politics, as the strong emphasis on methods indicates. Crucial questions about the relationship between democracy and affluence, the consequences of ethnic and religious fragmentation for state stability and the effects of alternative institutional frames for state performance, as well as the debate concerning the role of individual actors in macropolitical events, all touch upon this concept.

While not denying the heuristic value of case studies and comparative work, a Humean approach to macropolitical causation focuses on the equation same cause, same effect. Is it possible to arrive at causal generalizations about the impact of universal conditions on the state?

Eight sets of conditions have been identified looking at a large number of models that recognize a number of factors relevant for the explanation of the dependent variables. They are listed here with the indicators stated in parentheses. These are listed in Appendix 10.1.

(I)   Physical block: population (LNPOP), area (LNAREA) and type of climate (CLIMATE)

(II) Socio-economic block: agricultural employment (AGRI88), size of agricultural farms (FARMSIZE) and urbanization, 1960 (UR196)

(III) Economic block: logarithm of gross national product per capita (LNGNP), economic growth 1965–89 (EG6589), position in the world economy (COREP), openness of the economy (OPEN80) and external debt (DEBT/EXP)

Table 10.1   Physical block

	REG		CIVIC		HED86		TOP10	
	Beta	T	Beta	T	Beta	T	Beta	T
CLIMATE	.50	6.32	.23	2.62	.55	6.98	−.64	−5.51
LNPOP	−.09	−.90	.22	2.11	−.36	−3.69	−.24	−1.67
LNAREA	−.05	−.57	−.28	−2.70	.08	.86	.26	1.87
R²A	.22		.10		.31		.38	

(IV)   Economic system block: economic power concentration (ECONCON) and economic system type (ECOSYS)

(V)   Social block: ethno-linguistic fragmentation (ELF), ethno-linguistic domination (DOM1) and religious fragmentation (RF)

(VI)   Cultural block: Protestantism (PROT), Islamic culture (ISLAM), family structure (FAM), white settler culture (WHITESET)

(VII)   Institutional block: Electoral participation (TURNOUT), institutional sclerosis (SCLER1), parliamentarism (PARLAM), party system (PASIZE, MULTIPA), chamber system (UNICAM), federalism (FEDERAL), military rule (MILITGOV) and coalitions (GOVCOAL), military expenditure (MIE80) and trade union status (UNION)

(VIII)   Actor block: duration of leaders (AVELEAD), political party orientation (RIGHT2, NEWPOL), collective action (TRADEUD).

We look first at the explanatory relevance of each set of factors, and then proceed to formulate some theoretical notes that may account for the empirical findings.

Findings

The relevance of each block of conditions is indicated in tables 10.1 to 10.8, where the dependent variables are regressed one by one on the independent variables in the same block. Let us start with the physical block (see table 10.1).

The regression estimates indicate that the causal relevance for pure physical conditions for the state is low. State stability, civil and political rights and the size of welfare programmes has little to do with whether the state is large or small, in terms of population or territory. The only traces of a connection between size and state performance are the negative parameter for population size and welfare spending and the negative impact of a large area on state performance, which reflects the circumstance that welfare states tend to be rather small.

Surprisingly, the climate factor is revealed to be of relevance, following the

Table 10.2 Socio-economic block

| | REG | | CIVIC | | HED86 | | TOP10 | |
	Beta	T	Beta	T	Beta	T	Beta	T
FARMSIZE	.24	3.21	.40	6.20	.21	2.73	−.32	−2.33
AGRI88	−.23	−1.77	−.30	−2.70	−.40	−3.05	.23	.96
UR196	.35	2.73	.34	3.03	.18	1.39	−.14	−.55
R²A		.34		.50		.34		.19

Table 10.3A Economic block

| | REG | | CIVIC | | HED86 | | TOP10 | |
	Beta	T	Beta	T	Beta	T	Beta	T
COREP	.21	1.65	.22	1.94	.14	1.39	−.64	−2.22
EG6589	.12	1.56	−.01	−.02	.10	1.49	.09	.62
OPEN80	.26	3.09	−.15	−1.95	.41	5.77	−.23	−1.35
LNGNP	.36	2.59	.68	5.37	.39	3.36	.18	.53
R²A		.55		.63		.69		.33

Montesquieu model that a cold climate is more conducive to state stability and performance than a hot climate. It is also the case that income inequality tends to be higher in countries with a hot climate. But these relationships could be spurious. How about the frequently emphasized broad socio-economic variables? Table 10.2 offers an answer.

The interesting finding here is not that broad socio-economic factors, such as size of agricultural population or degree of urbanization, are relevant for state stability and performance. The forces of modernization are generally supportive of state stability and performance, although these factors in no way account for the variation. What is actually striking is that the FARMSIZE factor matters so much for REG and CIVIC, the latifundia system and its imitators reducing state stability and being conducive to poor state performance, whereas the tradition of a free peasantry has the opposite effect. Let us proceed to general economic factors (see table 10.3A).

Here, we have a few striking findings: politics and economics are strongly connected at the macropolitical level. One does not have to believe in economic determinism to acknowledge the strong impact of economic factors on regime durability, and for the institutionalization of civil and political rights and welfarism. The regression estimates are quite convincing on this point. Marx's emphasis on economic factors seems to be correct when it comes to the impact of major factors on the state, but it is not his special

Table 10.3B Economic block

	REG		CIVIC		HED86		TOP10	
	Beta	T	Beta	T	Beta	T	Beta	T
COREP	−.01	−.05	−.03	−.25	.11	1.04	.02	.06
EG6589	.29	2.09	−.13	−1.09	.11	.95	.09	1.13
OPEN80	.14	1.20	−.21	−2.01	.43	4.28	−.01	−.03
LNGNP	.16	1.12	.67	5.41	.36	2.99	.36	1.13
DEBT/EXP	.06	.45	−.03	−.33	.06	.63	−.02	−.08
R^2A	.09		.34		.38		.00	

Note: The OECD is not included in this analysis.

Table 10.4 Economic system block

	REG		CIVIC		HED86		TOP10	
	Beta	T	Beta	T	Beta	T	Beta	T
ECOSYS	.11	1.19	−.08	−1.41	.15	1.55	−.37	−1.91
ECONCON	−.71	−7.70	−.86	−15.71	−.68	−7.20	.57	2.97
R^2A	.42		.80		.38		.14	

model which is at stake here. The major finding is that the level of affluence is a major condition of state stability and two aspects of state performance, namely the respect for civil and political rights and welfare expenditure. But how about the debt factor (see table 10.3B)? Its impact on state stability and performance has to be identified in terms of a somewhat different selection of cases, since the debt data do not include the OECD countries.

The finding is that the variation in state stability and performance among all the states that are not members of the OECD set has little relationship to the debt problem, even though it is difficult to handle for several countries. The type of economic system in operation matters more (see table 10.4).

Most interestingly, the nature of the economic system is highly important for both state stability and state performance, in particular the institutionalization of civic and political rights. The more economic power is concentrated in the hands of the state or the more political control there is over the economy, the fewer civil and political rights there will be. There is some support for the hypothesis that economic systems which emphasize the state more than the market – state-capitalist systems and planned economies – tend not to respect human rights as much as regimes where the market plays an important role, such as decentralized capitalist systems

Table 10.5 Social block

	REG		CIVIC		HED86		TOP10	
	Beta	T	Beta	T	Beta	T	Beta	T
ELF	−.20	−1.51	−.07	−.55	−.24	−1.86	.71	4.01
RF	.05	.54	.03	.29	.15	1.53	−.15	−1.09
DOM1	.10	.72	.24	1.76	.27	1.99	.31	1.70
R²A	.04		.06		.16		.24	

Table 10.6 Cultural block

	REG		CIVIC		HED86		TOP10	
	Beta	T	Beta	T	Beta	T	Beta	T
PROT	.27	3.45	.24	3.17	.23	2.83	−.17	−1.32
ISLAM	.24	2.84	−.00	−.02	.23	2.57	−.35	−2.39
FAM	−.31	−3.49	−.46	−5.53	−.18	−1.92	.10	.75
WHITESET	.33	3.80	.16	1.92	.46	4.88	−.62	−4.35
R²A	.34		.42		.34		.37	

and mixed economies. But the relationship is by no means a universal one. There are capitalist economies in several countries that score low on CIVIC.

Regime durability, civil and political rights and welfare expenditure depend upon conditions such as level of affluence, an open economy and a small agricultural sector. Civil and political rights are difficult to introduce or maintain in societies where a large part of the population lives on the land, especially if the number of independent peasants is small. Surprisingly, economic factors seem to be of little relevance for income inequality. So how about the impact of social heterogeneity in terms of ethnic and religious fragmentation in the social structure? Table 10.5 has a few interesting findings.

Whereas the relevance of economic factors is beyond dispute, the findings are negative with regard to broad sociological models. Social fragmentation does not have such a strong connection with state stability or state performance as one might predict. This is a great surprise. The model that such social cleavages as ethnicity or religion, if wide enough, cause state instability is too simple. The mere presence of ethnic or religious fragmentation is not enough to shatter states. There is faint support for the hypothesis that the more ethnically homogeneous a society is, the less there would be of the institutionalization of civil and political rights. If ethnic or religious heterogeneity in themselves do not present major threats to regime duration and state performance, then what counts? Perhaps cultural factors (see table 10.6)?

Table 10.7 Institutional block

| | REG | | CIVIC | | HED86 | | TOP10 | |
	Beta	T	Beta	T	Beta	T	Beta	T
PASIZE	−.05	−.40	−.41	−6.19	−.06	−.43	−.00	−.00
MIE80	−.00	−.03	−.06	−1.31	.11	1.45	−.12	−.94
MILITGOV	−.33	−3.39	−.07	−1.24	−.24	−2.22	.00	.02
UNICAM	.09	1.06	−.00	−.05	.08	.80	−.00	−.01
TURNOUT	−.05	−.53	−.06	−1.18	.03	.27	−.21	−1.06
FEDERAL	.06	.76	−.01	−.12	.00	.01	.17	1.15
PARLAM	.25	2.46	.14	2.48	.11	.99	−.11	−.67
SCLER1	−.32	−2.94	−.10	−1.68	−.25	−2.12	.16	.78
UNION	−.00	−.03	.18	2.65	−.08	−.61	.11	.56
GOVCOAL	.38	1.86	−.04	−.31	.18	.80	−.43	−1.33
MULTIPA	−.32	−1.46	.29	2.43	.13	.56	.04	.10
R^2A	.48		.84		.41		.35	

Again, one hesitates: the cultural factors are much more relevant than the social ones. Yet it is not easy to interpret the findings of the regression analysis in a straightforward Humean manner. Religion is important for the state, as is the family structure, but is it causal relevance that we are talking about here? The high coefficients for family structure confirm the relevance of culture theory, but how to account for such strong interaction between one kind of family structure – liberty in obedience but inequality in inheritance (the Anglo-American system) – and state stability and strong state performance? Protestantism is conducive to both state stability and state performance, whereas an Islamic culture enhances only stability. There is also the indication of an impact from the spread of a white settler culture.

The discipline of comparative politics comprises the notion that social determinism is invalid and that structural conditions offer neither sufficient nor necessary conditions for state stability and performance. The logic here is that the economy and the structure of society present political man with a setting from which he may start building institutions as well as indulge in collective behaviour. How about institutional factors taken as a block or set of conditions (see table 10.7)?

Models including general institutional factors concur well. This pertains in particular to the explanation of the occurrence of civil and political rights, which quite naturally tend to accompany institutions such as parliamentarism and freedom of collective action. Their relevance for understanding state stability is obvious.

Several institutions are clearly relevant for understanding regime duration, civil and political rights and welfare expenditure. However, a truly interest-

Table 10.8 Actor block

	REG		CIVIC		HED86		TOP10	
	Beta	T	Beta	T	Beta	T	Beta	T
AVELEAD	.17	1.81	.51	6.04	.26	2.74	−.06	−.43
RIGHT2	−.31	−1.68	−.26	−1.59	−.10	−.53	−.26	−1.35
NEWPOL	.39	2.10	.28	1.69	−.01	−.07	.07	.32
TRADEUD	.27	2.85	−.02	−.20	.27	2.79	−.53	−3.38
R^2A	.09		.27		.13		.20	

ing finding in these regression estimates is that the relevance of institutional factors varies with the particular aspect of the state considered. They are particularly relevant to the understanding of the variation in the protection of civil and political rights: the positive experience of a parliamentary or multi-party system of government, freedom of collective action and the length of time that has elapsed since a modernized leadership was introduced.

The institutional age of the state and the absence of military government are most important for regime duration. Newly founded states tend to be unstable, particularly so if there is a risk of military intervention. Note that parliamentarism also appears to increase state stability. Whereas the impact of the experience of a military regime on state instability is obvious, given the way regime duration is measured, it remains to be seen whether the age of the state and parliamentary institutions still have an effect when controlling for other factors, mainly economic ones. Do actors also matter with regard to state stability and performance?

The general logic of comparative politics would lead us to assume that institutional factors are more important than actor-related factors. After all, when we are taking such a broad look at causality, with an analysis that covers a set of most general conditions applying to roughly 130 states, the personal element will probably be swamped. However, table 10.8 shows that actors are of consequence.

Two actor-related variables are important for state performance – the average number of leaders and the strength of the trade unions measured by their membership ratio. The latter is closely associated with the occurrence of welfare expenditure and greater income equality, as predicted in the 'does politics matter' literature. The former is strongly connected with the institutionalization of human rights. The average number of leaders tends to be large in states that honour civil and political rights, since rapid turnover is associated with a competitive atmosphere. Thus stability of leadership in the sense of a high average length of period in office may actually indicate poor state performance.

Causal principles

The formulation of causal models of state stability and performance may start from the circumstance that states are evaluated by the citizens in the country as well as on the international scene. State institutions are expected to operate in accordance with citizens' assumptions, and state actors face expectations about what they should do when functioning within public institutions. These expectations tend to be concentrated in a set of orientations clustering around the concept of legitimacy.

Legitimacy is a special belief in terms of which citizens orientate towards the state. A state may be regarded as legitimate from several points of view, one of which is the respect for human rights. When the state has a large degree of legitimacy, there is a special attitude among the citizens towards its public institutions, that is, the institutions are bestowed with a special quality, meaning that the regime is accepted as *valid in a moral sense*.

A model of the state also has to take into account how efficient the state is in terms of its operations. Whereas legitimacy refers to the value aspect, efficiency deals with the instrumental aspect. States have to be efficient in a number of activities if they are not to risk anarchy, anomie or annexation by another state. Efficient states deliver state capacity.

But efficiency is neutral in relation to ends. It may be employed for the sake of humanitarian objectives or for so-called reasons of state. Both legitimacy and efficiency have dark sides, as aggressively nationalistic regimes may be legitimized by their citizens and authoritarian regimes may employ massive amounts of repression to keep the state intact.

Where legitimacy is looking upon the state from the standpoint of the citizens, efficiency is looking upon the citizens from the standpoint of the state. Both offer different perspectives on the state, the first referring to political ends and the second to political means.

A simple model of state stability would point out efficiency and legitimacy as being of crucial importance. Efficiency is a necessary condition for state stability, but it is not a sufficient condition; legitimacy is a sufficient but not a necessary condition for state stability.

In the short term a legitimate state may manage to remain stable, even though it may perform poorly as a result of circumstances that are difficult to handle. A regime may have a considerable degree of legitimacy while at the same promising, but not actually delivering, policy outputs and outcomes considered acceptable by its citizens. However, in the long term legitimacy will be affected by state inefficiency, which reduces state stability.

A state may compensate for its lack of legitimacy by efficiency in holding back opposition to the regime. How long it may employ massive repression to resist the implications of a loss in legitimacy depends upon the circumstances, but a regime with a bad performance record, such as crushing human rights, will sooner or later find that its stability is at stake.

States may bolster their legitimacy by means of a special appeal to their citizens, such as propagating a populist ideology or nursing a culture with strong political overtones. For a time such a tactic may strengthen state stability, although the actual performance of the regime is poor. Yet, in the long term states cannot survive only on the basis of ideological ferment.

A stable state has to be an efficient state. It must possess resources and be capable of producing outcomes that make it legitimate in the eyes of its citizens or, alternatively, make it possible for it to suppress opposition. Thus state stability is a function of the factors that impact on state efficiency. Yet the factors that enhance legitimacy also matter for state stability, as in the end there is a limit to how long illegitimate states can survive.

A simple model of state performance would also include state efficiency, but it would have to underline legitimacy in the basic equation. Efficiency and legitimacy are necessary conditions for state performance, and a combination of the two constitutes a sufficient condition.

Both state capacity and legitimacy impact on state performance. When citizens face a poor performance record, then doubts about government legitimacy will arise. Similarly, good performance records sustain legitimacy. Governments look upon state performance as one basic tool for sustaining the legitimacy of the state.

The sources of state performance are to be found among, on the one hand, general social and economic conditions, and, on the other, specific political institutions that make for state capability or improve on state legitimacy. Thus citizens may regard the state as legitimate because the overall living conditions are endurable. Economic factors play a large role here. Higher levels of affluence are conducive to favourable attitudes towards the state, especially when state activities have been perceived as directed at citizen welfare for a long time.

Citizens require that the policy outputs or outcomes of the actions of their leaders result in decent standards of living. However, political legitimacy can be sustainable even in the midst of weak state performance if there are features that compensate for the negative impact of bad economic conditions. Special cultural factors may give the state an aura of self-evident existence, such as in Islamic fundamentalism. Institutions which have been in existence for some time or which offer participation and power-sharing may enhance state legitimacy. Finally, leaders in general and political actors in particular may provide the state with a temporary legitimacy by invoking charisma or a totalitarian ideology at the stage of mass mobilization.

Efficiency in state operations is crucial when performance is assessed by citizens. The concept of efficiency or effectiveness is tied up with the idea of accomplishing goals. Efficiency refers to means and not to ends. States may be efficient in relation to different ends. These state objectives extend all the way from the humanitarian, such as social welfare and human rights, to the classical reasons of state, in the form of geopolitical goals covering state power and territorial integrity.

When humanitarian objectives are at stake, the performance profile of a state is also at stake. It may be assessed in terms of general objectives such as the general values of politics since the French Revolution – liberté, egalité and fraternité. The humanitarian approach to state performance includes a vast number of state activities.

State performance requires not only the capacity for but also the commitment towards the promotion of the interests of the citizens in terms of a number of aspects, including human rights and quality of life. Looking at the state from the perspective of state interests, other objectives become the criteria for assessment. The worst outcome from this perspective would be the disintegration of the state, the collapse of the regime or the annexation of the state's territory by another foreign power. When states are evaluated from the standpoint of stability, then achieving legitimacy by means of a good performance record is not a *sine qua non*.

State stability and performance thus depend on state efficiency and legitimacy. States that are not efficient cannot be stable. States that are not legitimate can remain stable for a period of time by employing huge resources to counteract opposition. States that are not performing well can be efficient but lack the commitment to humanitarian aims. States that are not efficient cannot display a good performance record.

State stability depends on both environmental factors and institutional conditions. Economic factors are directly relevant for state efficiency as they offer vital means for the implementation of state objectives. What is at stake is the access to affluence, which may in turn depend on the type of economic system, trade patterns and the position of the country in the world economy, because all these may have an impact on economic growth. Cultural factors may also influence state efficiency. For example, the orientation of religious systems towards spiritual and material matters may make a crucial difference to both the ends and the means of state policies.

State performance is also related to environmental factors and institutions. Firstly, economic conditions must be such that good state performance is feasible. Secondly, there must also be legitimacy in the sense that the state is firmly committed to humanitarian objectives. This would tend to reflect values more than capacity, meaning that cultural and institutional conditions are particularly significant. State performance demands more than just efficiency, because it requires the state to promote its legitimacy not simply by enhancing its own existence but also by delivering social outcomes that are in the interests of the population.

Causal models

State stability and performance are both functions of legitimacy and efficiency, though in different ways. And state legitimacy and efficiency are affected by the three general sets of conditions identified here – environmental, institutional and actor-related conditions. State stability is endangered when the legitimacy of the state is declining or when its activities are becoming more inefficient. And state performance is reduced by lack of efficiency or conduct that reduces legitimacy.

Given that efficiency is important for state stability, we predict that economic resources will also have a profound impact. What counts is neither economic growth nor relative deprivation; it is the level of affluence that makes state capacity possible. Ethnic or religious fragmentation does not necessarily mean state inefficiency. Social heterogeneity may have a tremendous impact on politics in a country, but it does not translate automatically into state instability or a bad performance record. The emphasis on affluence and its political consequences is not meant as a new kind of economic determinism. It simply underlines economic factors, though not those prevalent in Marxist analysis.

Political institutions hamper state stability in so far as they reduce state legitimacy. Thus we predict that a transitory regime overthrowing an established institution would face profound legitimacy problems. Military governments, for example, result in state instability.

Legitimacy is especially important for state performance, although efficiency also enters the equation, because state performance results from efficient activities with regard to humanitarian ends. Certain institutions enhance political legitimacy, such as the recognition of a multi-party system, the existence of clear property rights and the dispersion of power to several independent centres.

State performance will be good only where the state is highly efficient, that is, in countries where there are abundant resources. But that is not enough. State performance will be good only in countries where there is a culture or a system of institutions that look upon state legitimacy as deriving from an emphasis upon the individual. Cultural factors, such as the occurrence of Islamic fundamentalism, may be decisive in directing the state towards performance in accordance with humanitarian objectives.

The factors that reduce state performance and state stability will be found among those that reduce efficiency or legitimacy, such as poverty, the concentration of political or economic power and certain cultural factors that reduce efficiency and legitimacy *per se*. We now move to the final step in the enquiry, looking at regression analyses which combine factors from the condition sets introduced above.

The theory about causality at the macrolevel of politics launched here implies three hypotheses. First, economic conditions, by strengthening state efficiency, should enhance both state stability and state performance. Second, institutional conditions, by enhancing state legitimacy, should bolster both state stability and state performance. Third, actor-related factors may have an impact only in so far as there exists a substantial degree of freedom for individual action when social forces and institutional conditions have been taken into account. It is an open question how great is the degree of

Table 10.9 Mixed model 1: REG

Variable	Beta	T
LNGNP	.35	1.79
FEDERAL	.08	1.00
PROT	.15	1.86
ECOSYS	−.02	−.20
ELF	.08	.87
OPEN80	.29	3.06
FAM	−.18	−1.48
WHITESET	.00	.01
CLIMATE	.16	1.34
SCLER1	.02	.17
AGRI60	.09	.45
R^2A = .53		

freedom, just as whether economic, cultural or institutional conditions matter most.

A number of mixed models are tested below, and these display surprisingly high empirical and systematic import. We will start with regime stability: the first model includes several of the factors that proved relevant in the analyses above; the following mixed model shows those factors that may be singled out as being important.

State stability (REG)

We have found a number of factors that tend to accompany state stability. Let us take these factors and regress state stability onto all of them simultaneously. Table 10.9 gives the results.

Regime duration has its sources in economic and cultural factors. The acceptable explanatory power of the combined model implies that we search for the conditions for state stability among economic factors such as level of affluence and openness of the economy, as well as the extent of individualism in the culture. It is notable that one type of religion – Protestantism in its various forms – and the type of climate also appear to be important. Yet one may examine another combined model which includes only the factors that have some significance in the model above (see table 10.10).

The most significant finding in table 10.10 is the importance of two economic factors, the openness of the economy and the level of affluence. A high level of affluence and a high level of exports and imports is conducive to both state efficiency and legitimacy, which both enhance stability from a general point of view. One should note that the economic system factor is

Table 10.10   Mixed model 2: REG

Variable	Beta	T
OPEN80	.30	3.30
ELF	.08	.87
FEDERAL	.08	.98
PROT	.14	1.89
CLIMATE	.15	1.54
FAM	−.15	−1.49
LNGNP	.29	2.12
R^2A = .55		

not relevant for understanding state stability; what matters is the overall level of affluence.

State stability stems in general from favourable economic conditions, including the openness of the economy. States which have considerable interaction with the international community tend to be more stable than states with a closed economy. It is not therefore the case that all the uncertainties resulting from the world economy spill over into state instability. The openness of the economy has an impact that is independent of the fact that many countries with an exceptionally open economy are also rich.

Again, there are results for climate and the family structure, which is all the more astonishing now that other factors are kept constant. Yet their impact must be explained by the fact that the difference in climate and family structure, mainly between Western Europe and Africa or Asia Minor, co-incides with an underlying cultural factor – principally individualism. We note that the findings allude to the fact that federalism as an institution has hardly any effect on the stability of the state.

Civil and political rights

Table 10.11 contains the first step in regressing the status of civil and political rights, including a number of factors that have proved to be relevant in the above analyses.

Here, interestingly, we arrive at the opposite conclusion to that of the stability models, namely that economic system factors are more important than the overall level of affluence. There is one institutional factor, the size of the largest party, which has a profound impact on democratic performance.

Two interpretations are possible here. Either states which do not respect civil and political rights install one-party systems in order to enhance the ruling regime, or one major political party consolidates its power by

Table 10.11 Mixed model 1: CIVIC

Variable	Beta	T
FEDERAL	.09	1.69
ECOSYS	−.13	−2.34
OPEN80	−.00	.10
ISLAM	−.01	−.20
ELF	−.07	−1.20
PASIZE	−.19	−2.57
SCLER1	.01	.06
CLIMATE	−.13	−1.77
FAM	.00	.05
ECONCON	−.41	−3.96
AGRI60	−.19	−1.50
LNGNP	.17	1.18

$R^2A = .84$

restricting civil and political rights. It may be argued, though, that the importance of the institutional factor – the size of the largest political party – is rather obvious, as there are clear institutional ramifications pertaining to political rights.

However, the finding that a dirigiste economic system is a strong threat to civil and political rights is not self-evident. Here we have a clue as to the resolution of Lipset's problem of accounting for the association between affluence and democracy. It has to do with the connection between the type of economic system and the protection of civil and political rights. In countries where the state has a pronounced influence over economic life, such as in capitalist-state or planned economy systems, civil and political rights are somewhat precarious. And these economic systems tend to prevail in countries with a low level of affluence. Besides, an economy with a substantial proportion of the population in agriculture seems to be characteristic of many dictatorships.

Perhaps it is somewhat startling to find that federalism turns out to be not as significant a factor as was predicted in the federal models. All other things being equal, a federal state enhances the institutionalization of civil and political rights and promotes democratic performance, but the impact of federalism is considerably less than the size of the largest party. Again, there is the finding that the climate matters, whereas the cultural factors, for example, an Islamic orientation, do not. This makes sense for the Fertile Crescent, as in this part of the world, which has a hot climate, there is a profound lack of civil and political rights.

Table 10.12   Mixed model 2: CIVIC

Variable	Beta	T
CLIMATE	−.12	−1.84
FEDERAL	.08	1.78
PASIZE	−.22	−3.12
ECOSYS	−.11	−2.05
LNGNP	.35	3.46
ECONCON	−.42	−4.35
R^2A = .84		

Table 10.12 confirms the thesis that the economic system, and not overall affluence, is the best predictor of the status of civil and political rights.

It should not be expected that the various modes of state performance have the same conditions. The classical political values of the French Revolution in their different expressions may be conditioned by economic, institutional and actor-related factors in different ways. Thus liberté expresses the status of human rights in general, whereas égalité reflects the capacity and willingness of the state to engage in policies that reduce the differences between rich and poor.

Welfare spending

Tables 10.13 and 10.14 show the regressions for the amount of welfare spending by the state.

Spending on welfare state programmes arises from Schumpeter's tax state, Keynes's demand-spurring government, utilitarianist welfarism or Wildavsky's equalitarianism. The famous Wagner model predicts that affluence is a necessary and sufficient condition for a state to be strongly orientated towards welfare spending. The regression estimates only partially confirm Wagner's law, as there is ample support here for the role of factors other than economic.

There is also corroboration of Cameron's model of the crucial importance of an open economy. Welfare programmes partly compensate small states for the strains and risks that are involved in an advanced economy. At the same time welfare spending depends on other factors, making affluence only a necessary condition but not a sufficient one. The importance of political factors such as the absence of a strong right and the presence of a strong left is a very neat finding.

Table 10.13 Mixed model 1: HED86

Variable	Beta	T
MILITGOV	−.16	−1.80
ISLAM	−.02	−.25
ELF	.02	−.24
LEFT2	.12	1.41
OPEN80	.28	3.16
FAM	−.09	−.78
ECOSYS	.00	.00
CLIMATE	.11	1.09
SCLER1	.03	.23
ECONCON	−.12	−.96
AGRI60	.17	.96
LNGNP	.39	1.98
R^2A = .58		

Table 10.14 Mixed model 2: HED86

Variable	Beta	T
LEFT2	.14	2.12
LNGNP	.56	6.98
OPEN80	.29	3.57
R^2A = .58		

As table 10.14 shows, state efficiency counts for much in relation to welfare spending, explaining the strong impact of economic factors. Yet here we also see the relevance of bringing in political actors and their ideological orientation when trying to understand state performance.

Income inequality

Tables 10.15 and 10.16 contain the regressions for income inequality. When analysing income inequality the number of cases drops considerably, as it is difficult to get access to data concerning income distribution in several countries. The regression models below are based on only 48 countries. Let us start with a general mixed model.

Income inequality is a performance aspect of the state that is less dependent on economic factors and more related to cultural and institutional ones. What matters for the extent of income inequality is not the overall level of

Table 10.15 Mixed model 1: TOP10

Variable	Beta	T
GOVCOAL	−.53	−2.30
ECOSYS	−.11	−.55
FAM	.27	1.62
ELF	.00	.01
ISLAM	−.36	−2.25
LEFT2	−.12	−.78
CLIMATE	−.49	−2.14
OPEN80	.09	.47
AGRI60	.07	.24
ECONCON	.01	.06
SCLER1	−.10	.22

$R^2A = .47$

Table 10.16 Mixed model 2: TOP10

Variable	Beta	T
GOVCOAL	−.46	−3.03
FAM	.20	1.47
ISLAM	−.42	−3.21
CLIMATE	−.34	−2.47
LEFT2	−.18	−1.51

$R^2A = .54$

affluence but the extent of power-sharing and the culture of the country. It is most interesting that the indicator on the extent to which government coalitions tend to be formed has such a clear negative impact on income inequality, since power-sharing reduces economic injustices.

Table 10.16 shows that countries which are run by means of political institutions that are inclined to reduce power-sharing tend to be characterized by extensive income inequality. Most interesting is the strong evidence for the climatic factor, pointing at income inequality particularly in hot areas of the world. Equally interesting is the finding that a stronger position for Islam is conducive to income equality. A few of the Islamic countries are rich, which makes greater income equality feasible, but the hostility of Islam towards acquisitiveness (for example, charging a high rate of interest when lending money) should also be emphasized. At the same time we note that there is little support for a direct link between affluence and income equality. Culture matters more than economics here.

Conclusion

State stability is affected by the overall level of affluence of a country in combination with a high degree of openness in the economy. Institutional sclerosis does not matter when other factors are taken into account. As stated in Chapter 8, the introduction of institutions associated with military regimes implies fundamental state instability, which, as we saw in this chapter, tends to occur in poor countries with weak and more or less closed economies.

State performance has a substantial economic footing, but institutions and actors are also of some consequence. The extent of civil and political liberties in a state is connected particularly with the position of the largest political party. Less party competition reduces the likelihood of establishing and maintaining human rights. A major finding is that the structure of the economic system has a profound impact on the occurrence of civil and political rights, as greater political involvement in the economy, especially in the form of state ownership and state control over markets, is negative.

Welfare state spending cannot exist without abundant economic resources, but affluence is not a sufficient condition for the rise of the welfare state. Politics as measured by the position of leftist movements has to be recognized as being of crucial importance. Cultural factors show up in several findings, such as the influence of the family structure – individualism – on state stability and the institutionalization of civil and political rights.

The major negative finding is that, in mixed models, we have little sign of any particularly detrimental effects of ethnic and religious fragmentation on state stability and performance. This is the more startling because it is not in agreement with the common-sense notion about ethnicity and religious heterogeneity on the one hand and causality in macropolitics on the other.

The relevance of a variety of economic factors for state stability and state performance is striking. State stability cannot be approached simply as a question of the choice of the appropriate institutions. There has to be a functioning economy whose operations result in a decent standard of living. The existence of civil and political rights has a strong connection with the nature of political institutions, such as the position of the largest political party, but the structure of the economic system matters more, in particular the role of the state in the economy (see tables 10.17 and 10.18).

Put another way, economic determinism is wrong, because economic conditions have to be complemented by other factors. Welfare spending is influenced by the political factors referring to the power of the left. The level of income equality proceeds from institutions that guarantee a high level of

Table 10.17 The conditions for state stability

Variable	Beta	T
PROT	.23	3.21
FAM	−.10	−1.15
LNGNP	.54	5.95
$R^2A = .50$		

Table 10.18 The conditions for civil and political rights

Variable	Beta	T
ECOSYS	−.22	−3.67
PROT	.13	2.19
FAM	−.35	−4.29
LNGNP	.26	3.23
SCLER1	−.16	−1.91
$R^2A = .69$		

power-sharing as well as from specific institutions in cooler parts of the world and a collectivist culture such as Islam.

The overall finding is that economic factors set the framework for state stability and performance. State efficiency deriving from affluence and an open economy is a *sine qua non*. These are at most necessary conditions, however. Both state stability and state performance are conditioned by specific institutional factors, such as military rule and the basic structure of the party system, which either decrease or increase state legitimacy. Political and civil rights are conditioned more by the type of economic system than by the level of affluence, especially the extent to which economic resources are concentrated in the hands of the state. What are the policy implications of these findings? Let us try to analyse transition models, focusing on the transformation of authoritarian regimes into democracies.

APPENDIX 10.1 Variables and measures

AGRI60, AGRI88: proportion of those working in the agricultural sector, 1960, 1988 (World Bank: *Social Indicators of Development 1990*, 1991).

AVELEAD: average number of years of leadership duration (Bienen and Van de Walle, 1991).

CIVIC: civil and political rights (Gastil; Freedom House); the higher the score, the greater the extent of civil and political rights (Appendix 5.1).

CLIMATE: 0 = tropical rainy; 1 = dry; 2 = temperate, warm, rainy; 3 = cool (*Shorter Oxford Economic Atlas*).

COREP: position in the world economy: 0 = periphery; 1 = semi-periphery; 2 = core (Terlouw, 1989).

DEBT/EXP: size of foreign debt as a percentage of exports (World Bank, 1992).

DEBT/GNP: size of foreign debt as a percentage of GNP (World Bank, 1992).

DOM1: size of dominant ethno-linguistic group (Rustow, 1967).

ECONCON: relative proportion of economic concentration: public sector, private sector and foreign (Vanhanen, 1990).

ECOSYS: type of economic system: 0 = decentralized capitalism; 1 = mixed capitalism; 2 = state capitalism; 3 = mixed socialism; 4 = socialism (Gastil, 1987).

EG6589: economic growth, 1965–89 (World Bank, 1991).

ELF: ethno-linguistic fractionalization (Taylor and Hudson, 1972).

FAM: Todd's classification orders eight different family systems. A higher score stands for greater collectivism: (1) absolute nuclear family; (2) anomic family; (3) authoritarian family; (4) egalitarian nuclear family; (5) anomic and egalitarian nuclear family; (6) exogamous community family; (7) endogamous community family; (8) African family system (Todd, 1983).

FARMSIZE: proportion of family-based farming, 1970–80, measuring the strength of a tradition of free peasants (Vanhanen, 1990).

FEDERAL: extent of federalism: 0 = non-federalism; 1 = federalism (Sullivan, 1991).

GOVCOAL: experience of coalition government: 0 = other kinds; 1 = one-party government; 2 = multi-party governments (Sullivan, 1991).

HDI: human development index for 1987 (United Nations Development Programme, 1990).

HED86: health and education expenditures (United Nations Development Programme, 1990); the higher the percentage figure, the greater the proportion of education and health spending as a percentage of GDP.

INF8090: average annual rate of inflation 1980–90 (World Bank, 1992).

ISLAM: proportion of Muslims around 1975 (Barrett, 1982).

LEFT1: electoral support for political parties that were centre-left or left-wing at an election at the end of the 1980s (*Encyclopedia Britannica Book of the Year*, 1990).

LEFT2: modification of LEFT1 to include authoritarian regimes (*Encyclopedia Britannica Book of the Year*, 1990).

LNAREA: logarithm for area of the state (*Encyclopedia Britannica Book of the Year*, 1990).

LNGNP: logarithm for GNP per capita, 1989 (World Bank, 1991; World Tables).

LNPOP: logarithm for population around 1980 (*Encyclopedia Britannica Book of the Year*, 1990).

MIE80: Military expenditure, 1980 (Sipri, 1990).

MILITGOV: experience of military leaders: 0 = no experience, 1 = existing; (Sullivan, 1991).

MULTIPA: extent of multi-party systems: 0 = non-multi-party; 1 = multi-party (Sullivan, 1991).

NEWPOL: left–right scale of regimes: −1 = left-wing authoritarian; −0.5 = left-wing domination; 0 = indifferent; 0.5 = right-wing domination; 1 = right-wing authoritarian (Derbyshire and Derbyshire, 1991).

OPEN80: Impex 1980 = import + export as a proportion of GNP (Summers and Heston, 1991).

PARLAM: extent of parliamentary system: 0 = non-parliamentary regimes; 1 = regimes with parliamentarism (Sullivan, 1991).

PARLSYS: 1 = parliamentarism; 2 = limited presidentialism; 3 = unlimited presidentialism; 4 = communist regime; 5 = military regime; 6 = traditional regime (Derbyshire and Derbyshire, 1991).

PASIZE: size of the largest party in elections during the 1980s (Vanhanen, 1990).

POLORI: modification of NEWPOL: left–right scales of regimes: −1 = left-wing authoritarian; 0 = non-authoritarian; +1 = right-wing authoritarian (Derbyshire and Derbyshire, 1991).

PROT: proportion of Protestants (Barrett, 1982).

REG: average duration of regimes in years since 1945; the higher the score, the more stable the state (authors' index).

RF: religious fragmentation (Barrett, 1982).

RIGHT1: electoral support for political parties that are centre-right or right-wing at an election at the end of the 1980s (*Encyclopedia Britannica Book of the Year*, 1990).

RIGHT2: modification of RIGHT1 to include authoritarian regimes (*Encyclopedia Britannica Book of the Year*, 1990).

SCLER1: consolidation of modernized leadership (Black, 1966).

SCLER2: starting-point for social and economic transformation (Black, 1966).

TOP10: income inequality; the higher the score, the greater the extent of income inequality (World Bank, *Social Indicators of Development 1990*, 1991).

TOP20: income inequality (income share of the top 20 per cent of the population); the higher the score, the greater the extent of income inequality (World Bank, *Social Indicators of Development 1990*, 1991).

TRADEUD: level of trade union membership (Sullivan, 1991).

TURNOUT: electoral participation in terms of the entire population (Vanhanen, 1990).

UNICAM: type of chamber system: 0 = other than single chamber system; 1 = single chamber system (Sullivan, 1991).

UNION: status of trade unions: 0 = banned; 1 = legal (Sullivan, 1991).

UR196, UR199: Urban population in 1960, 1990 (United Nations Development Programme, 1992).

WHITESET: countries with European cultural tradition of some kind: 0 = non-European settlement; 1 = European settlement (authors' index).

11

Transition to Democracy

Introduction

Hitherto, the analysis has been mainly static: we have been preoccupied primarily by cross-sectional analyses looking at the country variation in state properties during the postwar period. It is time now to consider the dynamic implications of some of these models, such as the major state transformations taking place in both Eastern Europe and the Third World since the late 1980s and early 1990s. Is it possible to draw on the findings in the cross-sectional analyses in order to enhance the understanding of the conditions for the transformation of authoritarian regimes or dictatorships into democracies?

This chapter discusses the logic of regime transformation at the level of macropolitics by employing a few of the findings presented earlier in order to portray transformation processes in Eastern Europe, Latin America, Africa and Asia. Following the models that specify the conditions for one crucial aspect of a democratic regime – the establishment of civil and political rights – the prospects for a successful transition to democracy depend on: (1) level of affluence, (2) type of economic system, and (3) choice and development of political institution (such as parliamentarism, presidentialism or federalism).

Democracy and the market economy

The transformation process faced by countries in both the former communist bloc and the Third World involves not just the transition to a democratic regime; in addition there is the basic choice of which economic system to adopt. Both problems are institutional ones, meaning that they require a long-term commitment from the state to support new rules.

It is true that this double problem is most acute in Eastern Europe, but in the Third World the transition towards new institutions also involves the

	Politics	
Economics	Democracy	Dictatorship
Market exchange mechanisms	I: USA, Switzerland, Japan	II: Chile (1973–88), Zaïre
Extensive state involvement	III: Scandinavian countries, Austria	IV: USSR, Argentina (1980), Brazil (1980)

Figure 11.1 Political and economic regimes

restructuring of economic systems. In addition, several of the dictatorships now seeking democratic rule wish to do away with economic institutions that are at odds with the smooth functioning of a market economy – either a planned economy or a state-capitalist framework.

Thus, when analysing the problems connected with the dismantling of authoritarian principles in favour of the institutionalization of democratic ones, it is also necessary to pay attention to the search for new economic system institutions: the two issues are closely linked. On the one hand, there is the distinction between democracy and dictatorship, and, on the other, that between market-dominated economic systems and systems where the state plays a major role. It is absolutely essential to recognize from the outset that these distinctions are not dichotomies, but always remain interrelated. There is a choice not only between alternative democratic formulas but also to some extent in the framing of economic institutions that may be more or less market orientated. This results in the system combinations shown in figure 11.1. A number of countries attempt to make the transition from type IV to type I, whether they formerly adhered to the planned economy model, as in Eastern Europe, or to the state-capitalist model, as in many Third World countries. Some countries, looking for some sort of mixed economy, wish to move from type IV to type III.

We have already seen that such general factors as affluence, culture and institutional elements constrain what is feasible with regard to the innovatory introduction of democratic institutions and market-type economic systems. Which conditions are necessary or sufficient for a stable democratic state is a matter of contention in the social sciences. Some scholars have underlined economic factors whereas others have emphasized political institutions. Tocqueville's position that the culture of a civil society is crucial is well known:

> If I have hitherto failed in making the reader feel the important influence of the practical experience, the habits, the opinions, in short, of the customs of the Americans upon the maintenance of their institutions, I have failed in the principal object of my work. (Tocqueville, [1835–40] 1990: 322–3)

The causal relevance of economic factors to politics in the system transformations that take place in authoritarian states comprises two different
links. Firstly, there are the implications of a transition from heavy state
involvement in the economy towards a *laissez-faire* or democratic system
(and vice versa, since these two transitions affect each other reciprocally).
Secondly, there is a causal connection between general economic factors such
as the level of affluence and the prospects for change in either the political or
the economic system.

Here, following the findings in Chapter 10, we wish to emphasize not only
the role played by general economic factors, but also the significance of the
creation of new economic institutions for the feasibility of a democratic
regime. We look at the logic of state transition and the interaction between
democracy and economic factors, and finally pay attention to a concrete
institutional problem – what kind of democracy is feasible?

From dictatorship to democracy

Theoretically, one may distinguish two ways of modelling transitions of
political regimes. On the one hand it is possible to focus on major economic
and social forces, as did Barrington Moore in his *Social Origins of Dictatorship and Democracy* (1966). Or one may pay attention to the very circumstances and events that play a major role in country-specific transition
processes, as in *Transitions from Authoritarian Rule: Tentative Conclusions
about Uncertain Democracies*, by Guillermo O'Donnell and Phillip
Schmitter.

It is important to underline, as Adam Przeworski does in his *Democracy
and the Market* (1991), that the breakdown of an authoritarian regime does
not mean that democracy will automatically follow:

> The central question concerning transitions is whether they lead to consoli-
> dated democracy, that is, a system in which the politically relevant forces
> subject their values and interests to the uncertain interplay of democratic
> institutions and comply with the outcomes of the democratic process.
> (Przeworski, 1991: 51)

Processes dismantling a dictatorship may be reversed, as in Czechoslovakia in 1968, in Brazil in 1974 and in Poland in 1981, or the change process
may get 'stuck' between dictatorship and democracy, as in Romania in
1990. In addition, a new authoritarian regime may take advantage of the
uncertainties from the breakdown of a dictatorship to install a new undemocratic regime, as happened in Iran after the fall of the Shah in 1979.

There are two aspects to the transfer from an authoritarian to a democratic regime. First, there is the short-term, almost technical, issue of establishing democratic institutions, such as introducing competitive elections and

writing a constitution. Second, there is the much more difficult problem of promoting factors that are conducive to long-term democratic stability. Whereas the actual replacing of dictatorial rule with democratic institutions tends to be dramatic if not spectacular, involving protest or violence as the old rulers try to hang on to their privileges, the accomplishment of democratic stability is a slow process that is not easily brought about by fiat.

One step in the political transformation process is the constitutional stage – a microperspective that focuses on the choice of institutions almost in a contractarian sense. Yet at the same there is the basic argument that political transformation is moulded by macroforces – for example, the degree to which civil society has developed is decisive for success (Diamond, Linz and Lipset, 1990; Rose, 1992), and reflects whether a country's society is backward or not.

One often encounters in the literature a distinction between two patterns of transition: that of Southern Europe and that in Latin America. As a consequence there is a debate about what system transition could mean in Eastern Europe, in particular whether there are great risks for a process that leads to so-called *dictablandas*, or a mixture of dictatorship and democracy. Typical of system transition in Latin America has been its circular pattern, the uncertainty both in the process and of the actual outcomes as well as the attending negative aspects of violence, political unrest and economic instability (O'Donnell, Schmitter and Whitehead, 1986; O'Donnell, 1994). However, the unique process of regime transition in Southern Europe involved not only the shift away from dictatorship but also the consolidation of democracy.

In Latin America authoritarian rule has typically been introduced after a putsch or coup from the military. The *causus belli* referred to by the military junta or its caudillo is the supposed threat to 'national security' by subversive or anti-national elements. The next stage is the implementation of a bureaucratic-authoritarian regime, which attempts to stabilize the overthrow of democracy by suppressing civil society and its voluntary organizations. However, force is not enough, as there is a constant surge for any kind of legitimacy that could motivate the prolongation of authoritarianism. Even though a dictatorship in Latin America may fall back on the forces of the state, employing a ruthless secret police to track down pockets of resistance, there is an assumption even among the adherents of authoritarian regimes that more openness of procedure must eventually be resorted to.

The first step towards dismantling dictatorship is most often initiated from within the regime, when it is looking for ways to increase its legitimacy by formal concessions to democratic principles. 'Tutelary' or 'protected' democracy may be the aim, in order to stem any opposition. Such new flexibility (*casuismo*) may also reflect internally competing factions. But the tradition of military *caudillismo* or *continuismo* in Latin America has not been able to break the commitment towards democratic legitimacy. A process of liberalization (*apertura*) is bound to follow such a long period of exceptional rule, if only to have non-authoritarian institutions to display internationally – *par Ingles ver* (for the English).

Regime transition processes contain a logic of their own, but it is seldom the logic of continuity and linear development. There are several uncertain stages between the first step towards liberalization and the final stage of fully institutionalized democracy. The processes in Southern Europe were different to those in Latin America, particularly with regard to the steady progression in the former and the many fluctuations in the latter. The distinction between the more general liberalization stage ending the authoritarian regime and the decisive point in time when democratic procedures *sensu stricto*, such as secret and free elections, are introduced was much shorter and less painful in Greece, Spain and Portugal than in Argentina, Brazil and Chile. It turned out to be possible both to confine the activities of the military to the barracks and restrict populist leaders to democratic procedures.

The regime transitions in Italy after the Second World War and in Spain after Franco's death were based explicitly on a negotiated pact (*reform pactada*) to change the prevailing system (*poderes de hecho*) in a piecemeal fashion. In both Portugal and Greece the regime transitions took the form of a *ruptura pactada*, or an agreement among major actors to overturn the established order in a radical fashion. The resurrection of civil society was much faster and more profound in Southern Europe than in Latin America, where the feeling of irreversibility is not that strong, reflecting the lingering threat from the right (*trama negra*) as well as the frustration of the left (*desencanto*) (Schmitter, 1986). The transition stages in Eastern Europe involved both types of process.

O'Donnell and Schmitter state, in concluding their analyses of transitions from authoritarian to democratic regimes:

> Political democracy, then, usually emerges from a nonlinear, highly uncertain, and imminently reversible process involving the cautious definition of certain spaces and moves on a multilayered board (of chess). (O'Donnell and Schmitter, 1986: 70)

This generalization does not seem to fit the recent transformations involving communist regimes. Here the process, thus far, has been irreversible, yet a truly consolidated democracy has not been reached. At the same time a few communist states linger on, meaning that not every communist country need crumble. The largest remaining state adhering to Marxist values, China, has initiated reform processes in order to reduce the impact of the Leninist model of party rule and a planned economy.

The democratization process may be affected if it involves the restoration of democracy: if there is a legacy of democracy, as, for example, in Czechoslovakia, then the legitimation problem will not be that difficult. The probability of dismantling the predecessor regime calls into question the legitimacy and efficiency of its successor. The road to democracy may appear to be a mixture of continuity and deliberate gradualism, as in Greece (Diamandouros, 1986), or it may entail a certain amount of vacillation back and forth between democracy and military rule, as in Turkey (Sunar and Sayari, 1986).

The concentration on political institutions may imply that important social conditions are neglected, in particular economic factors. A number of recent studies look at the interaction between the establishment of democracy and the spread of market institutions in the economy (Rueschemeyer et al., 1992). First we look at the interaction between democracy and the overall level of affluence, following the classical Lipset model (1959) of a strong association between the two (Cutright, 1963).

Economic conditions for democratic transition

In Chapter 7 we referred to the empirical association between a country's level of affluence and its democratic institutions, such as the establishment of civil and political rights. It is a widely debated question whether this correlation could be interpreted theoretically as a causal relationship – affluence being either a necessary or a sufficent condition for a democratic regime (Marks and Diamond, 1992).

If a high level of affluence is a necessary condition for a viable democracy, then the prospects for the third wave of democratization to succeed in the long term are grim indeed. The average income per capita in Eastern Europe and in most Third World countries is not large enough to maintain the momentum of democratization. If a high level of affluence is a sufficient condition for democratization, then we would not expect as many transition processes in the former communist countries or in Third World countries as in the super-rich oil states and in the South-East Asian Tigers (South Korea, Singapore, Taiwan and Hong Kong), but there are few if any signs of democratization there.

How the correlation is to be interpreted is actually a major issue in comparative politics. On the one hand, it has been argued that the causal pattern is one of interaction, or even democracy causing economic development. On the other hand, there has been a search for intervening variables that could explain why affluence and democracy tend to go together, although not in an interactive fashion. A third possibility is that the relationship could be merely accidental. But the finding in different tests is that the correlation tends to remain much the same for various points in time (Diamond, 1992a; Lipset et al., 1993).

One might conclude that affluence is most important when countries try to move towards democracy. General economic conditions such as the average level of income would be a highly relevant contributory condition, which in combination with other conditions makes democratic transition possible. Yet the relationship between affluence and democracy is too open-ended to

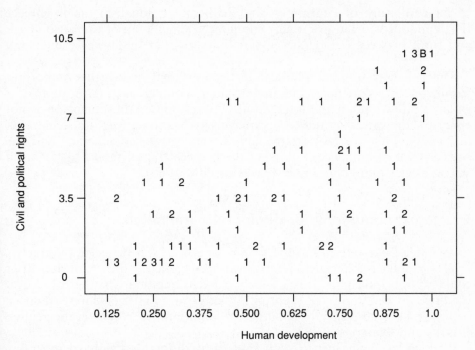

Figure 11.2 Human development and civil and political rights

Note: For explanation of figures, see Appendix II.

allow any policy conclusions about prospects for successful democratization.

Even though it may be true that the forces which accompany a high level of affluence – urbanization, industrialization, secularization – foster a democratic culture (Lipset, 1959; Almond and Verba, 1965; Inglehart, 1990), there is no guarantee that an authoritarian regime or dictatorial rule could not be introduced and sustained in an affluent society. There are too many examples of relatively rich societies turning authoritarian – Germany and Italy between the wars, Latin America after the Second World War – to contradict the hypothesis that there might be some causal mechanism that leads from affluence to democracy. We suggest that the well-known correlation between affluence and democracy be interpreted somewhat differently, based upon a few findings in this volume.

Firstly, we argue that it is not affluence *per se* that is the crucial factor, but the level of human development, building on the finding in Chapter 5 that quality of life in a country is not a proportional function of the variation in that country's prosperity. The human development index first rises sharply, with an increase in wealth from very low to medium, but then levels off, as the quality of life is almost independent of any further rise in affluence.

Looking at the relationship between democracy and the human development index (r = .59, N = 127), one may establish that democracy is not

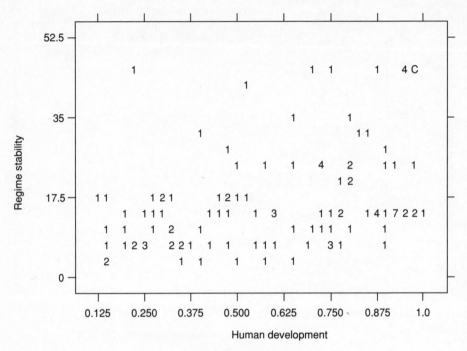

Figure 11.3 Regime stability and human development

Note: For explanation of figures, see Appendix II.

feasible at a low level of human development in a country (see figure 11.2). However, although a certain degree of human development is a necessary condition for democracy, a high level is not a sufficient condition.

A certain minimum quality of life is needed to make democracy possible, because no state can be stable in a situation of extreme poverty. A low level of human development excludes democracy, because it excludes any kind of stable regime (see figure 11.3). Thus one may account for the negative relationship between poverty and democracy by means of the impossibility for any state with a low level of human development to remain stable. The fact that a decent level of human development is a necessary but not a sufficient condition for democracy correctly implies that, after a certain level has been reached, democracy is an option, not a necessity.

Secondly, we argue that what matters for a democratic regime is the structure of the economic system, not previously mentioned in the debate about affluence and democracy.

In Chapter 10 we found that regime stability is to a significant extent brought about by the level of affluence, whereas the institutionalization of civil and political rights is strongly influenced by the structure of the economic system. This means that democracy would occur in relatively well-off

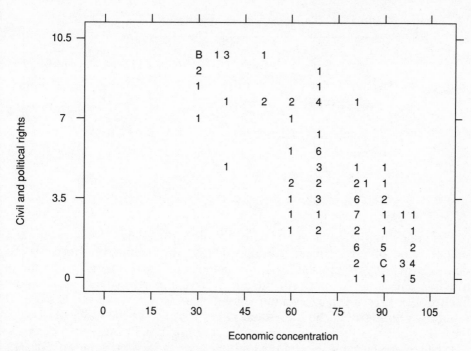

Figure 11.4 Concentration of economic resources and civil and political rights
Note: For explanation of figures, see Appendix II.

societies which adhere to an economic regime that is either of the decentralized capitalist or the mixed capitalist type.

In figure 11.4 the extent of democracy is plotted against the extent to which economic resources are concentrated as they tend to be in state-capitalist economic systems or economic statism and planned economies. One may interpret the strong correlation between the two in the following way: an economic system that is based on decentralized capitalism or a mixed economy, as in the welfare states, requires a number of institutions that emphasize the scope of individual responsibility and the range of personal incentives, such as property rights, market transaction rights, joint stock companies and a stock exchange. Such systems of individual rights will sooner or later tend to be combined with democratic rights.

The occurrence of democracy in the various types of economic systems is displayed by means of an analysis of variance in table 11.1. Since the category of decentralized capitalist systems includes many poor countries which are not stable, we know that they will tend to score low on democracy. A certain quality of life in a country is a necessary condition for regime stability, that is, also for the stability of democratic regimes. However, once a decent level of human development is reached, then the type of economic system matters more than affluence.

Table 11.1 Economic system and democracy

Economic system	CIVIC mean
1) Decentralized capitalist (N = 40)	4.16
2) Mixed capitalist (N = 21)	6.25
3) State-capitalist (N = 32)	4.32
4) Mixed socialist (N = 14)	1.68
5) Socialist (N = 21)	.68
$E^2 = .39$	

Source: Gastil (1987).

The policy implications are: (1) a certain level of human development is a *sine qua non* for the introduction of a democratic regime, but higher levels of affluence will not automatically bring about more democracy; (2) a move towards democracy without the introduction of a market economy will most likely not be successful, at least in the long term. State-capitalist and planned economy regimes defy the individual rights that are at the heart of democracy. To sum up: there are important economic conditions for democracy but they are to be found not in the GNP per capita indicator, but in a decent level of human development and in the establishment of the institutions of a stable market economy. How about political conditions?

Political conditions for democratic transformation

It is possible to distinguish between different types of democracies. The crucial question is whether one kind of democracy is a better model than another. The theory that parliamentarism works better than presidentialism when a state is to move out of dictatorship is much discussed in relation to the state transformation process (Lijphart, 1990, 1992a). Yet although it is true that more than half of all the presidential regimes are dictatorships, there are also democratic regimes with presidentialism. And not all states that adhere to parliamentarism are stable democracies.

The theoretical support for the hypothesis that parliamentary regimes are more conducive to a stable democracy is based on the perverted form of presidential rule – the risk that presidents try to undo the balance of powers to their own advantage (Linz, 1992). Thus it is claimed that parliamentary regimes result in more power diffusion. Yet this conclusion is not in accordance with the American model of presidentialism, which follows from the doctrine of the separation of powers (Ostrom, 1987, 1991). By separating the executive power clearly from the legislative and judicial powers, the ideal type of presidentialism would secure power diffusion. Moreover, the ideal model of parliamentarism aims at a fusion of power between the executive and legislative functions by entrusting both to parliament and its cabinet committee.

First, it is now argued in connection with the introduction of new constitutions in Eastern Europe that the Lijphartian consensus model of democracy is more stable or performs better than the Westminster type, because the former involves more power sharing. Second, it is asserted that strong presidential democracies tend more towards instability than parliamentary democracies, despite the fact that, in principle, presidential democracies belong to the set of consensus states, on account of their strong institutionalization of the doctrine of the separation of powers.

The distinction between presidential and parliamentary democracies emphasizes the fact that the new states have to make critical choices about what institutions to believe in and give support to. New constitutions have to be written and agreed upon. The critical question is whether one type of democratic institution leads to better democracy than another. When referring to presidential states, it is vital to make a distinction between weak and strong regimes. A weak presidential state is parliamentarism where the president functions only as the head of state; a strong regime has a president as the head of the executive branch of government. There are also a few border-line examples, such as France and Finland.

The problem of how to design the executive as well as how it is to be recruited has very important power implications. First, the single membership rule requires that no member of the executive is also active in the national assembly. Second, the double membership rule calls for all members of the executive to be members of the national assembly. This distinction does not coincide with that between parliamentary and presidential systems (see table 11.2), because mixtures of pure institutional ideal types are bound to occur.

When the new constitutions in Eastern Europe come to be written there will have to be a choice between these three principles for structuring the important relationships between the executive and the legislature. There are more basic principles operating here than simply the distinction between the power fusion of parliamentarism and the power diffusion of the consensus model. Thus even in the United Kingdom there has been since 1979 a restriction on the double membership principle; due to deliberations about conflict of interest (Drewry, 1985), in order to be independent of the influence of party and government (Ryle and Richards, 1988), the departmental select committees that scrutinize government are to be recruited from among backbenchers. As a matter of fact, it is not only executives that differ greatly, but also legislatures (Mezey, 1979).

It is interesting to note that some Eastern European countries, such as Hungary, Bulgaria and the Czech Republic, have made a firm commitment to the parliamentary type of democracy. All these countries have written constitutions that are followed more or less in detail. Other East European

Table 11.2 Executive and parliamentary membership

	Parliamentary regime	Presidential regime	Mixture or other
Double membership principle	United Kingdom, Australia, Canada, New Zealand, India, Malta, Trinidad	Tanzania, Kenya	–
Single membership principle	The Netherlands, Norway, Sweden	Argentina, Brazil, USA Mexico	France, Switzerland
Mixed forms of membership	Belgium, Denmark Spain, Italy, Greece, Germany	–	Finland, Peru

Source: Laundy (1989: 30–2); Shugart and Carey (1992).

states, such as Poland and Romania and the former states in the Soviet empire, have relied on the presidential type of democracy. But in Poland and the Ukraine no final constitutions have thus far been enacted, which seems to have impeded the establishment of stable democratic institutions.

On the other hand, there seems to be no such institutional choice in the Latin American transformation processes. The presidential model and its single membership principle remains the only possible institutional type in countries such as Brazil, Argentina, Venezuela and Mexico. In spite of all the bad historical experiences of presidential rule in Latin America since the American model was first imitated, the parliamentary model has little appeal on the continent (Linz, 1992). But it is a fact that the only country in Latin America with a stable democracy, Costa Rica, adheres to the presidential model.

The events in the state transformation processes in Southern Europe may be interpreted in terms of this theme. At first, Portugal and Greece enacted presidential-type democratic constitutions, but these failed in both countries. Not many years later there was a shift towards parliamentarism, first in Portugal (1983) and then in Greece (1986), institutionalized by means of constitutional provisions. If this concept is measured by the institutional-ization of civil and political rights, does parliamentarism work better than presidentialism with regard to democracy?

Table 11.3 presents a picture of the functioning of democracy in various types of state, which is relevant to the problem of presidentialism and parliamentarism. We note that parliamentarism clearly tends to be combined with democracy, whereas presidentialism also occurs among several non-

Table 11.3   Regimes and civil and political rights

	CIVIC *mean*
1) Parliamentary regimes (N = 26)	8.42
2) Limited presidentialism (N = 41)	5.10
3) Unlimited presidentialism (N = 25)	1.83
4) Communist regimes (N = 16)	.76
5) Military regimes (N = 13)	2.01
6) Traditional regimes (N = 7)	2.93
$E^2 = .67$	

Source: Derbyshire and Derbyshire (1991).

Note: Unlimited presidentialism is a regime where the president wields executive powers without firm constitutional constraints.

democratic states. The policy implication is rather obvious: the introduction of a parliamentary regime instead of a presidential one would be conducive to democratic stability, at least in a longer-term perspective.

Towards a market economy

Crucial in the transition towards a market economy is the time dimension. Should capitalist institutions be introduced quickly or slowly? Should the institutional framework for the economy be reformed comprehensively or in a marginal fashion? It is remarkable that we have less understanding of the transformation of economic systems than we do of the transformation of political regimes. Some scholars argue in favour of shock therapy for the communist countries (Aslund, 1992), but in reality we have examples both of quick and comprehensive reform, such as in East Germany, Poland, Mexico and Chile, and of a slow, marginalist approach, as in Russia, Hungary, Romania and Bulgaria (Clague and Rausser, 1992).

To devise strategies that one can rely on with some certainty or predictability to replace the command economy with a market economy has proved far more difficult than was anticipated in the wake of optimism during 1990. At first a list of recommendations was drawn up: deregulate prices and trade, make the currency convertible but check the money supply, and privatize state assets by copying other countries' legislation. However, it was soon realized that a better strategy would be to introduce new private firms and outperform the parastatals (Kornai, 1990).

What is the role of an economic system? Economic factors are relevant in two ways. First, they shape the transfer from authoritarian rule to democracy, as wealth and the openness of the economy are conditions that strongly favour a democratic regime. Second, there is the economic transformation process itself, the basic change to a decentralized market economy with the establishment of capitalist institutions. Perhaps there are connections between economic factors and the choice of an economic system, or perhaps such political factors as democracy bring economic system transformation in their wake?

It should be pointed out that, just as the movement from dictatorship to democracy involves not only several steps but also fusions of these state types, the distinction between capitalism and socialism is not clear-cut. Let us adopt Przeworski's definitions:

> By 'capitalism' I mean any economic system in which (1) the optimal division of labor is so advanced that most people produce for the needs of others, (2) the means of production and the capacity to work are owned privately, and (3) there are markets in both. By 'socialism' I mean any system in which (1) the division of labor is equally advanced, (2) the means of production are owned publicly, and (3) most productive resources, at least other than labor services, are allocated by centralized command. (Przeworski, 1991: 101)

Although the pure socialist model, the model of a planned economy with almost all resources in public ownership (implemented on a grand scale when the forced industrialization process was initiated in 1929 in the Soviet Union), is no longer a viable option, the interpretation of capitalism is not exactly straightforward.

Not all countries looking for economic change conform to the pure socialist model. There is actually a large number of countries that work towards decentralized capitalism from a state-capitalist base – countries whose economic systems, while recognizing the concept of private ownership, acknowledge a major role for the state in terms of both ownership and regulation. During the 1980s several countries, including Argentina, Brazil, Venezuela, Mexico, Zaïre, Ghana, Nigeria, India and Indonesia, began to put an end to extensive state involvement in the economy. How far this process of market reform will go depends not least upon the development of the world economy – in particular the temptation of free-trade regimes to resort to protectionism.

It has been claimed that there is more than one socialist model (Lindblom, 1977, 1988): in fact there are three socialist alternatives to decentralized capitalism. First, there is the existing welfare state model, which combines private ownership with large-scale public spending for allocative and redistributive purposes. Second, the market socialism model suggests that, while ownership remains public, resources could be allocated by means of market mechanisms; although such an economic system may be theoretically possible, it is hardly workable in practice. Thirdly, there is the planner sovereignty model, where ownership would be basically in the private sector

	Poor states	Affluent states
State dirigiste (e.g., import substitution at one stage)	Planned economies in Eastern Europe and state-capitalist systems in Latin America, Africa and Asia	Taiwan, South Korea, Singapore
Decentralized capitalism or the market economy (e.g., export orientation)	Capitalist states in Africa, Asia and Latin America	Welfare states, welfare societies, Hong Kong

Figure 11.5 Development strategies and affluence

but allocative decisions would be concentrated in the hands of state planners; again, the practicality of this model remains debatable.

The attempt to extend the range of markets does not only characterize the new states in Eastern Europe; it holds generally for Third World countries. Here we find a distinction between the type of economic system employed and the development or strategy for economic growth, which is essential to the understanding of the Third World states and their zest for reform. The efforts to increase the scope of the market follow upon decades of interventionist policies by the state. The main goal for many Third World countries is not so much comprehensive reform of economic systems *per se* as the search for improved economic outcomes – a sustained process of economic growth leading to a considerable rise in the level of affluence.

Thus we have a distinction between, on the one hand, decentralized capitalism or laissez-faire systems in the Adam Smith version and state dirigiste economies in the Friedrich List interpretation, and, on the other, affluence and poverty (see figure 11.5). And the crucial question concerning economic development remains: which strategy is the best guarantee of economic prosperity?

The Third World states, whether former communist orders or adherents of state-capitalism, seek a route towards long-term economic growth by means of institutional transformation. However, will the move towards greater domination by the market and less state intervention in itself result in a process leading to economic affluence? Table 11.4 looks at the relationship between type of economic system and level of affluence.

Now, if a decent level of human development is, as stated above, a necessary but not a sufficient condition for the establishment of a stable democracy, then the transformation of the economic system from regulation by the state to decentralized capitalism will not automatically bring forward the political transition from authoritarian to democratic rule. There are countries which have a decentralized capitalist regime but which are undemocratic because they are poor.

Table 11.4 Type of economic system and affluence

Economic regime	GNP/cap, 1989 (US dollars)
1) Decentralized capitalism	5,561 (37)
2) Mixed capitalism	9,445 (20)
3) State-capitalism	2,957 (31)
4) Mixed socialism	1,123 (13)
5) Communism	1,117 (7)

Source: Appendix 7.1 and World Bank (1991).

Third World transformation: governance crisis

The two forms of fundamental institutional change, from dictatorship to democracy and from public interference in the economy to decentralized capitalism, are equally relevant outside Eastern Europe. They concern not only Latin America but the entire set of Third World states, which face an absolute imperative in the form of economic development. There is a huge volume of literature on which development strategy is the best, which we cannot go into here. What we wish to emphasize is that the actual way of functioning of the Third World state has not been taken into account sufficiently in economic development models. The transition to democracy may be a *sine qua non* for the Third World countries if they are going to enhance state operations.

As a matter of fact, it is difficult to identify what type of state several of these countries have endured since independence from colonial rule; since it is hard to identify a few basic dimensions of the Third World state (Leftwich, 1994; Ayubi, 1991; Zubaida, 1993), the variation in regime cannot be covered in a comprehensive fashion. The Third World has seen personal dictatorships, one-party regimes and bureaucratic-authoritarian rule to an extent that was not predicted when colonial imperialism was dismantled after the Second World War (Kamrava, 1993; Bayart, 1993; Baxter et al., 1993).

It is interesting to note that there are some widely different interpretations of the Third World state: (1) personal rulership and patrimonialism (Roth, 1968), (2) 'soft' states (Myrdal, 1968), (3) overdeveloped states (Alavi, 1972), (4) bureaucratic bourgeois states (Shivji, 1976), (5) bureaucratic-authoritarian states (O'Donnell, 1973), (6) underdeveloped states (Medard, 1982), (7) strong states with weak regimes (Dominguez, 1987), (8) weak states in strong societies (Migdal, 1988) and (9) predatory states (Lundahl, 1991). Although the base from which the state transformation process starts in Africa and Asia is far from clear, the goal is democratization – but parliamentarism or presidentialism?

Firstly, in the Third World there has been little distinction between formally democratic presidential systems and real dictatorships. Despite the legacy of the Westminster model in the states that were formerly part of the British Empire, the prevailing trend is towards some kind of presidential regime. The explanation is that presidentialism offers the possibility of legitimizing the patrimonialism that has characterized many states in Africa and Asia. Harsh personal dictatorial regimes in presidential systems of government have been found in Uganda, Zaïre and Paraguay.

Secondly, military rule has been typical of the attempts to introduce party-centralism: Afghanistan, Angola, Benin, Cape Verde, the Congo, Cuba, Ethiopia, Ghana, Grenada, Guyana, Guinea-Bissau, Laos, Madagascar, Mozambique, Nicaragua, São Tomé and Príncipe, Surinam, Yemen, Vietnam and Zimbabwe. The failure to stimulate development on the basis of the model of a planned economy made military control all the more imperative, at the same time as civil war often made things even worse.

Thirdly, when there have been pluralist regimes, these have not necessarily been democratic. It is difficult to identify any stable democratic regimes in the large number of Third World states. However, democratic politics – bargaining between major social groups, compromise between government and opposition or the acceptance of reciprocity between contenders for political power – has not been totally absent. The legitimate acceptance, or at least the toleration, of opposition is crucial to a pluralist regime, as in Botswana, Mauritius, Senegal, Sri Lanka, Malaysia, Singapore and Thailand.

Fourthly, Marxist regimes have been authoritarian dictatorships embracing all kinds of social relationships, whereas personal dictatorship is less penetrating but equally if not more brutal. When the party rather than the individual is the main vehicle of political power, the regimen becomes less personalized and arbitrary, as party ideology substitutes for personal aggrandizement. Among the party regimes we would also categorize socialist regimes outside the Marxist set, such as Tanzania and Zimbabwe.

Finally, bureaucratic rule bypasses the search for ideological blueprints and concentrates on the day-to-day administration of the mundane business of government. At the same time, the potential capacity of bureaucracy to support hegemonic domination implies that there is a large step between bureaucratic rule and a pluralist regime. Bureaucratic regimes are found in Argentina, Venezuela, Kenya, Nigeria and Cameroon, and common to all these countries is that they suffer from political instability. The larger the Nigerian state becomes, the more complex and fragile it is.

The process of democratization in the Marxist and patrimonial states of the Third World will not be a smooth one. There is the ever-present danger of military coups, and the objective economic conditions are not favourable in several African and Asian countries because poverty implies state instability. A crucial test as to whether a country truly aspires to accept democracy comes when the party system is to be transformed. As long as the largest party accounts for over 50 per cent of the votes, the institutionalization of civil and political rights will be fragile. The prediction is then that the third

Table 11.5 Civil and political rights in new states

| | CIVIC scores | | |
	1991	1992	1993
Russia	6.7	5.8	5.8
Ukraine	6.7	6.7	5.0
Belarus	5.0	5.8	4.2
Uzbekistan	2.5	1.7	0.0
Kazakhstan	4.2	3.3	3.3
Georgia	2.5	4.2	3.3
Azerbaijan	3.3	3.3	1.7
Moldova	4.2	3.3	3.3
Kirghizstan	4.2	6.7	5.0
Tajikistan	3.3	2.5	0.0
Armenia	3.3	5.8	5.8
Turkmenistan	2.5	0.8	0.0
Lithuania	7.5	7.5	8.3
Latvia	7.5	6.7	6.7
Estonia	7.5	6.7	7.5
Slovenia	7.5	8.3	9.2
Croatia	5.8	4.2	5.0
Serbia	2.5	2.5	1.7

Source: Freedom House (1992, 1993, 1994).

wave of democratization will result in a roller-coaster process where there will be constant threats to its achievement.

What makes the problems of transition so difficult in many Third World countries is the bad shape of their economic system as a function of overall government. Whether a dictatorship of the right or the left, the role of the state in the economy is too large (Hyden and Bratton, 1992). The omnipresence of the parastatals has the consequence that economic efficiency is meagre but the politics of affection looms large. Extensive state involvement in the economy has meant clientilist policy-making, which hampers all efforts to increase the overall level of affluence. 'Central to the understanding of the essence of Third World politics is an appreciation of the fluid nature of state organisations and institutions' (Kamrava, 1993: 28).

It is argued that the Third World needs to implement more institutions pertaining to a market economy. Sometimes this is referred to as 'capitalism'. However, such a term is unfortunate as it often means colonialism; a distinction must be made between 'capitalism' to mean the market economy, or what is referred to here as 'decentralized capitalism', and other negative interpretations. At the same time, it is argued that what is fundamentally wrong in the Third World is the state (Chirkin, 1990; Berg-Schlosser, 1990;

Table 11.6 Civil and political rights, 1992

	CIVIC for old set	CIVIC for extended set
GNP/capita, 1989	.53 (N = 118)	.53 (N = 135)
LNGNP/capita	.60 (N = 118)	.57 (N = 135)
RF	−.01 (N = 127)	−.02 (N = 144)
ELF	−.21 (N = 127)	−.21 (N = 144)
PROT	.35 (N = 127)	.35 (N = 144)
ISLAM	−.46 (N = 127)	−.48 (N = 144)

Sources: Economic Commission for Europe (1992); Fleje (1991); Gotz and Halbach (1992); Marer et al. (1992); Freedom House (1992).

Welch, 1990; Hunneus, 1990; Schultz and Slater, 1990; Diamond, Linz and Lipset, 1990; Sakwa, 1993).

In particular, the focus has been on the shape of the bureaucracies in Third World countries, which often, in combination with rule by personal dictatorship, creates a profound crisis of governance in Africa. Instead of helping the process of economic development by such economic strategies as import-substitution or export-orientated growth, the state has become a major burden to society due to its *prebendal* characteristics (Joseph, 1987). It is at the same time too large and too weak, too independent, too underdeveloped and unstructured, and too malleable.

Events post 1989

Although the mere technical transformation of a state is not difficult to achieve once authoritarian forces have given up resistance to change, constitution-making is far from a sufficient condition for the consolidation of democracy. Democratic stability requires a firm institutionalization of a functioning party system as well as a clear demarcation of the borders between the executive, the legislative and the judicial branches of government. Several countries currently in transition have not yet introduced a constitution – and few countries actually operate according to a formal constitutional document.

Most interestingly, when one compares the CIVIC scores for the years 1991, 1992 and 1993 for several states undergoing transition, a number of countries score lower in the last year (see table 11.5). The progress towards a democratic regime has been halted in several African states due to either resistance to change by the incumbent ruler or the weak prevailing party system. And states in Latin America, such as Peru, Venezuela, Guatemala and Haiti, keep displaying signs of vacillation.

When the new states of the 1990s are added to the earlier set of states analysed, the overall structural conditions for democratic transition remain unchanged. Thus the correlations between the number of factors analysed in Chapter 7 are much the same (see table 11.6). The objective conditions for successful regime transition resulting in a consolidated democracy have not changed by the mere collapse of authoritarian systems. Although it is vital to understand the details of each transformation and how the participants view their roles, these subjective experiences will give rise to democratic legitimation and consolidation only when the objective conditions allow that to happen. We have emphasized the critical importance of a decent level of human development and the elimination of economic statism.

Conclusion

The models tested in Chapters 7 to 10 imply that democratic transition in Eastern Europe, Latin America, Africa and Asia hinges upon economic outcomes such as the amelioration of mass poverty, the pacification of the military and the emergence of a true multi-party system. Looking in this chapter, particularly at the transition from dictatorship to democracy, the major finding is that the type of economic system is very important.

Firstly, there are the negative implications of a low level of human development in combination with little prospect for rapid economic growth. Secondly, a decent level of human development does not automatically increase the prospects for long-term institutionalization of democracy. What matters is the introduction of economic institutions that decrease the concentration of economic power. Decentralized capitalism and mixed capitalism tend to enhance democracy, whereas a planned economy or a state-capitalist system is detrimental.

Finally, there is the choice of political institutions. The establishment of a firm distinction between politicians and military leaders has proved impossible in Third World states, which is extremely unfavourable to democratic transformation. Still, affluence and a low profile among the military is not enough to bring about democracy – as is shown in the interesting case of the highly affluent state of Singapore. As long as the largest political party (in the case of Singapore, the People's Action Party) is not willing to give up a hegemonic position, the opposition, competition, contestation and openness necessary to democracy will not be forthcoming. We also note, when the states undergoing transition enter the constitutional stage, that the choice between parliamentary and non-parliamentary institutions is a crucial variable (Lijphart, 1991a, 1992a).

Conclusion

Introduction

Comparative politics has a contested place within political science. There is disagreement about both its methodology and its substantive content. Much of the work in this field takes the form of area studies, which may be highly relevant for practical purposes; however, the theoretical implications of the case study approach are ambiguous. If one takes a Humean perspective, searching for general causal connections, the policy relevance may seem remote, but information about the relationship between society and state and among state institutions and actors based on models may offer a view about what the state can achieve in the short as well as the long term. It is possible to identify the degree of freedom for political actors to direct or change state activities.

In terms of its theoretical core, comparative government appears to be a mass of contested concepts and competing approaches. Perhaps it is timely to focus on the salient models, explicit or implicit, and structure this field of knowledge in terms of the formulation and testing of a number of them, which is what we outline in this concluding chapter. Recourse to models provides a better basis for description, understanding and explanation.

The model-driven approach

Turning to a model-driven approach would allow a more systematic presentation of knowledge in comparative politics and would also help the discipline to progress in a more cumulative manner. Models organize the search for knowledge in an efficient way, state relationships between factors, events or developments, and permit the formation of generalizations.

A model-driven approach to comparative politics is all the more relevant now that the employment of multivariate techniques for the analysis of huge data sets has become a real possibility. The limitations on methods or data that earlier made the case study or the comparative method a necessity no longer apply. In the methodology of comparison in relation to states, governments, polities or political systems it was necessary to move on just one step from the case study method to enquire into the most similar system design (in order to discover what is different among similarities) or the most different system design (in order to state what is similar among differences). The statistical method is another option that is far more available today.

Humean causality

Following David Hume's well-known approach to the problem of causality and applying it in comparative politics, it is vital to complement the strong orientation towards area studies with a search for lawlike generalizations. A general model needs to be formulated to take account of causal interaction observed in case studies stating (1) that a similar cause really brings about a similar effect, or (2) that a different effect is really brought about by a different cause. Such a model should be tested via a large number of cases.

In covering roughly 130 cases it is possible to divide all the variables studied into sets of dependent and independent variables and conduct a quasi-controlled enquiry. This way of approaching the difficult problem of causality in comparative government seems most promising, since there has always been much discussion about what kinds of factors matter most at the macrolevel of politics: social structure, economic conditions, cultural developments, institutional factors or the personal element.

States as the unit of analysis

When the field of comparative government was broadened from its narrow focus on Western societies, it was much discussed whether the concept of the state was the appropriate basic theoretical unit. Thus anthropologists spoke of 'stateless societies'. True, the concept of the state is an essentially contested notion. It is difficult not only to specify a set of semantically relevant properties but also to draw the boundary lines between such neighbouring concepts as 'society' and 'nation'.

Complicated questions arise when the state is analysed: no one would doubt that there was political authority in the Middle Ages, but were there states? Certainly Oriental despotism was a form of rule, but did the various dynasties in China, India and the Ottoman Empire govern states? And is it conceptually adequate to speak of huge states in Africa, such as the Kingdoms of Mali or Ethiopia, or in Latin America before the advent of European colonialism?

It has been argued that the concept of the nation-state presents fewer difficulties. There is an entire literature that focuses on the advent of nation-states, first in Europe and then throughout the world – the modernization and mobilization models. However, the concept of the nation-state is ambiguous. It would seem that nationality has become the key component in state building processes, which are referred to by political sociologists as 'nation-building'. Yet, not all existing states are the result of nation-building processes.

It would be a serious mistake to underestimate the impact of nationalism as an ideology on the politics of the twentieth century. The discovery, or the invention, of the concept of a national identity by Johann Gottfried Herder in the late eighteenth century has been implemented in practical politics throughout all continents. Its force remains immense, as was shown only recently in the division of Czechoslovakia. Actually, the political implications of nationalism remain stronger than its economic significance in Friedrich List's theory concerning the importance of each country's national economic development as a result of the ever-growing international economy.

Yet it is necessary to distinguish between states and nationalities. Although no one would challenge the proposition that there is a state in India or in Canada, we would be very hesitant to speak of a 'nation-state' in these cases. In no way are all the states of the world nation-states. And Woodrow Wilson's ideal of each nationality having its own state is still far from reality. Will there be a Kurdish state in the foreseeable future?

The concept of the Weberian state offers a starting-point for the comparative analysis of government. It underlines a few characteristics typical of the creation of modern states during the Renaissance period. Its core is the notion of 'stato' – the bureaucractic machinery – as the basis for sustainable political power, in contrast to the unpredictability of personal rule and the instability of negotiated feudal orders.

Here we encounter the complex question of what leads to state instability or bad state performance. Is social fragmentation or poverty more relevant? Can the significance of considerable ethnic or religious heterogeneity be offset by the introduction of special political institutions, such as a federal system of government where each one of the major minorities controls its own state, as in India? Since plausible theories about causal patterns have considerable policy implications, it is necessary to formulate such hypotheses in as general a form as possible and test them exhaustively. How is a viable state to be established in South Africa? By simple majority rule in a unitary state? By the employment of power-sharing mechanisms at the central level of government? Or is a federal or confederal solution allowing various cultural groups self-determination the safest device for reaching state stability? But perhaps economic factors are just as important as or even more significant than social fragmentation.

Framework of analysis

Starting from the definition of the Weberian state and underlining observable characteristics such as a compact territory, a system of law and order regulating the use of legitimate physical violence and a regime defining authority structures, we have looked for two kinds of model of the state for further empirical analysis – those of stability and performance. The first type dealt with how state regimes fare over time, whereas the second focused on how states deliver and what the consequences are. These two aspects of the state are not entirely unconnected.

When one begins to search for major models within the literature, one is often referred to theories that focus, implicitly or explicitly, on state stability and performance. Some approaches treat stability, such as in functionalism and systems theory, whereas others deal with performance, such as democracy or inequality. We could also have included other perspectives, but clarifing the conditions for aspects related to state stability and performance is a tangible task: it actually allows one to systematize a number of well-known models from Max Weber to modern comparative politics.

First, we defined the principal concepts in state stability and performance. If a causal approach is to be at all feasible, indicators must also be specified. In relation to the set of states included in our analysis – all those with a population larger than one million – we have collected information on a large number of indices that measure the occurrence of various phenomena during the period following the Second World War. As a matter of fact, the literature is full of indicators on political, economic and social factors that are highly relevant for putting comparative politics theory to the test.

Second, we introduced a general model that would allow us to test theories about the conditions for state stability and performance. The continuing institutionalist revolution in political science seems to be a promising starting-point for modelling the variety of independent variables that figure in hypotheses about stability and performance. Is it really true, as many now claim, that political institutions matter more in macropolitics than environmental conditions or the activities of political leaders in crucial positions of power?

State stability and performance reflect state efficiency and legitimacy to a considerable extent. It seems difficult for a state to enhance its efficiency if it lacks resources of various kinds, in particular economic resources, and it is possible to predict instability and weak state performance in poor countries. On the other hand, state efficiency does not necessarily result in stability and a good performance record, as a state's capability may be employed in counterproductive activities. Thus it is also necessary to take legitimacy into account, and institutions are of decisive importance for the legitimacy of the state.

Findings

In Chapter 10 we established a few interesting findings by means of regression analyses. The causal relevance of economic and institutional factors is beyond doubt, given the high R-squared scores for the models concerning regime duration, the existence of civil and political rights and welfare expenditure. Surprisingly, the social models do not explain as much as one might expect, considering the amount of attention given to ethnic and religious fragmentation. The cultural block contains a number of factors that are of significance both to state stability and state performance, which could hardly have been predicted from the present state of knowledge in comparative government. The actor set of models also display causal relevance.

State stability is rooted strongly in economics: a high level of affluence affects state stability decisively. Institutional sclerosis or the duration of uninterrupted modernized leadership are of little importance when other factors are taken into account, especially economic ones. Institutionally speaking, military government only adds to state instability.

State performance has a substantial economic footing but actor politics are also relevant. The extent to which civil and political rights are respected is closely related to the type of economic system; where economic power is wielded by the state, the regime is less likely to respect civil and political rights. Decentralized capitalism in itself is not enough to guarantee human rights, since affluence is also relevant for the stability of a state which respects civil and political rights. Several decentralized capitalist states exist on too low a level of human development, which makes any kind of stability precarious.

Welfare state spending cannot be undertaken without abundant economic resources, but affluence is not a sufficient condition for the rise of the welfare state. Politics as measured by party ideological orientation has to be recognized. The parameters for the variables here are worth noting, since they reveal the significance of actor conditions, particularly on welfare spending. Most interestingly, the explanation of income inequality takes institutional and cultural factors into account more than economic ones. Thus power sharing, the weak position of an individualist culture and possibly the presence of an Islamic culture matter more. Table 1 presents a summary of the findings from the block analyses of state stability and state performance.

In mixed models there is again little sign of any particularly detrimental effects of ethnic and religious fragmentation on state stability and performance. Actually, even the Montesquieu climate factor emerges as more important than social heterogeneity. This is unexpected since it is not in agreement with the common-sense notion about the role of social structure in macropolitics.

The relevance of a variety of economic factors for state stability and performance is striking. Institutional factors must be taken into account, as the experience of military rule appears to be particularly relevant to the

Table 1 Explanatory relevance of the condition sets (R²A-scores)

Blocks	REG	CIVIC	HED86	TOP10
Physical	.22	.10	.31	.38
Socio-economic	.34	.50	.34	.19
Economic	.55	.63	.69	.33
Economic system	.42	.80	.38	.14
Social structure	.04	.06	.16	.24
Cultural	.34	.42	.34	.37
Institutional	.48	.84	.41	.35
Actor	.09	.27	.13	.20

establishment of civil and political rights. State performance in the form of welfare spending is influenced by the basic political aspect of right versus left. One implication is that state stability cannot be guaranteed simply by the choice of the appropriate institutions, because the level of affluence and human development also play a role. And the existence of a commitment to civil and political rights is closely connected with specific economic institutions. Economic systems involving any kind of economic statism that plays down the role of private property institutions and minimizes the scope of market allocation tend to ignore human rights. Put another way, economic determinism does not work, as economic conditions, however strong, must be complemented by other factors in order to account for the variation in state stability and performance. Thus economic factors tend to have less relevance for the understanding of income inequality than institutional and cultural factors.

Looking at the politics of the postwar period, we find states with a good performance record – protecting human rights, enhancing economic growth and its derivatives to improve the quality of life, and securing support for the least well off in society by welfare programmes. Regrettably, we also encounter a large number of states which are experiencing poverty, inequality, misery and political oppression. Why is this so? Why are there lucky or fortunate states as well as unfortunate ones?

At the same time as political, economic and social performance vary tremendously from one continent to another, as well as between one state and another within continents, we also observe that states come and go. States are not very stable organizations. A significant minority of the states of the world today were established after the Second World War. Some recently founded states have already collapsed, and a record number of new states are being created in the early 1990s. Even if one recognizes that many states have survived for a long period of time, one must also remember that their internal structure – their regime – has almost certainly been transformed during the last hundred years. And in many states today the regime is under pressure, facing demands for system change.

Whether it has a good or bad performance record, a state often tries to survive – that is, to maintain its Weberian state properties: its territory and regime. However, regime stability is fragile. States may display regime continuation for decades but suddenly disintegrate, as happened to the communist states in Eastern Europe, or their regime may face a steady erosion of integrity, as in many states in Africa, from Algeria to the Republic of South Africa. Regimes are contested all over the globe, from China to Indonesia and from Brazil to Argentina, not to mention Zaïre, Liberia and Ethiopia.

Authoritarian states may be stable for many decades and face little opposition, as with the super-rich oil states, or the regime may be the focus of continuous political struggle, as in the states of the Fertile Crescent, such as Iraq, Iran and Egypt. States trying to introduce civil and political rights may be anything but stable, such as in Latin America, where numerous democratic regimes have been tried and overthrown. How strongly a state institutionalizes civil and political rights is closely related to the kind of economic system that is practised. Economic statism, whether of the right or the left, implies fewer political and economic rights, but states with such a huge stake in controlling the economy can be both rich and stable, as, for example, Taiwan and Singapore.

Policy implications

Some policy implications may be drawn from the major results which have relevance for the way in which stable democracy can be introduced, as discussed in Chapter 11. It would be very difficult to establish a democracy in extremely poor countries, as such states tend to be unstable whatever their regime. However, democracy is not a strict function of affluence. What matters is a decent level of human development, which may be reached at only a moderate level of affluence.

More important than great wealth is the structure of the economic system. Civil and political rights are difficult to establish in countries that do not fully recognize human rights in the form of economic institutions. The establishment of stable democracy may have to await the transformation of planned economies and state-capitalist economic systems into market economies of various kinds. The change of economic regime in moderately affluent countries is as relevant to democracy as the absolute necessity of raising the level of human development in very poor countries.

When a new state or a state in transformation towards democracy is making a choice between the various alternatives of political institution, it is vital to establish a firm non-political role for the military, thus denying any likelihood of a military coup. The best way of achieving this is to opt for a parliamentary regime rather than a presidential system. Although a presidential government can express polycentricity and a separation of powers to an extent not found in the Westminster model of government, it is also true that presidential systems, if not constrained by an efficient system of checks and balances, tend to slip towards dictatorship.

Epilogue

The concepts of state stability and state performance are general enough to give rise to a number of theories in comparative politics as this field of knowledge has developed since the painstaking analysis of authority by Weber. The first concept has yielded approaches that speak of state longevity, state persistence and state maintenance, although the teleological notions often accompanying these terms should be done away with. States are not organisms searching for a unique equilibrium; they are man-made organizations or social systems where the outcomes depend on the actions and decisions of the state actors. The second concept of state performance provides the evaluation perspective on what state leaders do as well as the unintended consequences of their decisions. It has proved possible to account for a substantial variation in these two crucial state aspects by means of Humean-type analysis that covers a large number of cases and factors. Why study comparative politics? Well, if one takes a truly Humean approach to causality in macropolitics, a model-driven framework makes it possible to delineate which conditions set limits for what states or elites can possibly accomplish. The question of determinism versus indeterminism is relevant to macropolitics. While not denying the scope for action by elites, we claim that predictability is not omnipresent. Thus Raymond Aron emphasized the degree of freedom for human action in relation to macroforces:

> And in the last analysis, sociologists of the Comtian and Marxian type are always inclined to do away with history; for when we seek to know history in advance, we deprive it of its own dimension, which is action; and, when we say action, we are also saying unpredictability. (Aron, 1968: 232)

Appendix I

Selection of States
(data from around 1990)

Number	Country	Continent	Area (km²)	Population (thousand)
001	Afghanistan	Asia	652,225	15,592
002	Albania	Europe	28,748	3,262
003	Algeria	Africa	2,381,741	25,337
004	Angola	Africa	1,246,700	10,002
005	Argentina	America	2,780,092	32,880
006	Australia	Oceania	7,682,300	17,073
007	Austria	Europe	83,857	7,623
008	Bangladesh	Asia	143,998	113,005
009	Belgium	Europe	30,518	9,958
010	Benin	Africa	112,600	4,741
011	Bhutan	Asia	47,000	1,442
012	Bolivia	America	1,098,581	7,322
013	Botswana	Africa	581,730	1,295
014	Brazil	America	8,511,965	150,368
015	Bulgaria	Europe	110,994	8,997
016	Burkina Faso	Africa	274,200	9,012
017	Burundi	Africa	27,834	5,451
018	Cambodia	Asia	181,916	8,592
019	Cameroon	Africa	465,458	11,900
020	Canada	America	9,970,610	26,620
021	Central African Republic	Africa	622,436	2,875
022	Chad	Africa	1,284,000	5,678
023	Chile	America	756,626	13,173
024	China	Asia	9,572,900	1,133,683
025	Colombia	America	1,141,748	32,978

Number	Country	Continent	Area (km²)	Population (thousand)
026	Congo	Africa	342,000	2,326
027	Costa Rica	America	51,100	3,015
028	Côte d'Ivoire	Africa	320,763	12,657
029	Cuba	America	110,861	10,603
030	Czechoslovakia	Europe	127,900	15,664
031	Denmark	Europe	43,092	5,139
032	Dominican Republic	America	48,443	7,170
033	Ecuador	America	269,178	10,782
034	Egypt	Africa	997,739	53,170
035	El Salvador	America	21,041	5,221
036	Ethiopia	Africa	1,223,500	50,341
037	Finland	Europe	338,145	4,978
038	France	Europe	543,965	56,647
039	Gabon	Africa	267,667	1,171
040	Germany	Europe	357,042	79,082
041	Germany, East	Europe	108,333	16,433
042	Germany, West	Europe	248,709	62,649
043	Ghana	Africa	238,533	15,020
044	Greece	Europe	131,957	10,038
045	Guatemala	America	108,889	9,197
046	Guinea	Africa	245,857	6,876
047	Haiti	America	27,400	5,862
048	Honduras	America	112,088	4,674
049	Hungary	Europe	93,033	10,437
050	India	Asia	3,166,414	853,373
051	Indonesia	Asia	1,948,732	180,763
052	Iran	Asia	1,648,196	56,293
053	Iraq	Asia	435,052	17,754
054	Ireland	Europe	70,285	3,509
055	Israel	Asia	20,700	4,666
056	Italy	Europe	301,277	57,512
057	Jamaica	America	10,991	2,391
058	Japan	Asia	377,835	123,530
059	Jordan	Asia	88,946	3,169
060	Kenya	Africa	582,646	24,872
061	Korea, North	Asia	122,370	22,937
062	Korea, South	Asia	99,237	42,793
063	Kuwait	Asia	17,818	2,143
064	Laos	Asia	236,800	4,024
065	Lebanon	Asia	10,230	2,965

Number	Country	Continent	Area (km²)	Population (thousand)
066	Lesotho	Africa	30,355	1,760
067	Liberia	Africa	99,067	2,595
068	Libya	Africa	1,757,000	4,206
069	Madagascar	Africa	587,041	11,980
070	Malawi	Africa	118,484	8,831
071	Malaysia	Asia	330,442	17,886
072	Mali	Africa	1,240,192	8,152
073	Mauritania	Africa	1,030,700	1,999
074	Mauritius	Africa	2,040	1,080
075	Mexico	America	1,958,201	81,883
076	Mongolia	Asia	1,566,500	2,116
077	Morocco	Africa	458,730	25,113
078	Mozambique	Africa	799,380	15,696
079	Myanmar (Burma)	Asia	676,577	41,675
080	Namibia	Africa	823,144	1,302
081	Nepal	Asia	147,181	18,910
082	Netherlands	Europe	41,863	14,934
083	New Zealand	Oceania	267,844	3,389
084	Nicaragua	America	130,700	3,871
085	Niger	Africa	1,186,408	7,779
086	Nigeria	Africa	923,768	119,812
087	Norway	Europe	323,878	4,246
088	Oman	Asia	300,000	1,468
089	Pakistan	Asia	879,811	122,666
090	Panama	America	75,517	2,418
091	Papua New Guinea	Oceania	462,840	3,671
092	Paraguay	America	406,752	4,279
093	Peru	America	1,285,216	22,332
094	Philippines	Asia	300,000	61,480
095	Poland	Europe	312,683	38,217
096	Portugal	Europe	92,389	10,388
097	Romania	Europe	237,500	23,265
098	Rwanda	Africa	26,338	7,232
099	Saudi Arabia	Asia	2,240,000	14,131
100	Senegal	Africa	196,722	7,317
101	Sierra Leone	Africa	71,740	4,151
102	Singapore	Asia	622	2,718
103	Somalia	Africa	637,000	7,555
104	South Africa	Africa	1,225,815	37,418
105	Spain	Europe	504,783	38,959

Number	Country	Continent	Area (km²)	Population (thousand)
106	Sri Lanka	Asia	65,610	17,103
107	Sudan	Africa	2,503,890	28,311
108	Sweden	Europe	449,964	8,529
109	Switzerland	Europe	41,293	6,756
110	Syria	Asia	185,180	12,116
111	Taiwan	Asia	36,000	20,221
112	Tanzania	Africa	945,037	24,403
113	Thailand	Asia	513,115	56,217
114	Togo	Africa	56,785	3,764
115	Trinidad and Tobago	America	5,128	1,233
116	Tunisia	Africa	154,530	8,182
117	Turkey	Asia	779,542	56,941
118	Uganda	Africa	241,040	16,928
119	USSR	Europe	22,403,000	290,122
120	United Arab Emirates	Asia	77,700	1,903
121	United Kingdom	Europe	244,110	57,384
122	United States	America	9,529,063	251,394
123	Uruguay	America	176,215	3,033
124	Venezuela	America	912,050	19,735
125	Vietnam	Asia	329,566	66,128
126	Yemen	Asia	531,869	11,240
127	Yemen, Aden	Asia	336,869	2,486
128	Yemen, Sana	Asia	195,000	9,060
129	Yugoslavia	Europe	255,804	23,800
130	Zaïre	Africa	2,345,095	34,138
131	Zambia	Africa	752,614	8,456
132	Zimbabwe	Africa	390,759	9,369

Appendix II

Statistical Terms and Symbols

Beta coefficient [standardized regression coefficient, beta weight]   This indicates the difference in a dependent variable associated with an increase (or decrease) of one standard deviation in an independent variable when controlling for the effects of other variables.

Between-group differences   These are usually contrasted to differences within the groups studied in an analysis of variance. A measure of the between-group differences is the between sum of squares, which is calculated by squaring and summing deviation scores from the mean or average score (for example, differences between the countries on the five continents versus the differences between the countries within each continent).

Correlation   The extent to which two or more properties (variables) are related (co-related) to one another, expressed as a correlation coefficient.

Correlation coefficient   A number showing the degree to which two variables are related. Such coefficients range from -1.0 to $+1.0$. If there is a perfect negative correlation (-1.0) between A and B, whenever A is high, B is low, and vice versa. If there is a perfect positive correlation ($+1.0$) between A and B, whenever one is high or low, so is the other. A correlation coefficient of 0 means that there is no relationship between the variables.

Pearson's correlation coefficient   [Pearson's product-moment correlation coefficient, Pearson's r]   This shows the degree of linear relationship between two variables measured on interval or ratio scales.

E^2 [Eta-squared]   The ratio of explained to unexplained variance in an analysis of variance, that is, the ratio of the between-group variance to the within-group variance. The higher the Eta-squared score, the larger the between-group variation and the smaller the within-group variation.

Mean [M]   The average. To get the mean, one adds up the values for each case and then divides the total by the number of cases.

N   Number of cases studied (e.g., countries or states). In the computer printout showing the distribution of cases (countries) along the X-axis and

Y-axis, the number of cases having the same score is indicated by a number larger than 1. Here A = 10; B = 11; C = 12; D = 13 cases.

r   Symbol for a Pearson's correlation, which is a bivariate correlation (between two variables).

R   Symbol for a multiple correlation, that is, a correlation between more than two variables.

R^2   The R-squared symbol stands for a coefficient of multiple determination between a dependent variable and two or more independent variables.

Adjusted R^2   An R-squared adjusted to give a true (smaller) estimate of how much the independent variable in a regression analysis explains the dependent variable. The adjustment is made by taking into account the number of independent variables.

Regression analysis   Method of explaining or predicting the variability of a dependent variable using information about one or more independent variables. It attempts to answer the question 'What values in the dependent variable can we expect given certain values of the independent variable(s)?'

Significance   The degree to which a research finding is meaningful or important.

Significance level   The probability of making a type I error, or incorrectly concluding that two variables are related when in fact they are not. The lower the probability, the higher the statistical significance.

T-test   A test statistic, also used to test the significance of correlation coefficients and regression coefficients. The higher the t-statistic, the higher the statistical significance.

References and Bibliography

Africa Demos (1991–): *A Bulletin of the Africa Governance Program*. The Carter Center of Emory University.

Agh, A. (1993): The 'comparative revolution' and the transition in Central and Southern Europe. *Journal of Theoretical Politics*, 5, 2, 231–52.

Alavai, H. (1972): The state in post-colonial societies: Pakistan and Bangladesh. *New Left Review*, 74, 59–81.

Allardt, E. and Rokkan, S. (eds) (1970): *Mass Politics: Studies in Political Sociology*. New York: Free Press.

Allison, G. T. and Beschel, R. P. (1992): Can the United States promote democracy? *Political Science Quarterly*, 107, 81–9.

Almond, G. A. (1960): Introduction: a functional approach to comparative politics. In Almond and Coleman (eds), 3–64.

Almond, G. A. and Coleman, J. S. (eds) (1960): *The Politics of the Developing Areas*. Princeton: Princeton University Press.

Almond, G. A. and Powell, B. (1966): *Comparative Politics*. Boston: Little, Brown.

Almond, G. A. and Verba, S. (1965): *The Civic Culture*. Boston: Little, Brown.

Almond, G. A., Powell, G. B. and Mundt R. J. (1993): *Comparative Politics: a Theoretical Framework*. New York: Harper Collins.

Althusius, J. ([1610] 1965): *The Politics of Johannes Althusius*, trans. F. S. Carney. London: Eyre & Spottiswoode.

Anderson, J. (ed.) (1986): *The Rise of the Modern State*. Atlantic Highlands, NJ: Humanities Press.

Apter, D. (1965): *The Politics of Modernization*. Chicago: University of Chicago Press.

Archer, C. (1992): *International Organizations*. London: Routledge.

Aron, R. (1968): *Main Currents in Sociological Thought*, I. Harmondsworth: Penguin.

Ash, T. G. (1990): *We the People: the Revolution of '89' Witnessed in Warsaw, Budapest, Berlin and Prague*. Cambridge: Granta.

Ashford, D. E. (ed.) (1978): *Comparing Public Policies: New Concepts and Methods*. Beverly Hills, CA: Sage.

Aslund, A. (1992): *Post-Communist Economic Revolutions: How Big a Bang?* Washington, DC: Center for Strategic and International Studies.

Atlas statistique: chiffres du monde (yearly). Paris: Encyclopaedia Universalis.

Ayubi, N. (1991): *Political Islam: Religion and Politics in the Arab World*. London: Routledge.

Bagehot, W. ([1867] 1993): *The English Constitution*. London: Fontana.

Balassa, B. (1991): *Economic Policies in the Pacific Area Developing Countries*. London: Macmillan.

Banac, I. (ed.) (1992): *Eastern Europe in Revolution*. Ithaca, NY: Cornell University Press.

Banks, A. S. (1971): *Cross-Polity Time-Series Data*. Cambridge, MA: MIT Press.

Barrett, D. B. (ed.) (1982): *World Christian Encyclopaedia: a Comparative Study of Churches and Religions in the Modern World, AD 1900–2000*. Nairobi: Oxford University Press.

Bartolini, S. (1993): On time and comparative research. *Journal of Theoretical Politics*, 5, 131–67.

Baxter, C. et al. (1993): *Government and Politics in South Asia*. Boulder, CO: Westview Press.

Bayart, J.-F. (1993): *The State in Africa: The Politics of the Belly*. London: Longman.

Bebler, A. (1990): Typologies based on civilian-dominated versus military-dominated political systems. In Bebler and Seroka (eds), 261–74.

Bebler, A. and Seroka, J. (eds) (1990): *Contemporary Political Systems: Classifications and Typologies*. Boulder, CO: Lynne Rienner.

Bell, D. (1976): *The Cultural Contradictions of Capitalism*. New York: Basic Books.

Bendix, R. (1978): *Kings or People: Power and the Mandate to Rule*. Berkeley: University of California Press.

Bennett, A. L. (1988): *International Organizations: Principles and Issues*. Englewood Cliffs, NJ: Prentice-Hall.

Berglund, S. and Dellenbrant, J. A. (eds) (1994): *The New Democracies in Eastern Europe: Party Systems and Political Cleavages*. Aldershot: Edward Elgar.

Berg-Schlosser, D. (1990): Typologies of third world political systems. In Bebler and Seroka (eds), 173–201.

Bermeo, N. (ed.) (1991): Liberalization and democratization in the Soviet Union and Eastern Europe. *World Politics*, 44, 1.

Bienen, H. S. and van de Walle, N. (1991): *Of Time and Power: Leadership Duration in the Modern World*. Stanford, CA: Stanford University Press.

Bill, J. and Hardgrave, R. (1973): *Comparative Politics: the Quest for Theory*. Columbus, OH: Charles Merrill.

Black, C. (1966): *The Dynamics of Modernization*. New York: Harper & Row.

Blais, A., Blake, D. and Dion, S. (1993): Do parties make a difference? Parties and the size of government in liberal democracies. *American Journal of Political Science*, 37, 40–62.

Blondel, J. (1969): *An Introduction to Comparative Government*. London: Weidenfeld & Nicolson.

Blondel, J. (1980): *World Leaders: Heads of Government in the Postwar Period*. Beverly Hills, CA: Sage.

Blondel, J. (1990): *Comparative Government: an Introduction*. Hemel Hempstead: Philip Allan.

Boahen, A. Adu (1987): *African Perspectives on Colonialism*. Baltimore: Johns Hopkins University Press.

Bogdanor, V. (ed.) (1988): *Constitutions in Democratic Politics*. Aldershot: Gower.

Bollen, K. A. (1980): Issues in the comparative measurement of political democracy. *American Sociological Review*, 45, 370–90.

Bollen, K. A. (1986): Political rights and political liberties in nations: an evaluation of human rights measures, 1950 to 1984. *Human Rights Quarterly*, 8, 567–91.

Bollen, K. A. (1990): Political democracy: conceptual and measurement traps. *Studies in Comparative International Development*, 25, 7–24.

Bollen, K. A. (1993): Liberal democracy: validity and method factors in cross-national measures. *American Journal of Political Science*, 37, 1207–30.

Borcherding, T. E. (1977): *Budgets and Bureaucrats: the Sources of Government Growth*. Durham, NC: Duke University Press.

Braudel, F. (1993): *Civilization and Capitalism, 3: The Perspective of the World*. New York: Fontana.

Brownlie, I. (1975): *Basic Documents in International Law*. Oxford: Clarendon Press.

Brownlie, I. (1990): *Principles of Public International Law*. Oxford: Oxford University Press.

Bryce, J. (1921): *Modern Democracies*. London: Macmillan.

Budge, I. and Keman, H. (1990): *How Party Government Works: Testing a Theory of Formation, Functioning and Termination in 20 Democracies*. Oxford: Oxford University Press.

Burgess, M. and Gagnon, A.-G. (eds) (1993): *Comparative Federalism and Federation: Competing Traditions and Future Directions*. London: Harvester Wheatsheaf.

Calhoun, J. C. ([1853] 1953): *A Disquisition on Government*. Indianapolis: Bobbs-Merrill.

Cameron, D. R. (1978): The expansion of the public economy: a comparative analysis. *American Political Science Review*, 72, 1243–61.

Cammack, P., Pool, D. and Tordoff, W. (1993): *Third World Politics: A Comparative Introduction*. London: Macmillan.

Cardoso, F. H. and Faletto, E. (1979): *Dependency and Development in Latin America*. Berkeley: University of California Press.

Castles, F. G. (1978): *The Social Democratic Image of Society: a Study of the Achievements and Origins of Scandinavian Social Democracy in Comparative Perspective*. London: Routledge & Kegan Paul.

Castles, F. G. (ed.) (1982): *The Impact of Parties: Politics and Policies in Democratic Capitalist States*. London: Sage.

Castles, F. G., Lehner, F. and Schmidt, M. G. (1988): Comparative public policy analysis: problems, progress and prospects. In Castles (ed.), *Managing Mixed Economies*. Berlin: de Gruyter, 197–223.

Chazan, N. (1988): *The Early State in African Perspective: Culture, Power and Division of Labor*. Leiden: E. J. Brill.

Chazan, N., Mortimer, R., Ravenhill, J. and Rothchild, D. (1992): *Politics and Society in Contemporary Africa*. Boulder, CO: Lynne Rienner.

Chilcote, R. H. (1981): *Theories of Comparative Politics: the Search for a Paradigm*. Boulder, CO: Westview Press.

Chilcote, R. H. (1984): *Theories of Development and Underdevelopment*. Boulder, CO: Westview Press.

Chilcote, R. H. (1991): Alternative approaches to comparative politics. In Wiarda (ed.), 154–69.

Chirkin, V. (1990): The comparative study of third world political systems. In Bebler and Seroka (eds), 159–69.

Cipolla, C. M. (1965): *The Economic History of World Population*. Harmondsworth: Penguin.

Clague, C. and Rausser, G. C. (eds) (1992): *The Emergence of Market Economies in Eastern Europe*. Oxford: Blackwell.

Clark, J. and Wildavsky, A. (1990): *The Collapse of Communism: Poland as a Cautionary Tale*. San Francisco: ICS Press.

Coase, R. (1988): *The Firm, the Market and the Law*. Chicago: University of Chicago Press.

Cohen, M. and Middleton, K. (1967): *Comparative Political Systems*. New York: Natural History Press.

Cohen, R. and Nagel, E. (1934): *An Introduction to Logic and Scientific Method*. London: Routledge & Kegan Paul.

Coleman, J. S. (ed.) (1965): *Education and Political Development*. Princeton, NJ: Princeton University Press.

Collier, D. (ed.) (1979): *The New Authoritarianism in Latin America*. Princeton, NJ: Princeton University Press.

Collier, D. (1991): The comparative method: two decades of change. In Rustow and Erickson (eds), 7–31.

Collins, R. (1986): *Weberian Sociological Theory*. Cambridge: Cambridge University Press.

Collins, R. and Waller, D. (1993): Der Zusammenbruch von Staaten und die Revolutionen im sowjetischen Block: welche Theorien machten zutreffende Voraussagen? In Joas, H. and Kholi, M. (eds), *Der Zusammenbruch der DDR: soziologische Analysen*. Frankfurt am Main: Suhrkamp, 302–25.

Coppedge, M. and Reinecke, W. H. (1990): Measuring polyarchy. *Studies in Comparative International Development*, 25, 51–72.

Curtis, G. L. (1988): *The Japanese Way of Politics*. New York: Columbia University Press.

Cutright, P. (1963): National political development: measurement and analysis. *American Sociological Review*, 32, 562–78.

Dahl, R. A. (1956): *A Preface to Democratic Theory*. Chicago: University of Chicago Press.

Dahl, R. A. (1958): A critique of the ruling elite model. *American Political Science Review*, 52, 463–9.

Dahl, R. A. (1961): The behavioural approach in political science: epitaph for a monument to a successful protest. *American Political Science Review*, 55, 763–72.

Dahl, R. A. (1971): *Polyarchy: Participation and Opposition*. New Haven, CT: Yale University Press.

Dahl, R. A. (1989): *Democracy and its Critics*. New Haven, CT: Yale University Press.

Dahl, R. A. and Tufte, E. R. (1973): *Size and Democracy*. Stanford, CA: Stanford University Press.

Davidson, B. (1989): *Modern Africa: a Social and Political History*. Harlow: Longman.

Decalo, S. (1992): The process, prospects and constraints of democratization in Africa. *African Affairs*, 91, 7–35.

DeFronzo, J. (1991): *Revolutions and Revolutionary Movements*. Boulder, CO: Westview Press.

d'Entreves, A. P. (1967): *The Notion of the State*. Oxford: Oxford University Press.

Derbyshire, J. D. and Derbyshire, I. (1991): *World Political Systems: an Introduction to Comparative Government*. Edinburgh: Chambers.

Deutsch, K. W. (1961): Social mobilization and political development. *American Political Science Review*, 55, 493–514.

Deutsch, K. W. (1963): *The Nerves of Government: Models of Political Communication and Control*. New York: Free Press.

Deutsch, K. W. (1980): *Politics and Government: how People Decide their Fate*. Boston: Houghton Mifflin.

Diamandouros, P. N. (1986): Regime change and the prospects for democracy in Greece, 1974–1983. In O'Donnell et al. (eds), 138–64.

Diamond, L. (1988): Introduction: roots of failure, seeds of hope. In Diamond et al. (eds), 1988a, 1–32.

Diamond, L. (1992a): Economic development and democracy reconsidered. In Diamond (ed.), 450–99.

Diamond, L. (ed.) (1992b): Comparative perspectives on democracy: essays in honour of Seymour Martin Lipset. *American Behavioral Scientist*, 35, 4–5, 349–606.

Diamond, L. and Linz, J. (1989): Introduction: politics, society and democracy in Latin America. In Diamond et al. (eds).

Diamond, L., Linz, J. and Lipset, S. M. (eds) (1988a): *Democracy in Developing Countries*, Vol. 2: *Africa*. Boulder: Lynne Rienner.

Diamond, L., Linz, J. and Lipset, S. M. (eds) (1988b): *Democracy in Developing Countries*, Vol. 3: *Asia*. Boulder: Lynne Rienner.

Diamond, L., Linz, J. and Lipset, S. M. (eds) (1989); *Democracy in Developing Countries*, Vol. 4: *Latin America*. Boulder: Lynne Rienner.

Diamond, L., Linz, J. and Lipset, S. M. (eds) (1990a): *Democracy in Developing Countries*, Vol. 1: *Persistence, Failure and Renewal*. Boulder: Lynne Rienner.

Diamond, L., Linz, J. J. and Lipset, S. M. (1990b) *Politics in Developing Countries: Comparing Experiences with Democracy*. Boulder: Lynne Rienner.

Dicey, A. V. ([1885] 1924): *Introduction to the Study of the Constitution*. London: Macmillan.

Di Palma, G. (1990): *To Craft Democracies: an Essay on Democratic Transitions*. Berkeley: University of California Press.

Dispute, R. (1993): *The Australian Form of Government*. Melbourne: Macmillan.

Dogan, M. (ed.) (1988): *Comparing Pluralist Democracies: Strains on Legitimacy*. Boulder, CO: Westview Press.

Dogan, M. and Kasarda, J. D. (1988): Introduction: How Giant Cities will multiply and Grow. In Dogan and Kasarda (eds), *The Metropolis Era*, Vol. 2: *Mega-Cities*. London: Sage, 12–29.

Dogan, M. and Pelassy, D. (1984): *How to Compare Nations: Strategies in Comparative Research*. Chatham, NJ: Chatham House.

Dominguez, J. I. (1987): Political change: Central America, South America, the Caribbean. In Weiner and Huntington (eds), 65–99.

Donnelley, J. (1989): *Universal Human Rights in Theory and Practice*. Ithaca, NY: Cornell University Press.

Downs, A. (1957): *An Economic Theory of Democracy*. New York: Harper & Brothers.

Doyal, L. and Gough, I. (1991): *A Theory of Human Need*. London: Macmillan.

Drewry, G. (1985): *The New Select Commitees: a Study of the 1979 Reform*. Oxford: Clarendon Press.

Dreyer, J. T. (1993): *China's Political System: Modernization and Tradition*. London: Macmillan.

Duchacek, I. D. (1970): *Comparative Federalism: the Territorial Dimension of Politics*. New York: Holt, Rinehart & Winston.

Dunleavy, P. and O'Leary, B. (1987): *Theories of the State: the Politics of Liberal Democracy*. London: Macmillan.

Dunn, J. (ed.) (1992): *Democracy: the Unfinished Journey*. Oxford: Oxford University Press.

Duverger, M. (1954): *Political Parties: their Organization and Activity in the Modern State*. London: Methuen.

Dye, T. R. and Gray, V. (eds) (1980): *The Determinants of Public Policy*. Lexington, MA: Lexington Books.

Easton, D. (1965a): *A Systems Analysis of Political Life*. New York: Wiley.

Easton, D. (1965b): *A Framework for Political Analysis*. Englewood Cliffs, NJ: Prentice-Hall.

Eccleston, B. (1993): *State and Society in Post-War Japan*. Cambridge: Polity Press.

Eckstein, H. (1966): *Division and Cohesion in Democracy: a Study of Norway*. Princeton, NJ: Princeton University Press.

Eckstein, H. (1971): *The Evaluation of Political Performance: Problems and Dimensions*. Beverly Hills, CA: Sage.

Eckstein, H. and Apter, D. E. (eds) (1963): *Comparative Politics*. New York: Free Press.

Eckstein, H. and Gurr, T. R. (1975): *Patterns of Authority: a Structural Basis for Political Inquiry*. New York: Wiley.

Economic Commission for Europe (1992): *Economic Survey of Europe in 1991–92*. New York: United Nations.

Eggertsson, T. (1990): *Economic Behaviour and Institutions*. Cambridge: Cambridge University Press.

Eide, A. and Hagtvet, B. (eds) (1992): *Human Rights in Perspective*. Oxford: Blackwell.

Eisenstadt, S. N. (1963): *The Political Systems of Empires*. New York: Free Press.

Eisenstadt, S. N. (1966): *Modernization: protest and Change*. Englewood Cliffs, NJ: Prentice-Hall.

Eisenstadt, S. N. (1973): *Tradition, Change and Modernity*. New York: Wiley.

Elazar, D. J. (1972): Federalism. In *International Encyclopedia of the Social Sciences*. New York: Free Press.

Elazar, D. J. (ed.) (1984): *Federalism and Political Integration*. Landham, MD: University Press of America.

Elazar, D. J. (ed.) (1991): *Federal Systems of the World: A Handbook on Federal, Confederal and Autonomy Arrangements*. Harlow: Longman.

Encyclopedia Britannica (yearly): *Britannica Book of the Year: Britannica World Data*. Chicago: Encyclopedia Britannica.

Esping-Andersen, G. (1985): *The Three Worlds of Welfare Capitalism*. Cambridge: Polity Press.

L'état du monde (yearly, 1982–). Paris: La Découverte.

Etzioni-Halevy, E. (1993): *The Elite Connection: Problems and Potential of Western Democracy*. Cambridge: Polity Press.

Eulau, H. (1963): *The Behavioral Persuasion in Politics*. New York: Random House.

Europa Yearbook (yearly). London: Europa Publications.

Evans, P. B., Rueschemeyer, D. and Skocpol, T. (eds) (1985): *Bringing the State Back In*. Cambridge: Cambridge University Press.

Ferdinand, P. (1991): *Communist Regimes in Comparative Perspective*. Hemel Hempstead: Harvester-Wheatsheaf.

Finer, H. (1950): *The Theory and Practice of Modern Government*. London: Methuen.

Finer, S. E. (1970): *Comparative Government*. London: Allen Lane.

Finer S. E. (1976): *The Man on Horseback: the Role of the Military in Politics*. Harmondsworth: Penguin.

Finer, S. E. (1988): Notes towards a history of constitutions. In Bogdanor (ed.), 17–32.

Der Fischer Welt Almanach (yearly, 1959–): Frankfurt am Main: Fischer Taschenbuchverlag.

Fleje, S. (1991): Denominational affiliation in Yugoslavia, 1931–1987. *East European Quarterly*, 2, 145–65.

Forsyth, M. (1981): *Union of States: the Theory and Practice of Confederation.* Leicester: Holmes & Meier.

Forsyth, M. (ed.) (1989): *Federalism and Nationalism.* Leicester: Leicester University Press.

Fortes, M. and Evans-Pritchard, E. E. (eds) (1940): *African Political Systems.* Oxford: Oxford University Press.

Frank, A. G. (1967): *Capitalism and Underdevelopment in Latin America: Historical Studies of Chile and Brazil.* New York: Monthly Review Press.

Freedom House (ed.) (1992): *Freedom in the World: Political Rights and Civil Liberties, 1991–1992.* New York: Freedom House.

Freedom House (1993): The comparative survey of freedom: 1993. *Freedom Review*, 24, 1, 14–16.

Freedom House (1994): The comparative survey of freedom: 1994. *Freedom Review*, 25, 1, 13–15.

Frey, B. (1978): *Modern Political Economy.* London: Macmillan.

Friedrich, C. (1950): *Constitutional Government and Democracy: Theory and Practice in Europe and America*, rev. edn. Boston: Ginn.

Friedrich, C. (1963): *Man and his Government: an Empirical Theory of Politics.* New York: McGraw-Hill.

Galtung, J. (1971): A structural theory of imperialism. *Journal of Peace Research*, 8, 81–117.

Gastil, R. D. (ed.) (1987): *Political Rights and Civil Liberties 1986–1987.* New York: Greenwood Press.

Gastil, R. D. (ed.) (1990a): *Freedom in the World: Political Rights and Civil Liberties 1989–1990.* New York: Greenwood Press.

Gastil, R. D. (1990b): The comparative survey of freedom: experiences and suggestions. *Studies in Comparative International Development*, 25, 25–50.

Gastil, R. D. and Sussman, L. R. (eds) (1987): *Freedom in the World: Political Rights and Civil Liberties, 1986–1987.* New York: Greenwood Press.

George, S. (1992): *The Debt Boomerang.* Boulder, CO: Westview Press.

Giner S. (1986): Political economy, legitimation and the state in Southern Europe. In O'Donnell et al. (eds), 11–44.

Glenny, M. (1990): *The Rebirth of History: Eastern Europe in the Age of Democracy.* Harmondsworth: Penguin.

Goldstone, J. A., Gurr, T. R. and Moshiri, F. (eds) (1991): *Revolutions of the Late Twentieth Century.* Boulder, CO: Westview Press.

Gotz, R. and Halbach, U. (1992): *Politisches Lexikon GUS.* Munich: Beck.

Gregory, P. R. and Stuart, R. C. (1989): *Comparative Economic Systems.* Boston: Houghton Mifflin.

Gurr, T. R. (1970): *Why Men Rebel.* Princeton, NJ: Princeton University Press.

Gurr, T. R. (ed.) (1980): *Handbook of Political Conflict: Theory and Research.* New York: Free Press.

Gurr, T. R. (1990): *Polity II: Political Structures and Regime Change, 1800–1986.* Boulder, CO: Center for Comparative Politics [computer file].

Gurr, T. R. (1993): Why minorities rebel: a global analysis of communal mobilization and conflict since 1945. *International Political Science Review*, 14, 161–201.

Gurr, T. R. and McClelland, M. (1971): *Political Performance: a Twelve-Nation Study*. Beverly Hills, CA: Sage.

Hadenius, A. (1992): *Democracy and Development*. Cambridge: Cambridge University Press.

Hague, R., Harrop, H. and Breslin, R. (1992): *Comparative Government and Politics*. London: Macmillan.

Hall, J. A. (1985) *Powers and Liberties: the Causes and Consequences of the Rise of the West*. Harmondsworth: Penguin.

Hall, J. A. (ed.) (1986) *States in History*. Oxford: Blackwell.

Hall, J. A. and Ikenberry, G. J. (1989): *The State*. Milton Keynes: Open University Press.

Hamilton, A., Madison, J. and Jay, J. ([1787–8] 1961): *The Federalist Papers*. New York: New American Library.

Hayek, F. A. von (ed.) (1935): *Collectivist Economic Planning*. London: Routledge & Kegan Paul.

Hayek, F. A. von (1944): *The Road to Serfdom*. London: Routledge.

Heady, F. (1979): *Public Administration: a Comparative Perspective*. New York: Dekker.

Heidenheimer, A. J., Heclo, H. and Admas, C. T. (1990): *Comparative Public Policy: the Politics of Social Choice in America, Europe, and Japan*. New York: St Martin's Press.

Held, D. (1987): *Models of Democracy*. Cambridge: Polity Press.

Held, D. (1989): *Political Theory and the Modern State*. Cambridge: Polity Press.

Held, D. (ed.) (1991): *Political Theory Today*. Cambridge: Polity Press.

Held, D. (ed.) (1993): *Prospects for Democracy: North, South, East, West*. Cambridge: Polity Press.

Held, D. et al. (eds) (1983): *States and Societies*. Oxford: Blackwell.

Hibbs, D. A. (1987): *The American Political Economy: Macroeconomics and Electoral Politics*. Cambridge, MA: Harvard University Press.

Hicks, A. and Swank, D. H. (1992): Politics, institutions, and welfare spending in industrialized democracies, 1960–82. *American Political Science Review*, 86, 658–74.

Higley, J. and Gunther, R. (eds) (1992): *Elites and Democratic Consolidation in Latin America and Southern Europe*. Cambridge: Cambridge University Press.

Hirschman, A. O. (1982): *Shifting Involvements: Public Interest and Public Action*. Oxford: Martin Robertson.

Hobsbawm, E. J. (1990): *Nations and Nationalism since 1970*. Cambridge: Cambridge University Press.

Hollis, M. and Smith, S. (1990): *Explaining and Understanding International Relations*. Oxford: Clarendon Press.

Holt, R. T. and Turner, J. E. (eds) (1970): *The Methodology of Comparative Research*. New York: Free Press.

Horowitz, D. L. (1985): *Ethnic Groups in Conflict*. Berkeley: University of California Press.

Horowitz, D. L. (1991): *A Democratic South Africa? Constitutional Engineering in a Divided Society*. Berkeley: University of California Press.

Hourani, A. (1991): *A History of the Arabic People*. London: Faber & Faber.

Humana, C. (1986): *World Human Rights Guide*, 2nd edn. London: Economist Publications.

Hunneus, C. (1990): Latin American political systems. In Bebler and Seroka (eds), 337–51.

Huntington, S. P. (1962): *Changing Patterns of Military Politics*. New York: Vintage Books.

Huntington, S. P. (1965): Political development and political decay. *World Politics*, 17, 386–430.

Huntington, S. P. (1968): *Political Order in Changing Societies*. New Haven, CT: Yale University Press.

Huntington, S. P. (1991): *The Third Wave: Democratization in the Late Twentieth Century*. Norman: University of Oklahoma Press.

Huntington, S. P. (1993): The clash of civilizations? *Foreign Affairs*, 72, 3, 22–49.

Huntington, S. P. and Dominguez, J. I. (1975): Political development. In Green-stein, F.-I. and Polsby, N. W. (eds), *Handbook of Political Science*, Vol. 3: *Macropolitical Theory*. Reading, MA: Addison-Wesley, 1–114.

Hyden, G. and Bratton, M. (eds) (1992): *Governance and Politics in Africa*. Boulder, CO: Lynne Rienner.

ILO (1991): *Yearbook of Labour Statistics*. Geneva: ILO.

Inglehart, R. (1990): *Culture Shift in Advanced Industrial Society*. Princeton, NJ: Princeton University Press.

Ionescu, G. (1988) The theory of liberal constitutionalism. In Bogdanor (ed.), 33–52.

Jackman, R. W. (1993): *Power without Force: the Political Capacity of Nation-States*. Ann Arbor: University of Michigan Press.

Jalali, R. and Lipset, S. M. (1993): Racial and ethnic conflicts: a global perspective. *Political Science Quarterly*, 107, 585–606.

Janowitz, M. (1964): *The Military in the Political Development of New Nations*. Chicago: University of Chicago Press.

Jellinek, G. ([1901] 1966) *Allgemeine Staatslehre*. Bad Homburg: Max Gehlen.

Jennings, I. (1951): *Cabinet*. Cambridge: Cambridge University Press.

Jennings, I. (1961): *Parliament*. Cambridge: Cambridge University Press.

Jessop, B. (1982): *The Capitalist State: Marxist Theories and Methods*. Oxford: Blackwell.

Jones, R. E. (1967): *The Functional Analysis of Politics*. London: Routledge & Kegan Paul.

Joseph, R. (1987): *Democracy and Prebendal Politics in Nigeria: the Rise and Fall of the Second Republic*. Cambridge: Cambridge University Press.

Kamrava, M. (1993): *Politics and Society in the Third World*. London: Routledge.

Kaplan, A. (1964): *The Conduct of Inquiry: Methodology for Behavioral Science*. San Francisco: Chandler.

Kazancigil, A. (1991): Democracy in Muslim islands: Turkey in comparative perspective. *International Social Science Journal*, 43, 341–59.

Kellas, J. (1991): *The Politics of Nationalism and Ethnicity*. London: Macmillan.

Kelsen, H. (1945): *General Theory of Law and State*. New York: Russell & Russell.

Keman, H. (ed.) (1993): *Comparative Politics: New Directions in Theory and Method*. Amsterdam: Free University Press.

Kennedy, P. (1987): *The Rise and Fall of the Great Powers*. New York: Random House.

Kennedy, P. (1993): *Preparing for the Twenty-First Century*. New York: Harper Collins.

Keohane, R. O. (1984): *After Hegemony: Cooperation and Discord in the World Political Economy*. Princeton, NJ: Princeton University Press.

Kluckhohn, C. (1962): *Culture and Behavior*. New York: Free Press.

Kluckhohn, C. and Leighton, D. (1946): *The Navaho*. Cambridge, MA: Harvard University Press.

Korany, B. (1990): Arab political systems. In Bebler and Seroka (eds), 303–29.

Kornai, J. (1990): *The Road to a Free Economy*. London: Norton Press.

Korpi, W. (1989): Power, politics, and state autonomy in the development of social citizenship: social rights during sickness in eighteen OECD countries since 1930. *American Sociological Review*, 54, 308–28.

Krasner, S. (1982): *International Regimes*. Ithaca, NY: Cornell University Press.

Krejci, J. (1990): *The Civilizations of Asia and the Middle East before the European Challenge*. London: Macmillan.

Kriek, D. J., Kotze, D. J., Labuschange, M. P. and O'Malley, K. (1992): *Federalism: The Solution?* Pretoria: HSRC.

Kuhn, T. (1962): *The Structure of Scientific Revolutions*. Chicago: University of Chicago Press.

Kuznets, S. (1955): Economic growth and income inequality. *American Economic Review*, 45, 18–25.

LaPalombara, J. (1974): *Politics within Nations*. Englewood Cliffs, NJ: Prentice-Hall.

Laundy, P. (1989): *Parliaments in the Modern World*. Aldershot: Dartmouth.

Laver, M. and Schofield, N. (1990): *Multiparty Government: the Politics of Coalition in Europe*. Oxford: Oxford University Press.

Leftwich, A. (1990): Politics and development studies. In Leftwich (ed.), *New Developments of Political Science: an International Review of Achievements and Prospects*. Aldershot: Edward Elgar, 82–106.

Leftwich, A. (1994): States of underdevelopment: the third world state in theoretical perspective. *Journal of Theoretical Politics*, 6, 1, 55–74.

Lehmbruch, G. (1979): Liberal corporatism and party government. In Schmitter, P. and Lehmbruch, G. (eds), *Trends Towards Corporatist Intermediation*. London: Sage, 147–83.

Lerner, D. (1958): *The Passing of Traditional Society: Modernizing the Middle East.* New York: Free Press.

Levy, M. (1952): *The Structure of Society.* Princeton, NJ: Princeton University Press.

Lijphart, A. (1968): Typologies of democratic systems. *Comparative Political Studies*, 1, 3–44.

Lijphart, A. (1971): Comparative politics and the comparative method. *American Political Science Review*, 65, 682–93.

Lijphart, A. (1974): Consociational democracy. In McRae (ed.), 70–89.

Lijphart, A. (1975a): *The Politics of Accommodation: Pluralism and Democracy in the Netherlands*, 2nd edn. Berkeley: University of California Press.

Lijphart, A. (1975b): The comparable-cases strategy in comparative research. *Comparative Political Studies*, 8, 158–77.

Lijphart, A. (1977): *Democracy in Plural Societies: a Comparative Exploration.* New Haven, CT: Yale University Press.

Lijphart, A. (1984): *Democracies: Patterns of Majoritarian and Consensus Government in Twenty-One Countries.* New Haven, CT: Yale University Press.

Lijphart, A. (1990): The Southern European example of democratization: six lessons for Latin America. *Government and Opposition*, 25, 1, 68–84.

Lijphart, A. (1991a): Constitutional choices for new democracies. *Journal of Democracy*, 2, 1, 72–84.

Lijphart, A. (1991b): Double-checking the evidence. *Journal of Democracy*, 2, 3, 42–8.

Lijphart, A. (1992a): Democratization and constitutional choices in Czecho-Slovakia, Hungary and Poland, 1989–91. *Journal of Theoretical Politics*, 4, 2, 207–23.

Lijphart, A. (ed.) (1992b): *Parliamentary versus Presidential Government.* Oxford: Oxford University Press.

Lijphart, A. (1994a): *Electoral Systems and Party Systems: a Study of Twenty-Seven Democracies, 1945–1990.* Oxford: Oxford University Press.

Lijphart, A. (1994b): Democracies: forms, performance, and constitutional engineering. *European Journal of Political Research*, 25, 1–17.

Lindblom, C. E. (1977): *Politics and Markets: the World's Political-Economic Systems.* New York: Basic Books.

Lindblom, C. E. (1988): *Democracy and Market System.* Oslo: Norwegian University Press.

Lindblom, C. E. (1990): *Inquiry and Change.* New Haven, CT: Yale University Press.

Linz, J. J. (1975): Totalitarian and authoritarian regimes. In Greenstein, F.-I. and Polsby, N. W., (eds), *Handbook of Political Science*, Vol. 3: *Macropolitical Theory*. Reading, MA: Addison-Wesley, 175–411.

Linz, J. J. (1990): Transitions to democracy. *Washington Quarterly*, 13, 143–64.

Linz, J. J. (1992): The virtues of parliamentarism. In Lijphart (ed.) (1992b), 212–16.

Lipset, S. M. (1959): *Political Man: the Social Bases of Politics.* New York: Doubleday-Anchor.

Lipset, S. M. and Rokkan, S. (eds) (1967): *Party Systems and Voter Alignments: Cross-National Perspectives*. New York: Free Press.

Lipset, S. M., Seong, K. R. and Torres, J. C. (1993): A comparative analysis of the social requisites of democracy. *International Social Science Journal*, 45, 155–75.

Lively, J. (1975): *Democracy*. Oxford: Blackwell.

Loewenstein, K. (1965): *Political Power and the Governmental Process*. Chicago: University of Chicago Press.

Luciani, G. (ed.) (1990): *The Arab State*. London: Routledge.

Lundahl, M. (1991): *Peasants and Poverty: a Study of Haiti*. London: Croom Helm.

McLennan, G., Hall, J. A. and Held, D. (1984): *The Idea of the Modern State*. Milton Keynes: Open University Press.

MacPherson, S. and Midgley, J. (1987): *Comparative Social Policy and the Third World*. Brighton: Wheatsheaf.

McRae, K. (ed.) (1974): *Consociational Democracy: Political Accommodation in Segmented Societies*. Toronto: McClelland & Stewart.

Macridis, R. C. (1955): *The Study of Comparative Government*. New York: Random House.

Macridis, R. C. and Burg, S. L. (1991): *Introduction to Comparative Politics: Regimes and Changes*, 2nd edn. New York: Harper Collins.

Madsen, E. S. and Paldam, M. (1978): *Economic and Political Data for the Main OECD Countries, 1948–1975*. Århus: University Institute of Economics.

Mainwaring, S. (1993): Presidentialism, multipartism, and democracy: the difficult combination. *Comparative Political Studies*, 26, 198–228.

Malinowski, B. (1922): *Argonauts of the Western Pacific*. London: Routledge.

Mannheim, K. (1936): *Ideology und Utopia: an Introduction to the Sociology of Knowledge*. London: Routledge & Kegan Paul.

Mansbridge, J. J. (1983): *Beyond Adversary Democracy*. Chicago: University of Chicago Press.

Maravall, J. M. and Santamaria, J. (1986): Political change in Spain and prospects for democracy. In O'Donnell et al. (eds), 71–108.

March, J. G. and Olsen, J. P. (1989): *Rediscovering Institutions: the Organizational Basis of Politics*. New York: Free Press.

Marer, P. et al. (1992): *Historically Planned Economies: a Guide to the Data*. Washington, DC: World Bank.

Marks, G. and Diamond, L. (1992): Seymour Martin Lipset and the study of democracy. In Diamond (ed.), 352–62.

Marshall, G. (1971): *Constitutional Theory*. Oxford: Clarendon Press.

Maxwell, K. (1986): Regime overthrow and the prospects for democratic transition in Portugal. In O'Donnell et al. (eds), 109–37.

Mayer, L. C. (1972): *Comparative Political Inquiry*. Homewood, IL: Dorsey Press.

Mayer, L. C. (1989): *Redefining Comparative Politics: Promise versus Performance*. Newbury Park, CA: Sage.

Medard, J.-F. (1982): The underdeveloped state in tropical Africa: political clientelism or neo-patrimonialism. In Clapham, C. (ed.), *Private Patronage and Public Power*. London: Pinter.

Meinecke, F. ([1908] 1962): *Weltbürgertum und Nationalstaat*. Munich: Oldenbourg.

Meinecke, F. ([1925] 1963): *Die Idee der Staatsräson*. Munich: Oldenbourg.

Merkl, P. H. (1970): *Modern Comparative Politics*. New York: Holt, Rinehart & Winston.

Merkl, P. H. (1977): *Modern Comparative Politics*, 2nd edn. Hinsdale, IL: Dryden Press.

Merkl, P. H. (1993): Which are today's democracies? *International Social Science Journal*, 45, 257–70.

Mezey, M. L. (1979): *Comparative Legislatures*. Durham, NC: Duke University Press.

Migdal, J. (1988): *Strong Societies and Weak States: State–Society Relations and State Capabilities in the Third World*. Princeton, NJ: Princeton University Press.

Mill, J. S. ([1862] 1986): *Considerations on Representative Government*. Cambridge: Cambridge University Press.

Mill, J. S. ([1843] 1884): *A System of Logic*. London: Longman.

Modelski, G. and Perry, G. III (1991): Democratization in long perspective. *Technological Forecasting and Social Change*, 39, 23–34.

Montesquieu, C. de ([1748] 1989): *The Spirit of the Laws*. Cambridge: Cambridge University Press.

Monthias, J. M. (1976): *The Structure of Economic Systems*. New Haven, CT: Yale University Press.

Moon, B. E. (1991): *The Political Economy of Basic Human Needs*. Ithaca, NY: Cornell University Press.

Moore, B. (1966): *Social Origins of Dictatorship and Democracy*. Harmondsworth: Penguin.

Morlino, L. (1990): Authoritarianism. In Bebler and Seroka (eds), 91–110.

Morris, M. D. (1979): *Measuring the Conditions of the World's Poor: the Physical Quality of Life Index*. New York: Pergamon Press.

Musgrave, R. and Jarrett, P. (1979): International redistribution. *Kyklos*, 32, 541–58.

Myrdal, G. (1957): *Economic Theory and Underdeveloped Regions*. London: Duckworth.

Myrdal, G. (1968): *Asian Drama*, 3 vols. New York: Pantheon.

Needler, M. C. (1991): *The Concepts of Comparative Politics*. New York: Praeger.

Nordlinger, E. A. (1977): *Soldiers in Politics: Military Coups and Governments*. Englewood Cliffs, NJ: Prentice-Hall.

Nordlinger, E. A. (1981): *The Autonomy of the Democratic State*. Cambridge, MA: Harvard University Press.

North, D. (1990): *Institutions, Institutional Change and Economic Performance*. Cambridge: Cambridge University Press.

Norton, P. (ed.) (1992): *Legislatures*. Oxford: Oxford University Press.

Oakeshott, M. J. (1991): *On Human Conduct*. Oxford: Oxford University Press.

O'Donnell, G. (1973): *Modernization and Bureaucratic-Authoritarianism: Studies in South American Politics*. Berkeley, CA: Institute of International Studies.

O'Donnell, G. (1988): *Bureaucratic Authoritarianism: Argentina, 1966–1973, in Comparative Perspective*. Berkeley: University of California Press.

O'Donnell, G. (1994): Delegative democracy. *Journal of Democracy*, 5, 1, 55–69.

O'Donnell, G. and Schmitter, P. C. (1986): *Transitions from Authoritarian Rule: Tentative Conclusions about Uncertain Democracies*. Baltimore: Johns Hopkins University Press.

O'Donnell, G., Schmitter, P. C. and Whitehead, L. (eds) (1986): *Transitions from Authoritarian Rule: Prospects for Democracy*, Vol. I: *Southern Europe*; Vol. II: *Latin America*; Vol. III: *Comparative Perspectives*. Baltimore: Johns Hopkins University Press.

OECD (1968): *National Accounts, 1950–1968*. Paris: OECD.

OECD (1979): *National Accounts, 1960–1977*. Paris: OECD.

OECD (1983): *National Accounts, 1964–1981*. Paris: OECD.

OECD (1988): *Labour Force Statistics*. Paris: OECD.

OECD (1992a): *Economic Outlook*, 51, December.

OECD (1992b): *National Accounts, 1978–1990*. Paris: OECD.

Olsen, J. P. (1988): *Statsstyre og Institusjonsutforming*. Oslo: Universitetsforlaget.

Olson, M. (1963): Rapid growth as a destabilizing force. *Journal of Economic History*, 23, 529–52.

Olson, M. (1982): *The Rise and Decline of Nations: Economic Growth, Stagflation and Social Rigidities*. New Haven, CT: Yale University Press.

Ostrom, V. (1987): *The Political Theory of a Compound Republic: Designing the American Experience*. Lincoln: University of Nebraska Press.

Ostrom, V. (1991): *The Meaning of American Federalism: Constituting a Self-Governing Society*. San Francisco: ICS Press.

Owen, R. (1992): *State, Power and Politics in the Making of the Modern Middle East*. London: Routledge.

Öyen, E. (ed.) (1990): *Comparative Methodology: Theory and Practice in International Social Research*. London: Sage.

Page, E. (1991): *Localism and Centralism in Europe: the Political and Legal Bases of Local Self-Government*. Oxford: Oxford University Press.

Page, E. (1992): *Political Authority and Bureaucratic Power*. New York: Harvester Wheatsheaf.

Parry, G. (1969): *Political Elites*. London: Allen & Unwin.

Parsons, T. (1951): *The Social System*. Glencoe, IL: Free Press.

Pasquino, G. (1986): The demise of the first fascist regime and Italy's transition to democracy, 1943–1948. In O'Donnell et al. (eds), 45–70.

Pateman, C. (1970): *Participation and Democratic Theory*. Cambridge: Cambridge University Press.

Peacock, A. and Wiseman, J. (1961): *The Growth of Public Expenditure in the United Kingdom*. Princeton, NJ: Princeton University Press.

Peters, B. G. (1987): *The Politics of Bureaucracy: A Comparative Perspective*. New York: Longman.

Poggi, G. (1978): *The Development of the Modern State*. London: Hutchinson.

Poggi, G. (1990): *The State: its Nature, Development and Prospects*. Stanford, CA: Stanford University Press.

Polsby, N. W. (1963): *Community Power and Political Theory*. New Haven, CT: Yale University Press.

Pommerance, M. (1982): *Self-determination in Law and Practice*. The Hague: Martinus Nijhoff.

Pourgerami, A. (1988): The political economy of development: a cross-national causality test of development-democracy-growth hypothesis. *Public Choice*, 45, 123–41.

Przeworski, A. (1991): *Democracy and the Market: Political and Economic Reforms in Eastern Europe and Latin America*. Cambridge: Cambridge University Press.

Przeworski, A. and Teune, H. (1970): *The Logic of Comparative Social Inquiry*. New York: Wiley.

Putnam, R., Leonardi, R. and Nanetti, R. (1993): *Making Democracy Work: Civic Traditions in Modern Italy*. Princeton, NJ: Princeton University Press.

Pye, L. W. (1966): *Aspects of Political Development*. Boston: Little, Brown.

Radcliffe-Brown, A. R. (1952): *Structure and Function in Primitive Society: Essays and Addresses*. London: Cohen & West.

Rae, D. W. and Taylor, M. (1970): *The Analysis of Political Cleavages*. New Haven, CT: Yale University Press.

Ragin, C. (1987): *The Comparative Method: Moving Beyond Qualitative and Quantitative Strategies*. Berkeley: University of California Press.

Randall, V. (ed.) (1987): *Political Parties in the Third World*. London: Sage.

Ranney, A. (ed.) (1962): *Essays on the Behavioural Study of Politics*. Urbana: University of Illinois Press.

Riker, W. H. (1962): *The Theory of Political Coalitions*. New Haven: Yale University Press.

Riker, W. H. (1964): *Federalism: Origin, Operation, Significance*. Boston: Little, Brown.

Riker, W. H. (1975) Federalism. In Greenstein, F.-I. and Polsby, N. W. (eds), *The Handbook of Political Science*, Vol. 5. Reading, MA: Addison-Wesley.

Riker, W. H. (1982): *Liberalism against Populism*. San Francisco: Freeman.

Roberts, G. K. (1971): *Dictionary of Political Analysis*. London: Longman.

Roberts, G. K. (1972): *What is Comparative Politics?* London: Macmillan.

Rokkan, S. (1966): Norway: numerical democracy and corporate pluralism. In Dahl, R. A. (ed.), *Political Oppositions in Western Democracies*. New Haven, CT: Yale University Press, 70–115.

Rokkan, S. and Urwin, D. (1983): *Economy, Territory, Identity: Politics of West European Peripheries*. London: Sage.

Rokkan, S., Campbell, A., Torsvik, P. and Valen, H. (1970): *Citizens, Elections, Parties: Approaches to the Comparative Study of the Processes of Development*. Oslo: Universitetsforlaget.

Rose, R. (1984): *Understanding Big Government: the Programme Approach*. London: Sage.

Rose, R. (1989): *Ordinary People in Public Policy: a Behavioural Analysis*. London: Sage.

Rose, R. (1992): Escaping from absolute dissatisfaction: a trial and error model of change in Eastern Europe. *Journal of Theoretical Politics*, 4, 371–93.

Roskin, M. G. (1991): *The Rebirth of East Europe*. Englewood Cliffs, NJ: Prentice-Hall.

Rossiter, C. (1963): *Constitutional Dictatorship: Crisis Government in the Modern Democracies*. New York: Harcourt, Brace.

Rostow, W. W. (1960): *The Stages of Economic Growth*. New York: Cambridge University Press.

Roth, G. (1968): Personal rulership, patrimonialism and empire-building in the new states. *World Politics*, 20, 195–206.

Rousseau, J. J. ([1762] 1993): *The Social Contract*. London: Everyman.

Rowat, C. L. (1988): *Public Administration in Developed Democracies*. New York: Marcel Dekker.

Rueschemeyer, D., Stephens, E. H. and Stephens, J. D. (1992): *Capitalist Development and Democracy*. Cambridge: Polity Press.

Russett, B. R., Singer, J. D. and Small, M. (1968): National political units in the twentieth century. *American Political Science Review*, 62, 930–51.

Rustow, D. A. (1967): *A World of Nations: Problems of Political Modernization*. Washington, DC: Brookings.

Rustow, D. A. and Erickson, K. P. (eds) (1991): *Comparative Political Dynamics: Global Research Perspectives*. New York: Harper Collins.

Ryle, M. and Richards P. G. (1988): *The Commons Under Scrutiny*. London: Routledge.

Sakwa, R. (1993): *Russian Politics and Society*. London: Routledge.

Sanders, D. (1981): *Patterns of Political Instability*. London: Macmillan.

Sartori, G. (1969): From sociology of politics to political sociology. In Lipset (ed.), *Politics and the Social Sciences*. New York: Oxford University Press, 65–100.

Sartori, G. (1976): *Parties and Party Systems*, Vol. 1. Cambridge: Cambridge University Press.

Sartori, G. (1987): *The Theory of Democracy Revisited*. Chatham, NJ: Chatham House.

Sartori, G. (1991): Comparing and miscomparing. *Journal of Theoretical Politics*, 3, 243–57.

Sawyer, G. (1976): *Modern Federalism*. Carlton, Vic.: Pitman.

Scalapino, R. A. (1993): Democratizing dragons: South Korea and Taiwan. *Journal of Democracy*, 4, 3, 70–83.

Scarrow, H. A. (1969): *Comparative Political Analysis: an Introduction*. New York: Harper & Row.

Schmidt, M. G. (1982): *Wohlfartsstaatliche Politik unter bürgerlichen und sozialdemokratischen Regierungen: ein internationaler Vergleich*. Frankfurt am Main: Campus.

Schmitter, P. C. (1983): Democratic theory and neo-corporatist practice. *Social Research*, 50, 885–928.

Schmitter, P. C. (1986): An introduction to Southern European transitions from authoritarian rule: Italy, Greece, Portugal, Spain and Turkey. In O'Donnell et al. (eds), 3–10.

Schultz, B. M. and Slater, R. O. (1990): *Revolution and Political Change in the Third World*. Boulder, CO: Lynne Rienner.

Schumpeter, J. A. (1944): *Capitalism, Socialism and Democracy*. London: Allen & Unwin.

Sen, A. (1986): *Poverty and Famines: an Essay on Entitlement and Deprivation*. Oxford: Clarendon Press.

Shapiro, I. and Reeher, G. (eds) (1988): *Power, Inequality and Democratic Politics*. Boulder, CO: Westview Press.

Sharpe, L. J. (1978): *Decentralist Trends in Western Democracies*. London: Sage.

Sharpe, L. J. and Newton, K. (1984): *Does Politics Matter?* Oxford: Oxford University Press.

Shils, E. (1975): *Center and Periphery*. Chicago: University of Chigaco Press.

Shivji, I. (1976): *Class Struggle in Tanzania*. New York: Monthly Review Press.

Shugart, M. S. and Carey, J. M. (1992): *Presidents and Assemblies: Constitutional Design and Electoral Dynamics*. Cambridge: Cambridge University Press.

Singer, H. W. and Sharma, S. (1989): *Economic Development and World Debt*. New York: St Martin's Press.

SIPRI (1990): *World Armaments and Disarmaments*. Oxford: Oxford University Press.

Skidmore, T. E. and Smith, P. H. (1992): *Modern Latin America*. New York: Oxford University Press.

Skocpol, T. (1979): *States and Social Revolutions*. Cambridge: Cambridge University Press.

Smith, A. D. (1983): *State and Nation in the Third World: the Western State and African Nationalism*. Brighton: Wheatsheaf.

Smith, A. D. (1991): *National Identity*. Harmondsworth: Penguin.

Smith, A. D. (ed.) (1992): *Ethnicity and Nationalism*. New York: Brill.

Smith, T. (1991): The dependency approach. In Wiarda (ed.), 118–30.

Sörensen, G. (1993): *Democracy and Democratization: Processes and Prospects in a Changing World*. Boulder, CO: Westview Press.

Spindler, Z. A. (1991): Liberty and development: a further empirical perspective. *Public Choice*, 69, 197–210.

Statesman's Yearbook (yearly). London: Macmillan.

Stepan, A. and Skach, C. (1993): Constitutional frameworks and democratic consolidation: parliamentarianism versus presidentialism. *World Politics*, 46, 1–21.

Strom, K. (1990): *Minority Government and Majority Rule*. Cambridge: Cambridge University Press.

Sullivan, M. J. III (1991): *Measuring Global Values: the Ranking of 162 Countries*. New York: Greenwood Press.

Summers, R. and Heston, A. (1988): A new set of international comparisons of real product and price level estimates for 130 countries, 1950–1985. *Review of Income and Wealth*, 34, 1–25.

Summers, R. and Heston, A. (1991): The Penn world table (mark 5): an expanded set of international comparisons, 1950–1988. *Quarterly Journal of Economics*, May, 327–68.

Sunar, I. and Sayari, S. (1986): Democracy in Turkey: problems and prospects. In O'Donnell et al. (eds), 165–84.

Szentes, T. (1983): *The Political Economy of Underdevelopment*. Budapest: Akadémiai Kiadó.

Szporlouk, R. (1988): *Communism and Nationalism: Karl Marx versus Friedrich List*. New York: Oxford University Press.

Tarschys, D. (1975): The growth of public expenditures: nine modes of explanation. *Scandinavian Political Studies*, 10, 9–31.

Taylor, C. L. (1983): *World Handbook of Political and Social Indicators*, 3rd edn. New Haven, CT: Yale University Press.

Taylor, C. L. and Hudson, M. (1972): *World Handbook of Political and Social Indicators*, 2nd edn. New Haven, CT: Yale University Press.

Terlouw, C. P. (1989): World-system theory and regional geography: a preliminary exploration of the context of regional geography. *Tijdschrift voor economische en sociale geografie*, 80, 206–21.

Thompson, J. (1989): *Theories of Ethnicity: a Critical Appraisal*. New York: Greenwood Press.

Thompson, M., Ellis, R. and Wildavsky, A. (1990): *Cultural Theory*. Boulder, CO: Westview Press.

Tilly, C. (ed.) (1975): *The Formation of National States in Western Europe*. Princeton, NJ: Princeton University Press.

Tilly, C. (1978): *From Mobilization to Revolution*. Reading, MA: Addison-Wesley.

Tingsten, H. (1965): *The problems of democracy*. Totowa, NJ: Bedminster Press.

Tocqueville, A. ([1835–40] 1990): *Democracy in America*, 2 vols. New York: Vintage.

Tocqueville, A. ([1856] 1988): *The Ancien Regime*. London: Dent.

Todd, E. (1983): *La troisième planète: structures familiales et systèmes idéologiques*. Paris: Seuil.

Tordoff, W. (1984): *Government and Politics in Africa*. London: Macmillan.

Unger, A. L. (1981): *Constitutional Development in the USSR: a Guide to the Soviet Constitutions*. London: Methuen.

United Nations Development Programme (yearly, 1990–): *Human Development Report*. New York: Oxford University Press.

Valenzuela, A. (1993): Latin America: presidentialism in crisis. *Journal of Democracy*, 4, 4, 3–16.

van den Berghe, P. L. (1981): *The Ethnic Phenomenon*. New York: Praeger.

Van Dyke, V. (1985): *Human Rights, Ethnicity and Discrimination*. Westport, CT: Greenwood Press.

Vanhanen, T. (1990): *The Process of Democratization: a Comparative Study of 147 States, 1980–1988*. New York: Crane Russak.

Vincent, A. (1987): *Theories of the State*. Oxford: Blackwell.

Wallerstein, I. (1974): *The Modern World-System: Capitalist Agriculture and the Origins of the European World-Economy in the Sixteenth Century*. New York: Academic Press.

Weber, M. ([1904] 1965): *The Sociology of Religion*. London: Methuen.

Weber, M. ([1922] 1978): *Economy and Society: an Outline of Interpretive Sociology*, 2 vols. Berkeley: University of California Press.

Weiner, M. (1987): Empirical democratic theory. In Weiner and Ozbudun (eds), 3–34.

Weiner, M. and Huntington, S. P. (eds) (1987): *Understanding Political Development*. Boston: Little, Brown.

Weiner, M. and Ozbudun, E. (eds) (1987): *Competitive Elections in Developing Countries*. Durham, NC: Duke University Press.

Welch, C. E. (1990): African political systems. In Bebler and Seroka (eds), 281–97.

Wesson, R. (ed.) (1987): *Democracy: a Worldwide Survey*. New York: Praeger.

Wheare, K. C. (1947): *Federal Government*. New York: Oxford University Press.

Whiteley, P. (ed.) (1980): *Models of Political Economy*. London: Sage.

Whiteley, P. (1986): *Political Control of the Macroeconomy: the Political Economy of Public Policy Making*. London: Sage.

Wiarda, H. J. (1981): *Corporatism and National Development in Latin America*. Boulder, CO: Westview Press.

Wiarda, H. J. (ed.) (1991): *New Directions in Comparative Politics*. Boulder, CO: Westview Press.

Wildavsky, A. (1979): *Speaking Truth to Power: the Art and Craft of Policy Analysis*. Boston: Little, Brown.

Wildavsky, A. (1986): *Budgeting: a Comparative Theory of Budgetary Processes*, 2nd edn. New Brunswick, NJ: Transaction.

Wilensky, H. (1975): *The Welfare State and Equality: Structural and Ideological Roots of Public Expenditures*. Berkeley: University of California Press.

Williamson, E. (1992): *The Penguin History of Latin America*. Harmondsworth: Penguin.

Williamson, O. (1985): *The Economic Institutions of Capitalism*. New York: Free Press.

Wilson, G. K. (1990): *Interest Groups*. Oxford: Blackwell.

Wittfogel, K. (1957): *Oriental Despotism: A Comparative Study of Total Power*. New Haven, CT: Yale University Press.

Wolf, E. R. (1982): *Europe and the People without History*. Berkeley: University of California Press.

World Bank (yearly, 1978–) *World Development Report*. New York: Oxford University Press.

World Bank (1984): *World Tables*, 3rd edn. Baltimore: Johns Hopkins University Press.

World Bank (1991): *Social Indicators of Development 1990*. Baltimore: Johns Hopkins University Press.

Woytinsky, W. S. and Woytinsky, E. S. (1953): *World Population and Production: Trends and Outlook*. New York: Twentieth Century Fund.

Wright, L. M. (1982): A comparative survey of economic freedoms. In Gastil, R. D. (ed.), *Freedom in the World: Political Rights and Civil Liberties, 1982*. Westport, CT: Greenwood Press, 51–90.

Zubaida, S. (1993): *Islam, the People and the State*. London: Tauris.

Index